Edited by Timothy Green Beckley and William Kern

Hounds of the Baskervilles

From Demon Dogs To Sherlock Holmes

HOUNDS of the Baskervilles

From Demon Dogs To Sherlock Holmes

by Sir Arthur Conan Doyle

with additional material by

Timothy Green Beckley, Nick Redfern,

Andrew Cable and Claudia Cunningham,

with a Short Story By William Kern

HOUNDS of the Baskervilles
From Demon Dogs To Sherlock Holmes

New Edition And Cover Art Copyright

ISBN-13 9781606111253
ISBN 1606111256

Timothy Green Beckley: Editorial Director
Carol Rodriguez: Publisher's Assistant
Associate Editors: Sean Casteel & Tim Swartz
Special Thanks: William Kern

For Free Subscription To The Conspiracy Journal Write:
Timothy Green Beckley
Box 753, New Brunswick, NJ 08903
Sign Up On Line: MRUFO8@hotmail.com
www.ConspiracyJournal.Com
www.TeslasSecretLab.Com

SIR ARTHUR CONAN DOYLE - CREATOR OF SHERLOCK HOLMES, AUTHOR OF HOUND OF THE BASKERVILLES AND PARANORMAL AUTHORITY EXTRAORDINAIRE.
(Graphic created by Tim Swartz)

CONTENTS

ENTER THE HOUNDS –
DON'T BE AFRAID, THEY WON'T HARM YOU,
OR WILL THEY?
By Timothy Green Beckley

Oh my, *The Hound of the Baskervilles*. How the mere mention of this title brings back fond memories.

As far as I am concerned, this has to be the most brilliant book in the Sherlock Holmes series, written by that brilliant man whom I admire so much, Sir Arthur Conan Doyle. In fact, I wish he were alive today so that I could shake his hand and thank him for all the wonderful hours I spent reading the seemingly unsolvable mysteries he brought to the world, not only as the creator of the greatest detective of all time, but as one of the world's leading investigators of the paranormal.

For those who know the history of psychic phenomena, few others have been so influential in promoting a belief in life after death, spiritualism, levitation, spirit photography and for the overall conviction that anything is possible in the kingdom of the supernatural. At one point he wanted to give up his highly successful profession as a writer and delve into the realm of the mystical fulltime. He went on extensive lecture tours to promote numerous mediums who were being attacked by the likes of the great magician/escape artist Harry Houdini, who said that spiritualism was nothing more than a scam, a matter of "hocus pocus." Doyle went so far as to state his belief in a sensational series of photographs taken by two young girls of purported fairies beside a stream in the woods behind their home. He spent a good portion of his life trying to verify the case for the existence of the paranormal and scripted several works heavily laden with quotes from members of the scientific community who actively supported his belief in the Summerland, a sort of heavenly paradise where we go when we die if we have lead a relatively civil life and shown compassion to others not as fortunate as perhaps you and I.

Frankly, I cannot acquire an adequate amount of Sir Arthur Conan Doyle's paranormal writings. For some reason, I seem to have an overwhelming aspiration to return to print those creations of his on the subject which for the most part have been impossible to obtain during the course of the last several decades. These include:

"The Charismatic, Martyred Life of Joan Of Arc," a sort of channeled essay received by psychic means through the mediumship of Leon Denis.

"Revealing The Bizarre Powers of Harry Houdini – As Exposed By Sir Arthur Conan Doyle," which suggests that Houdini's fanatical debunking of psychics and mediums was a subterfuge to conceal his own remarkable paranormal powers.

"The Paranormal World of Sherlock Holmes: Sir Arthur Conan Doyle First Ghost Buster and Psychic Sleuth," includes a cool selection of photographs from the period in which Doyle studied the enigmas of the unknown.

As for *The Hound of the Baskervilles*, I read the literary version when I was but a tender youth, and I must have seen the original 1939 version of the film adaptation starring Basil Rathbone a half dozen times. It would come on from time to time late on a Friday or Saturday night on one of the independent stations broadcasting out of Manhattan or Philadelphia, and I happened to live just about halfway between the two mega cities. In the rafters while I was growing up was a talented performer named John Zacherle, who was hired to host some of the worst movies imaginable in the hope that the programs he made a spectacle of himself on would somehow attract an audience. Zacherle created a name for himself in no time by donning some cheap stylistic horror makeup while sleeping in a coffin and befriending a giant amoeba that he slung around the dungeon he lived in as if he were fighting the blob. On Saturday, August 2, 1958, Zacherle aired the *The Hound of the Baskervilles* for the first time and hooked me and an entire generation on what many consider to be Sir Arthur Conan Doyle's best work. If it weren't for this broadcast "way back when," there is a good chance this very book would never have been published.

Though there is no way of knowing, it is estimated that between 40 and 50 movie and TV adaptations of *The Hound of the Baskervilles* have been made, going back as early as 1915 with a silent German version <u>Der Hund von Baskerville</u>. The most recent one was released only a few months ago (circa 2012) in the United Kingdom under the slightly altered title, *The Hounds of Baskerville*.

But this book is mainly about the real hounds, the bona fide devil dogs, the crazed phantom canines of the night that influenced Doyle to pen his most well-received Sherlock Holmes thriller.

In order to strengthen the case for the reality of the hounds, we have called upon several top cryptolzologists to document the beasts' uncomfortable existence. Nick Redfern was born in England and has done a thorough job of creating an accurate timeline of the hounds' appearances throughout the British Isles, while blogger Andrew Gable hunkers down in the U.S. as he concentrates on sightings of the hounds in several eastern states.

And finally, before presenting a wonderfully illustrated version of Doyle's _The Hound of the Baskervilles_, we call upon our friend and fellow Fortean enthusiast Claudia Cunningham, who has personally heard many strange stories of the hounds in upstate New York, especially those which center about the very cemetery where Charles Fort is buried. DoDoDoDo – your next stop, the Twilight Zone!

Timothy Green Beckley, Publisher
New York City
August, 2012

mrufo8@hotmail.com

AIN'T NOTHING BUT A HOUND DOG —
OR IS IT?

There is no way of knowing for sure how many editions of Sir Arthur Conan Doyle's book The Hound Of the Baskervilles have been published around the world. It is estimated, however, that somewhere near 50 motion pictures and TV adaptations have been produced, starting with the earliest 1914 silent version.

Here is but a small collection of film art, posters, TV stills and DVD box covers — in various languages — to show the immense popularity of Sherlock Holmes and his demonic canine adversary from hell.

With signature pipe in hand, Peter Cushing plays Holmes
in the Hammer version of this classic.

Even the comics cannot escape the dastardly deeds of the Hound.

A rare set of theatrical one sheets illustrating quite nicely the horror of it all.

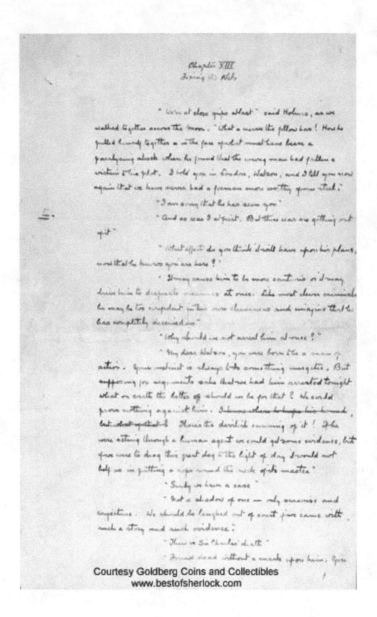

A copy of one page of the original hand-written text, valued at over one-hundred thousand dollars, from Doyle's "Hound Of The Baskervilles."

Holmes examines the victim in this rare still from the first
"Hound" film, circa 1914.

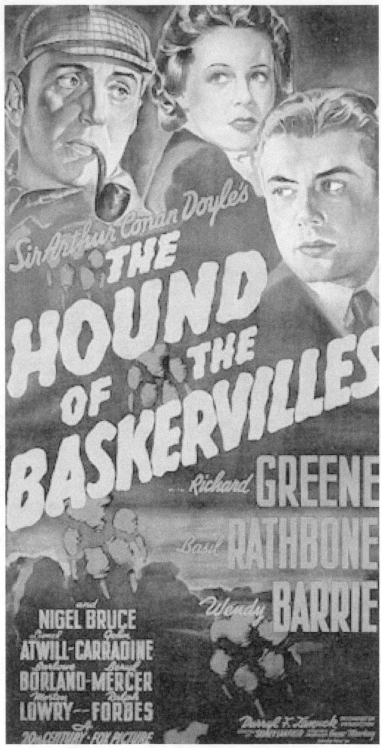

A promotion sheet for the most well known of the "Hounds" films, featuring Basil Rathbone as the famous sleuth, and Nigel Bruce as his faithful sidekick. The first English language adaptation of the Hound of the Baskervilles was an instant success.

There is only one original Sherlock Holmes as far as the author is concerned, and that is Basil Rathbone, who appeared as the detective in numerous films throughout his career.

On the Trail of Britain's Terrifying Phantom Black Dogs:
Folklore, Reality, Sherlock Holmes
and The Hound of the Baskervilles
By
Nick Redfern

Beware of the black dog
© Sidney Paget

BEWARE OF THE DOG!

Imagine the scene: it's late one cold, dark, winter's eve in a little old hamlet in central England. You're walking home, along a winding, tree-shrouded old road with only the light of an eerie full moon to illuminate your path. But, as you continue on your trek to your centuries-old cottage, you begin to feel uneasy.

For reasons that you are unable to fathom, as the icy wind sends a deep chill through your body, you develop the distinct feeling that you are not alone. Rather, you sense that you are being watched and followed by something terrible, something malignant, something nightmarish, and something as ancient as it is mysterious.

Then something truly ominous occurs: you begin to hear the

vague sound of panting – animalistic panting, no less – and the unmistakable sound of heavy, beastly paws hitting the road behind you. A terrible realization suddenly hits you hard: you are being followed, *or stalked*, by some sort of large, predatory animal. It's an animal that – even though you have yet to see it up close and personal – you know deep in your heart has you firmly in its sights.

You quicken your pace, but it's no good. The panting gets louder and closer, as do those paws hitting the road. A low, guttural growl issues forth and, by now crazed with fear, you turn around to face your foe. As you do so, you are instantly frozen to the spot by the immense creature before you.

Without doubt, it is a dog. But, it's unlike any dog you have ever seen before. This hound is huge, close to the size of a small donkey. Its coat is utterly black in color. Its limbs are thick and muscular. And its giant jaws are of a definitive bone-crushing nature. But it's the eyes that are most terrifying of all: they blaze like a pair of hot coals. Fiery, red and fiendish, they bore into your soul as easily as a hot knife would cut through butter.

Summoning up all your strength, and against all the odds, you manage to make a run for it. The local inn is only a quarter of a mile away and you know you can make it. You *have* to make it. After all, you're running for your life with a definitive hellhound on your tail.

You feel the beast's hot breath on your neck as it closes in and you prepare for the absolute worst. But it doesn't come. As you reach the door of the village tavern, the animal suddenly vanishes in a flash of light. Gone, melted away, or dematerialized; however you wish to word it.

Shaking with fear, you stagger into the pub and practically collapse into an old oak chair situated near a flaming fireplace. Your friends all look on in fear: the sheer terror on your pale face has immediately caught their attention.

After a couple of pints of hearty ale to calm your nerves, you finally splutter out the incredible and awful facts of what has just occurred. And an ominous silence grips the entire clientele, barmaids and inn-keeper as you do so.

While the specific nature of the experience is shrouded in mystery, one and all know exactly what has taken place: you have had a close encounter with one of Britain's most notorious, nightmarish and devilish beasts; a creature that, for centuries, has been a staple part of the nation's folklore, mythology, culture and history: the hellhound.

The story I have related above is not fiction. Nor did it occur, as you might imagine, in the distant, fog-shrouded past of ye olde Britain. Not at all: the event in question occurred in a small, centuries-old village in central England called Ranton, which is situated in the county of Staffordshire. And, it took place in 1997, no less.

But what are these infernal creatures? Are they legend, reality, or both? And how, and under what circumstances, did they inspire the most famous, cherished and much-loved Sherlock Holmes adventure-story of all time: Sir Arthur Conan Doyle's *The Hound of the Baskervilles*? Read on: the answers to those questions – and many more – will become terrifyingly clear as we go on a wild and fear-filled hunt for hounds supernatural, horrific and, sometimes, even deadly.

A NOVEL APPROACH

Published in 1902, Conan Doyle's *The Hound of the Baskervilles* tells the memorable and atmosphere-filled saga of the noted and wealthy Baskerville family that has called Dartmoor, Devonshire, England its home for centuries. Truly, a wild, expansive, foggy and boggy locale, Dartmoor is filled with supernatural tales of terror, horror and intrigue – but leading them all is the legend of the terrible hound that haunts the Baskervilles.

After the mysterious death of Sir Charles Baskerville, the only surviving heir to the family fortune – Sir Henry Baskerville – travels to Dartmoor from Canada to take his rightful place as master of Baskerville Hall and as local, revered dignitary. And that's when darkness, murder most foul, mayhem and horror all surface from the murky depths of those old, mystery-saturated moors.

As a result, we see Sherlock Holmes and ever-faithful Dr. Watson hot on the trail of the seemingly supernatural canine that has cursed the family for generations. But, all is not as it seems in a fantastically entertaining saga that pits Holmes and Watson against a brilliant foe who has exploited the folklore of the terrible hound for equally terrible gain.

If you have not yet read *The Hound of the Baskervilles*, then you are in for a big treat. It is, without doubt, a classic unrivaled. But, there's an important question that needs answering: from where did Sir Arthur Conan Doyle find his inspiration for the story? Was it all merely his own, personal invention and imagination?

No, it most certainly was not. Conan Doyle took the lead from all-too-real supernatural occurrences of the paranormal hound variety on Dartmoor. Sometimes, the old saying that truth is stranger than fiction really is true.

It surprises many to learn that Conan Doyle took the lead from a family who owned a huge, old hall near Hay-on-Wye, a small, centuries-old town in Powys, Wales. And, being a friend of the family, Conan Doyle was a regular visitor. Thus the atmospheric abode quickly became – in Conan Doyle's mind – the ideal place for his novel to be set. So, with a few changes here and there to name and location, Baskerville Hall was duly born.

Coupled with that, the legendary creator of Sherlock Holmes had been exposed to the stories surrounding one Richard Cabell, an evil squire whose remains can be found in the Devonshire town of Buckfastleigh. So, as Devonshire folklore tells it, Cabell was a monstrously evil character – possibly one who had even entered into a pact with the Devil himself, and sold his soul for personal gain in the process.

And, when, on July 5, 1677, Cabell finally shuffled off this mortal coil and into the terrible embrace of his fork-tailed, horned master, a pack of supernatural hounds materialized on the old moors and raced for Cabell's tomb, where they howled ominously all night long, and struck cold fear into one and all that called the land their home.

Thus, the story began to develop in Conan Doyle's mind and imagination. He moved the location of the old hall that he so often frequented to Dartmoor, and changed Richard Cabell to the evil Hugo Baskerville. In the process, literary history was made and *The Hound of the Baskervilles* was born.

But there is one important factor to remember: Conan Doyle did not invent Britain's phantom, fiery-eyed hounds. He merely brought them to the attention of the public in spectacularly entertaining, fictional style.

In reality, however, the creature had been prowling around the British countryside for centuries; and particularly so Dartmoor – the fictional home of the world's most famous hound of horror, as we shall now see, in all its awful glory.

DARTMOOR'S REAL DEVIL DOGS

Bowerman's Nose is a large stack of weathered granite on Dartmoor. It can be found on the northern slopes of Hayne Down, about a mile from the intriguingly named Hound Tor and close to the village of Manaton.

According to local legend, a huntsman named Bowerman lived on the moor around one thousand years ago; and while out one day chasing a hare, he and his pack of dogs unwittingly ran into a coven of witches, overturned their cauldron and catastrophically disrupted their dark ceremony. The witches decided that punishment was due.

The next time he was out hunting, one of the witches shape-shifted into a hare, and cunningly led both Bowerman and his hounds into a deadly mire of quicksand-like proportions. And if that was not enough, as a final punishment, the old crone turned Bowerman and his dogs to stone. So the legend goes, today the dogs can be seen as a jagged chain of rocks on top of Hound Tor, while the huntsman himself became the rock formation now known as Bowerman's Nose. Notably, with a little imagination, it is indeed possible to see a human face in the rocky outline.

And the intrigue did not end

Beware of the Wild Hunt
© Frederick Wilhelm Hein

there.

The same area is also rife with ancient tales and legends of a group of diabolical and unholy creatures known as the Wisht Hounds – fearsome devil-dogs with glowing eyes and large fangs. They are said to have a taste for both human flesh and human souls, and ride with the Devil himself, as he crosses the windswept wilds of Dartmoor late at night - and atop a headless, black horse, no less.

According to legend, the Wisht Hounds inhabit the nearby Wistman's Woods – a sacred grove where, in centuries past, ancient druids held pagan rituals in honor of a veritable multitude of old Earth gods and goddesses.

As I know from personal experience, even today Wistman's Woods is a strange and atmospheric locale: situated in a valley on the eastern slopes of Dartmoor's West Dart River, it is comprised of densely-packed, gnarled and dwarfish oak-trees that invoke graphic imagery of a distinctly Lovecraftian nature.

But, such creatures are not limited to Dartmoor. Rather, their exploits have been recorded across pretty much the entirety of the British Isles. As a prime example, I now invite you to accompany me on a journey to the ancient English county of Staffordshire where I grew up, the origins of which date back to around 650AD.

"...the biggest bloody dog I have ever seen in my life..."

Late one evening in the early weeks of 1972, a man named Nigel Lea was driving blissfully across the Cannock Chase woods that dominate much of Staffordshire when his attention was suddenly drawn to a strange ball of glowing, blue light that seemingly came out of nowhere and slammed violently into the ground some short distance ahead of his vehicle and amid nothing less than a veritable torrent of bright, fiery sparks.

Needless to say, Lea quickly slowed his car down to what was a literal snail's pace. And, as he cautiously approached the approximate area where the light had seemingly fallen, was both shocked and horrified to the absolute core to see looming before him, "the biggest bloody dog I have ever seen in my life."

Very muscular and utterly black in color, with a pair of large, pointed ears and huge, thick paws, the creature seemed to positively ooze both extreme menace and overpowering negativity, and had a crazed, staring look in its yellow-tinged eyes.

For twenty or thirty seconds or so, both man and beast alike squared off against each other in classic stalemate fashion, after which time the animal both slowly and carefully headed for the darkness and the camouflage of the tall, surrounding trees, not even once taking its penetrating eyes off of the petrified driver as it did so.

Somewhat ominously it might be said, and only around two or three weeks later at the most, says Lea, a very close friend of his who he had known since his earliest schooldays was killed in an industrial accident, under very horrific circumstances, in the West Midlands town of West Bromwich.

Which today, Lea firmly believes – after having deeply studied, almost to the point of total obsession, the history of British Black Dog lore and the creature's associations with both deep tragedy and death – was directly connected with his strange and unsettling encounter on that tree-shrouded road back in 1972 – as do many others, as we shall later learn.

It is also interesting to note that this was not the only British-based phantom black dog encounter of 1972: on April 19 of that same year, at Gorleston, Norfolk, England, for example, a coastguard named Graham Grant was witness to a huge black dog that was seen charging along the nearby beaches – until it vanished into thin air, that is, never ever to return.

Then, at around 3.20-3.30 a.m. on a particular day in the latter part of September 1972, a nurse returning home from a late-shift at a Sheffield, England, hospital encountered a glowing-eyed, ghostly dog briefly padding around – in what was perceived by the witness as a "disturbed or confused" fashion – on her doorstep, before leaping off into the ethereal, autumn darkness.

Perhaps not merely a coincidence is the revelation that only hours earlier, the nurse had been directly involved in a tragically-unsuccessful attempt to save the life of a young car-accident victim who had been fatally injured in a head-on crash on a main road situated on the fringes of the city of Sheffield.

In a somewhat highly synchronistic fashion, today the now-retired nurse and her husband make their home in the Staffordshire town of Hednesford, right in the heart of the Cannock Chase, where Nigel Lea had his very own terrifying close encounter of the black dog kind more than forty years ago.

THE GHOST HOUND OF BRERETON

In the early-to-mid 1980s, truly surreal and sinister reports began to surface of a creature that became known at a local level as the Ghost Dog of Brereton – a reference to the specific area of Staffordshire from where most of the sightings originated. Brereton once had its very own identity; but today it is considered to be a part of the town of Rugeley – or Rudgeley, as it was originally known, according to the *Domesday Book*, and which translates as "the hill over the field."

With specific respect to the Brereton encounters, the phantom dog at issue was described as being both large and frightening, and on at least two occasions it reportedly vanished into thin air after having been seen by terrified members of the public on lonely stretches of ancient road late at night. In direct response to an article that appeared in the *Cannock Advertiser* newspaper during the winter of 1984/5 on the sightings of Brereton's infamous ghost dog, a member of the public from a local village, one Sylvia Everett, wrote to the newspaper thus:

"On reading the article my husband and I were astonished. We recalled an incident which happened in July some four or five years ago driving home from a celebration meal at the *Cedar Tree* restaurant at about 11.30 p.m. We had driven up Coal Pit Lane and were just on the bends before the approach to the *Holly Bush* when, from the high hedge of trees on the right hand side of the road, the headlights picked out a misty shape which moved across the road and into the trees opposite."

Mrs. Everett continued with her account:

"We both saw it. It had no definite shape, seeming to be a ribbon of mist about 18in. to 2ft. in depth and perhaps nine or 10ft. long with a definite beginning and end. It was a clear, warm night with no mist anywhere else. We were both rather stunned and my husband's first words were: 'My goodness! Did you see that?'

"I remember remarking I thought it was a ghost. Until now we had no idea of the history of the area or any possible explanation for a haunting. Of course, this occurrence may be nothing to do with the 'ghost dog' or may even have a natural explanation. However, we formed the immediate impression that what we saw was something paranormal."

Another person who may very well have seen the phantom hound of Brereton was Sally Armstrong. It was shortly after the breaking of dawn one day in late March 1987, and Armstrong, a now-retired employee of a Shropshire, England-based auctioneering company, was on her way to meet with a client, then living in Brereton, who was employed in the antiques trade. For a while at least, all was completely and utterly normal. But, things were only destined to change - and for the absolute worst, too, it can be convincingly argued.

Shortly before she arrived at the old cottage of the man in question, Armstrong was witness to a monstrous black-hued dog with wild, staring eyes that was sitting at the edge of the main road that runs through the locale of Brereton, and which was staring intently at her as she passed by it.

Somewhat unsettling: as Armstrong drove by the huge beast, she slowed down, quickly looked in her rear-view mirror, and could see that its head had now turned in her direction. It was, apparently, still focusing upon her each and every move.

Armstrong concedes that there was nothing to definitively suggest an air of the supernatural or the paranormal about the fiend-dog she saw more than a quarter of a century ago; however, that its huge presence seemed to both surprise and unsettle her for reasons that she cannot to this day readily explain or rationalise properly, leads Armstrong to conclude that: "...there was just something about it that makes me remember it this much later."

MAN AND ANIMAL

Possibly of deep relevance to the tale of the ghost dog of Brereton was the story of a man named Ivan Vinnel. In 1934, as a twelve-year-old, he had a very strange encounter indeed in his hometown of nearby Burntwood, Staffordshire. The sun was beginning to set and the young Ivan and a friend were getting ready to head home after an afternoon of playing hide-and-seek.

Suddenly, however, the pair was stopped dead in its tracks by the shocking sight of a ghostly "tall, dark man," who was "accompanied by a black dog" that had seemingly materialized out of a "dense hedge" situated approximately ten yards from the boys' position. Both man and animal passed by in complete and utter silence before disappearing – in typical and classic ghostly fashion, no less.

Ivan later happened to mention the details of the unsettling incident to his uncle, who then quietly and guardedly proceeded to tell him that he, too, had actually seen the ghostly dog on several occasions when he was a young child.

And, as is typically the case with ghostly hounds all across the British Isles, the beast was always reportedly seen in the same location: namely, faithfully pacing along the old road that stretches from the village of Woodhouses to an area of Burntwood situated near the town's hospital. And: weird reports from Staffordshire's out-of-place, dog-like beasts continue to surface to this very day.

A MYSTERIOUS DOG ON THE M6 MOTORWAY

It was in the latter part of June 2006 that all hell metaphorically broke loose, when reports flew wildly around the town of Cannock to the effect that nothing less than a fully-grown wolf was roaming and rampaging around the area.

Early on the morning of June 28, motorists on Junction 10A of the M6 Motorway near Cannock, Staffordshire jammed Highways

The site of Nigel Lea's black dog encounter of 1972. Copyright Nick Redfern.

Agency telephone-lines with reports of a "wolf-like creature" that was seen "racing between lanes at rush hour." Gob-smacked motorists stared with complete disbelief as the immense beast, described as being "grayish-black," raced between lanes, skilfully dodging cars, before leaping for cover in the nearby trees.

Highways Agency staff took the reports very seriously at the time, but publicly concluded that the animal was most "probably a husky dog." However, a spokesperson for *Saga Radio* – which was the first media outlet to arrive on the scene – said in reply to the statement of the Highways Agency that: "Everyone who saw it is convinced it was something more than a domestic dog. I know it sounds crazy but these people think they've seen a wolf."

The local newspaper, the *Chase Post*, which has always been *very* quick off-the-mark to report on incidents of mystery animals seen in the vicinity of Staffordshire's old woods, stated on July 6 in an article titled *Great Beast Debate on Net* that: "Internet message boards are being flooded with debates on our front-page revelation last week that a 'wolf-like' creature was spotted by dozens of motorists on the M6 hard-shoulder."

The *Chase Post* further noted, with justified pride and perhaps even a little welcome surprise, that: "Our own website has been thrown into overdrive by the story, which received around 2,600 hits from fans of the unexplained across the globe in the last week alone."

While the highly mystifying affair was certainly never ultimately resolved to the satisfaction of everyone involved – or, it might reasonably be said, to the satisfaction of *anyone* involved, for that matter - the final words went to the Highways Agency, a spokesperson for whom stated that:

"We have received a number of reports that the animal was captured. But we don't know where, who by, or what it was." Of course, this truly open-ended and somewhat vague statement did nothing to resolve the matter, at all.

Perhaps the event had indeed been due to the mistaken sighting of an escaped Husky; however, that does not in any way come close to explaining the eerie encounter of Jim Broadhurst and his wife that occurred while the pair was out for a morning stroll on the Cannock Chase, only a matter of days before the memorably-monstrous events of June 28, 2006 took place.

Broadhurst states that he and his wife had seen, at a distance of about one hundred and fifty feet, what looked very much like "a giant dog" striding purposefully through an opening in the woods. Broadhurst added that deep fear firmly gripped the pair when the creature suddenly stopped and looked intently and menacingly in their direction.

That fear was amplified even further, however, when the beast reportedly, and bizarrely, reared up onto two powerful hind legs and backed away into the thick trees, never to be seen again. The husband and wife, unsurprisingly, fled those dangerous and eerie woods – and have not returned since; ever-fearful of what they believe to be some form of "monster" lurking deep within the mysterious depths of the Cannock Chase.

Interestingly, and certainly unfortunately, in the weeks that followed the encounter, the Broadhurst family was cursed with a seemingly never-ending run of bad luck and disaster that did not abate until well into September of that same year.

THE CREATURE OF THE CATHEDRAL

Moving away from the Cannock Chase, there is the story of the Bradley family of Leeds, England who had the very deep misfortune to encounter one of the now-familiar hounds of hell in early 2009: at no less a site than the Staffordshire city of Lichfield's famous and historic cathedral; which has the distinction of being the only English cathedral to be adorned with three spires.

According to the Bradleys, while walking around the outside of the cathedral one pleasant Sunday morning they were startled by the sight of a large black dog racing along at high speed, and adjacent to the side of the cathedral. The jaw-dropping fact that the dog was practically the size of a pony ensured their attention was caught and held.

Lichfield Cathedral, Black Dog Territory

But that attention was rapidly replaced by overwhelming fear when the dog allegedly "charged the wall" of the cathedral and summarily vanished right into the brickwork as it did so! Perhaps understandably, the Bradleys chose not to report their mysterious encounter to cathedral officials, to the police, or to local media outlets.

Interestingly, a very similar beast – if not, perhaps, the very *same* one - is believed to have been seen only a short distance from the cathedral by a Scottish family with the surname of either Dobson or Robinson way back in the early-to-mid-1950s. The details of this encounter are admittedly vague, scant and hazy in the extreme, however, and were passed on to me, merely as an aside and nothing else really, in the autumn of 1997 by a now-retired journalist who was working in the area at the time.

"...the size of a lioness..."

There is also the following, very significant story. In an article titled *Fresh Sighting of UFOs and Werewolves on Cannock Chase* that appeared in the *Birmingham Post* newspaper on January 15, 2010, it was reported that: "Resident, Jane McNally, recently had a run-in with a mysterious canine creature while out walking with her partner on Cannock Chase."

The *Birmingham Post* quoted McNally as saying: "I was walking with my partner and his dog. We put the dog back on the lead as we thought in the distance there was an enormous dog. As we approached the animal we realised this wasn't a dog and it just stared at us for a while – I said it looked like a fox, but the size of a lioness – it then turned into the wooded area, and we proceeded to walk on. As it turned its long, bushy black tipped tail, we realised it was definitely not a dog. I have just logged onto the net and went on to images of wolves, and can honestly say whatever we saw yesterday was the closest thing to a wolf."

SWYTHAMLEY'S NIGHTMARE

Two further stories of ghostly hounds seen in the county of Staffordshire come from paranormal investigator Tim Prevett, the first of which is focused around Swythamley Hall; a late-18th century country house that can be found near Leek, Staffordshire, and which, today, is classified as a Grade II listed building that has been converted into four separate residences.

The manor of Swythamley was held by the Crown following the dissolution of

Dieuclacres Abbey and, thereafter, had several owners. It was acquired by the Trafford family in 1654, who replaced the original manor-house with a new construction around 1690. The family remained in residence until Edward Trafford Nicholls – who was the High Sheriff of Staffordshire in 1818 - sold the estate to Sir Philip Brocklehurst in 1832.

And, of the particular ghost-hounds of Swythamley, Prevett says: "One of the Traffords of Swythamley, while out hunting with dogs, is said to have leaped over a chasm. Having successfully cleared the precipice with his horse, the hunting hounds were not so lucky. The fell and perished in Lud's Church, where their spectral howls are still heard on occasion today. Their owner is also said to return."

Prevett adds: "A little way to the south west is Gun Hill, past which Bonnie Prince Charlie and his army passed in December 1745. The hill was also the site of a gallows. A black dog haunts this spot, and elsewhere en route to Derby via Leek and Ashbourne, where members of the Highlanders' rebellion perished. It is said the black dogs either mark or guard the Jacobites' final resting places."

THE CREEPY CANINE OF THE CEMETERY

One of the strangest of all sagas began in April 2007, when a local, well respected group of paranormal investigators – the *West Midlands Ghost Club* – traveled out to the Cannock Chase woods of Staffordshire to investigate newly-surfaced reports of what some witnesses described as a large, hairy creature very much resembling a wolf and others a giant, fiendish hound.

Creepy canines haunt Staffordshire's German Cemetery. Copyright Nick Redfern

But, there was something extremely weird about this particular dog or wolf: as well as walking like any normal animal would, this one had the amazing and uncanny ability to rear up onto its hind limbs, which it invariably did when anyone had the distinct misfortune to cross its malevolent path.

One of those whose encounter caught the attention of one of the club's investigators, Nick Duffy, was a mailman who was riding past the cemetery on a motorbike when he became spellbound by the sight of what, at first, he assumed was a large, wild wolf on the loose.

This would be extraordinary enough in itself, as the wild wolf is generally acknowledged as having become extinct in the British Isles centuries ago. That the creature was no mere normal wolf, however, became very obvious to the shocked man when it caught his eye, raised itself upwards on its back legs, and bounded away into the countless trees that envelop the cemetery.

The next witness to come forward to Nick Duffy and his colleagues was a local scout-leader who was walking around the cemetery when he experienced something profoundly similar. Quite understandably not wanting to speak out on the record, Duffy's source, too, initially assumed that the creature he saw lurking among the graves was a wolf - or possibly even a large dog, such as a Husky. It was neither.

On realizing that the animal was large and seemingly running wild, the man slowly and carefully retreated to the safety of his car and slammed the door, at which point, on hearing the noise, the beast rose up on its back legs - to an incredible height of around seven-feet, no less - and raced off into the heart of the woods. The shocking encounter was over. The controversy, however, was just getting started.

The local newspaper, the *Chase Post*, soon got in on the action and began publishing reports suggesting the werewolf secretly made its lair deep amid the many natural caverns and winding, old, man-made mines and shafts that exist deep below the surface of the Cannock Chase.

The beast, some speculated, possibly had a point of entrance and exit somewhere close to the cemetery – something which hardly generated much cheer in those that lived nearby. And that the sightings of the monstrous thing coincided with the mysterious disappearance of a sizeable number of pet dogs in the area, and that several deer had been found horribly mutilated and with significant organs torn out and flesh viciously removed too, only served to increase the escalating anxiety over the presence of the monster of the cemetery.

As the sightings of the creature continued, and the dog disappearances duly escalated, so did the controversy. Derek Crawley, the chairman of the *Staffordshire Mammal Society*, expressed his view that while a wolf could, in theory at least, make a home for itself on the Cannock Chase, in this case there were a couple of problems. First, there was that not insignificant fact that wolves should not have been running wild anywhere in Britain during the first decade of the 21st Century.

Plus, as Crawley also noted, wolves are very much pack-animals. But, the dog-like beast of the German cemetery seemed to be an overwhelmingly solitary beast. No one walking around the graves had ever seen more than one such creature on any given occasion.

Crawley did note, quite correctly, that there were a number of people, locally, who owned Huskies, and he opined that this may have been what people were seeing. Indeed, such a theory might have been considered not just a possibility, but a downright probability, had it not been for that troubling issue of the beast seen running on two legs as well as four.

Thus, with the witnesses steadfastly standing by their claims and assertions, the mystery remained. Or, it's correct to say it remained until the late summer of 2007, when the strange animal vanished either into the ether, some dark and mysterious realm of paranormal origins, or those shadowy tunnels beneath the old woods.

THE HOUND OF THE CASTLE

And then we have the account of Marjorie Sanders. Although Sanders' account can be considered a new one – at least, in the sense that it only reached my eyes and ears in August 2009, during which time I was on a week-long return trip to England – it actually occurred back in the closing stages of the Second World War, when the witness was a girl of ten or eleven.

At the time, Sanders was living in a small village not too far from the ancient and historic Tamworth Castle – which overlooks the River Tame, and which has stood there since it was built by the Normans in the 11th Century; although an earlier, Anglo-Saxon castle is known to have existed on the same site, and which was constructed by the forces of Ethelfreda, the Mercian queen and the eldest daughter of King Alfred the Great of Wessex.

According to Sanders, "probably in about early 1945," her grandfather had "seen a hellhound parading around the outside of the castle that scared him half to death when it vanished in front of him." For reasons that Sanders cannot now remember or comprehend, her grandfather always thereafter memorably referred to the animal in question as "the furnace dog."

Whether or not this is an indication that the spectral dog had the seemingly-ubiquitous fiery red eyes that so many witnesses have reported remains unfortunately unknown; but, it would not at all surprise me if that was one day shown to be the case.

Then, we have the brief but highly thought-provoking account of Gerald Clarke, a Glasgow baker, whose father claimed to have briefly seen a phantom hound with bright, electric-blue-coloured eyes on the grounds of a military base called Royal Air Force Stafford (which is situated only a short distance from the Cannock Chase) in the late 1950s, and while on patrol late one winter's evening.

As was the case with so many other witnesses to such disturbing entities, the elder Clarke quietly confided in his son that the creature "just vanished: first it was there and then it wasn't." And, now it's time to move even further afield.

EAST COAST BLACK DOGS

Perhaps the most famous of all of the phantom hounds of old Britain are those that are said to have frequented – and, in some cases, *still* frequent - the ancient roads and pathways of Norfolk, Essex, Suffolk, and Sussex. Their many and varied names include Black Shuck, the Shug Monkey, and the Shock. The Shuck and the Shock are classic black dogs; whereas, interestingly enough, the Shug Monkey is described as being a combination of spectral monkey and immense hound.

Even their very names have intriguing origins: While some researchers consider the possibility that all of the appellations had their origins in the word *Shucky* – an ancient east-coast term meaning *shaggy* – others suggest a far more sinister theory; namely that Shock, Shuck, and Shug are all based upon the Anglo-Saxon *scucca*, meaning *demon*; a most apt description, for sure.

THERE'S SOMETHING IN THE FOREST

Back in the winter of 1983, Paul and Jayne Jennings of Woodbridge, Suffolk, England, had an encounter of the black dog kind in – of all places - Rendlesham Forest, which was home to Britain's most famous UFO encounter of all; a December 1980 event in which numerous military personnel from the nearby Royal Air Force Bentwaters military base encountered a UFO in the woods. But, UFOs aside, back to the matter of a certain black dog.

Both in their early twenties at the time of the incident, the Jennings were walking along a trail when they saw what Jayne Jennings described as "a big black dog that kept appearing and disappearing." When I asked her to elaborate, she explained to me that they had been walking along a pathway and on rounding a bend in the path came face to face with the dog.

It was a huge creature and, strangely, she said that while the head was unmistakably that of a large hound, the body was more feline in nature. For a moment the Jennings and the dog stared at each other. The dog was not aggressive, Jayne Jennings said. In fact, it had a mournful expression on its face.

But they were shocked when it vanished in the blink of an eye. They were even more shocked, however, when a moment later it reappeared and proceeded to "flicker on and off" four or five times before vanishing permanently. Paul Jennings told me that after the dog's final disappearance, the air was filled with a strange smell that resembled "burning metal."

It was hardly what you could call a positive experience for the terrified pair, and certainly not one they ever wanted repeating – which, most fortunately for them, it was not.

THE BUNGAY BEAST

It was August 4, 1577, when a terrifying event occurred at the village church in Bungay, Suffolk. An account written shortly afterwards, which can be found at the Parish Church of St. Mary in Bungay, tells the story of what took place. Although written in old English – which, to a degree, differs from today's English - its contents are decipherable.

Titled "*A Straunge and Terrible Wunder wrought very late in the parish Church of Bungay*," it reads as follows:

"Immediately hereupon, there appeared in a most horrible similitude and likeness to the congregation then and there present a dog as they might discerne it, of a black colour; at the site whereof, together with the fearful flashes of fire which they were then seene, moved such admiration in the minds of the assemblie, that they thought doomsday was already come.

"This black dog, or the divil in such a likenesse (God hee knoweth all who worketh all) running all along down the body of the church with great swiftnesse and incredible haste, among the people, in a visible forum and shape, passed betweene two persons, as they were kneeling upon their knees, and occupied in prayer as it seemed, wrung the necks of them bothe at one instant clene backward, in so much that even at a moment where they kneeled, they strangely died.

"There was at ye same time another wonder wrought; for the same black dog, still continuing and remaining in one and the self same shape, passing by another man of the congregation in the church, gave him such a gripe on the back, that therewith all he was presently drawn together and shrunk up, as it were a peece of lether scorched in a hit fire; or as the mouth of a purse or bag, drawen together with string. The man albeit hee was in so strange a taking, dyed not, but as it is thought is yet alive; whiche thing is marvelous in the eyes of men, and offereth much matter of amasing the minde."

It was only shortly afterwards that the beast appeared at the church at nearby Blythburgh: "Placing himself upon a maine balke or beam, whereon some ye Rood did stand, sodainly he gave a swinge downe through ye church, and there also, as before, slew two men and a lad, and burned the hand of another person that was there among the rest of the company, of whom divers were blasted."

Black Dog of Bungay.

Today, the people of Bungay continue to celebrate and promote the legend of their very own equivalent of the Loch Ness Monster or Bigfoot. Indeed, even the local football team takes its name from the legendary animal that roamed around town all those centuries earlier.

"...both of them saw it..."

Then there is a manuscript housed at Nottingham County Library, England. Dating from 1952, it tells the brief but intriguing story of a Mrs. Smalley:

"Her grandfather, who was born in 1804 and died in 1888, used to have occasion to drive from Southwell to Bathley in a pony and trap. This involved going along Crow Lane, which leaves South Muskham opposite the school and goes to Bathley. Frequently, along that lane he saw a black dog trotting alongside his trap. Round about 1915 his great-grandson, Mrs. Smalley's son Sydney, used to ride out from Newark on a motorcycle to their home at Bathley. He went into Newark to dances and frequently returned at about 11 o'clock at night. He too often saw a black dog in Crow lane; he sometimes tried to run over it but was never able to. One night Sidney took his father on the back of the motorcycle especially to see the dog, and both of them saw it."

BLACK DOGS OF LONDON

Neil Arnold is one of Britain's most respected of all paranormal authors and sleuths, and whose research for his book *The Mystery Animals of the British Isles: London* has turned up some notable data on the city's black dog legends. Neil says:

Nick Redfern and Neil Arnold.
Copyright Nick Redfern.

"The old Newgate Prison, built in 1188 on the orders of Henry II, was situated just inside the City at the corner of Newgate Street and Old Bailey. The site was said to harbour one of London's most terrifying apparitions, that of an evil black hound. Legend dates back to the reign of Henry III, during a period of extreme famine, where holed up prisoners were alleged to have gorged upon one another to survive!

"One of these victims was said to have been a sorcerer of the darkest arts, who claimed near death that he would seek revenge on the inmates. Although the jail was demolished in 1902, the most fascinating account originates from the pen of a Luke Hutton, who was an inmate in the 1500s, and hanged in 1598.

"This oft-repeated version of the beast comes from 1638, entitled *The Discovery of a London Monster, called the Blacke Dogg of Newgate* in which the narrator tells of entering a pub where he gets into a conversation about the dog, which reads as follows (word for word): 'I maintained that I had read an old Chronicle that it was a walking spirit in the likeness of a blacke Dog, gliding up and down the streets a little before the time of Execution, and in the night whilst Sessions continued, and his beginning thus. In the raigne of King Henry the third there happened such a famine through England, but especially in London, that many starved for want of food, by which meanes the Prisioners in Newgate eat up one another altue, but commonly those that came newly in . . . there was a certain scholar brought tither, upon suspicion of Conjuring, and that he by Charmes and devilish Whitchcrafts, had done much hurt to the kings subjects, which Scholler, mauger his Devil Furies, Spirits and Goblins, was by the famished prisoners eaten up. . .'"

Neil continues:

"With vengeance promised by the prey: '. . . nightly to see the Scholler in the shape of a black Dog walking up and downe the Prison, ready with ravening Jawes to teare out their bowles; for his late human flesh they had so hungerly eaten, and withal they hourely heard (as they thought) strange groanes and cries, as if it had been some creature in great paine and torments, whereupin such a nightly feare grew amongst them, that it turned into a Frenzie, and from a Frenzie to Desperation, in which desperation they killed the keeper, and so many of them escaped forth, but yet whither soever they came or went they imagined a Blacke Dog to follow, and by this means, as I doe thinke, the name of him began.'"

THE REALM OF THE BLACK DOG

Moving on, Neil Arnold adds: "Richard Jones in *Haunted London* writes of 'The Realm Of The Black Dog' at Amen Court, Warwick Lane stating, 'Amen Court is a delightful, hidden enclave of seventeeth to nineteenth century houses, where the Dean and Chapter of St Paul's Cathedral live. At the rear of the court a large and ominous dark wall looms. Behind it once stood the fearsome bulk of Newgate Prison . . . . there remains a tiny passage, which was known as Deadman's Walk. The passage took its name from the fact that prisoners were led along it to their executions, and were buried beneath it afterwards.'"

Neil expands further: "With reference to the phantom hound Jones writes, 'This shapeless, black form slithers along the top of the wall, slides sloppily down into the courtyard and then melts away. Its manifestations are always accompanied by a nauseous smell, and the sound of dragging footsteps.'"

SOUTHERN BLACK DOGS

Turning our attentions away from London, Neil Arnold has more to discuss of a black dog nature from his home-county of Kent, in the south of England. He begins: "In my *Mystery Animals Of The British Isles: Kent* I wrote, 'A black hound was seen during the 1960s on the Wandsworth Road. Researchers claimed that the form was the ghost of an animal killed on the road. The hound would often be seen disappearing into 523 Wandsworth Road, and the haunting occurred for more than four months.'

"In the December of 1962 a proprietor of a fish restaurant situated at the sight of the haunting wrote a letter to the Society for Psychical Research commenting, 'I respectfully bring to your notice a phenomenon that has occurred at the above address, and trust that it may be of sufficient interest for your investigation, which I would welcome.

"In the last six or seven weeks of that period, a large black and beautiful dog was seen to pass from the rear rooms of the premises through the shop, and out into the street, from whence it would turn right, and lope away up the main road and out of sight.

"This visitation occurred six or seven times, always between 6:00 and 6:30 pm, and when we were sitting at a table, in the then empty shop, and with the rear door locked. On one occasion he brushed solidly against my wife's leg, and on each appearance was seen by three of us clearly.'

"Similar harmless ghost dogs have been seen in South East London where a phantom dog was said to prowl the Anchor Tavern, and another pub, the Spanish Galleon of Greenwich, was also said to be haunted by a large mastiff hound. However, the lore of the black dog often concerns hounds which are sinister, often appearing as omens of death or ill luck as discussed. Meanwhile a dog resembling a dachshund is said to haunt an area of Baker Street.

"A large, yellow-colored dog was once said to haunt the old Motley Club at Dean Street, in Soho. It was mentioned by Elliot O' Donnell that a man named Dickson, present at the premises before it shut down, observed on at least three occasions a yellow dog which confronted him on the staircase. On the first occasion the witness threw the dog a biscuit which it ignored and wandered by. On the second occasion the same thing happened but this time Dickson was startled to see the dog vanish into thin air. On the third occasion Dickson threw the dog a piece of meat, which it ignored, and so the man decided to prod the creature with his stick but the object passed through and the animal faded into nothing."

THE BLACK DOG IN THE SECOND WORLD WAR

Cryptozoologist Jon Downes. Copyright Nick Redfern.

Jon Downes, of the British-based Center for Fortean Zoology – one of the very few full-time groups in the world dedicated to the study of unknown animals such as the Chupacabras, lake monsters and sea serpents - says:

"Clues to the emotional *zeitgeist* of a community can be found in the most unlikely places. For example, during the long, hot summer that saw Europe plodding slowly and inexorably towards the most terrible war that mankind had ever known, a country and western song called 'Riders in the Sky' was extremely popular on both sides of the Atlantic. It told the story of an airborne `ghost rider` who drove a herd of cattle whose 'brands were still on fire and their hooves were made of steel,' and whose 'horns were black and shiny and their hot breath he could feel.'

"The hapless observer described how: 'A bolt of fear went through him as they thundered through the sky, For he saw the riders coming hard and heard their mournful cry. Yi-pee-yi-ay, Yi-pee-yi-oh, Ghost Riders in the sky.'"

Downes continues: "This haunting song was revived as an instrumental twenty-two years later by a group called *The Ramrods*, and it is this wordless version that is perhaps most well known today. What is far more important, however, is that the events recounted in the song are an almost exact account of a paranormal event called `The Wild Hunt` which has been reported from all over the Celtic lands of Europe."

THE WILD HUNT AND WILDER HOUNDS

Jon Downes elaborates further: "Belief in the Wild Hunt is found not only in Britain but also on the Continent, and the basic idea is the same in all variations: a phantasmal leader and his men accompanied by hounds who 'fly' through the night in pursuit of something. What they are pursuing is not clear; although Norse legend has various objects such as a visionary boar or wild-horse and even magical maidens known as Moss Maidens.

"Greek myth has Hecate roaming the Earth on moonless nights with a pack of ghostly, howling dogs and the phenomenon has also been reported from Germany, where, according to folklore, the procession includes the souls of unbaptised babies in the train of 'Frau Bertha,' who sometimes accompanied the Wild Huntsman, and which in the Franche Comte was believed to be King Herod pursuing the Holy Innocents.

"The Wild Huntsman everywhere was a demonic figure, who would throw unsuspecting peasants their share of 'game' with horrific consequences. This savage and tricky being is generally thought to be an aspect of Woden, a god who was characterized by his duplicity - as in parts of Germany and Scandinavia the Wild Hunt was known as 'Woden's Hunt.'"

Downes expands on the presence of the black dog at a time of death and disaster: "Certainly, the hounds are universally believed to be portents of war, death and disaster, and a belated traveler hearing them would fling himself face downward on the ground to avoid seeing them. The Devil`s hunting pack, and the related phenomenon of the black Devil Dogs which are sometimes seen singly away from the Wild Hunt, are phenomena that have been reported on more occasions during the war years than on any other occasion - before or since.

"According to historian, Eric L. Fitch: 'A historical personage reputed to lead the Hunt is a character named Wild Edric, who held lands in the Welsh Marches in the eleventh century. In 1067 he led an uprising against the Normans and in 1069 sacked Shrewsbury. It appears that he was never defeated in battle and eluded capture altogether; in fact he made peace with William the Conqueror and actually joined his side. His death is not recorded and tradition has it that he did not die at all, but had to suffer eternal punishment for changing sides by leading a Wild Hunt. It is said that, along with his fairy wife Godda and his band of followers, he races across country in a furious ride."

Downes notes: "It would be interesting to find out whether German observers reported seeing their wild hunt, with 'Frau Bertha,' who seems to be the Germanic equivalent of Godda, during the months preceding the Second World War."

MORE WARTIME ENCOUNTERS

Jon Downes also offers us the following, thought-provoking statement: "Perhaps the most interesting thing about the sightings of the Devil Dogs - either *en masse* or singly during the war years - is the number of sightings by people who could not have been aware of the occult significance of the entity which they had been fortunate (or unfortunate) enough to encounter.

Downes cites the words of one such witness: "At the time, because of the war, my mother and I usually stayed with an elderly gentleman, who had kindly taken us in as 'refugees.' We only went back to the capital when the bombing ceased. The cottage where we lived is still in existence, in Bredon, Worcestershire. My encounter took place one late afternoon in summer, when I had been sent to bed, but was far from sleepy.

"I was sitting at the end of the big brass bedstead, playing with the ornamental knobs, and looking out of the window, when I was aware of a scratching noise, and an enormous black dog had walked from the direction of the fireplace to my left. It passed round the end of the bed, towards the door.

"As the dog passed between me and the window, it swung its head round to stare at me - it had very large, very red eyes, which glowed from inside as if lit up, and as it looked at me I was quite terrified, and very much aware of the creature's breath, which was warm and as strong as a gust of wind.

"The animal must have been very tall, as I was sitting on the old-fashioned bedstead, which was quite high, and our eyes were level. Funnily enough, by the time it reached the door, it had vanished. I assure you that I was wide awake at the time, and sat on for quite some long while wondering about what I had seen, and to be truthful, too scared to get into bed, under the clothes and go to sleep.

"I clearly remember my mother and our host, sitting in the garden in the late sun, talking, and hearing the ringing of the bell on the weekly fried-fish van from Binningham, as it went through the village! I am sure I was not dreaming, and have never forgotten the experience, remembering to the last detail how I felt, what the dog looked like, etc."

ADDITIONAL OBSERVATIONS OF THE BLACK DOG VARIETY

Commenting on the above, Jon Downes says:

"Events like this one are particularly interesting to the fortean investigator - primarily because they seem to provide supportive evidence for the theory that these `creatures` are, in fact, independent entities rather than hallucinations or delusions (caused, it has been suggested, by the witness having prior or preconceived knowledge of the folklore surrounding such `creatures.' In the case of a small child, however, this is almost certainly impossible.

"In East Anglia, there have been sightings of the local Devil Dog, known as *Black Shuck* for centuries. Unlike their counterparts elsewhere in Britain, these 'creatures' are often perceived as being particularly malevolent, and are often described as being physical manifestations of the Devil.

"The black dog which attacked Bungay Church in Suffolk in August 1577, for example, and which left several members of the congregation dead (and tell-tale demonic claw marks which can still be clearly seen on the wooden door of the church), is often considered to be one of these earthly visitations by the Lord of Darkness.

"None of the sightings of Black Shuck during the Second World War are as terrifying as the events chronicled in the previous paragraph, but they do tell us a great deal about the human psyche."

Downes cites the words of author and researcher, Graham McEwan:

"A curious case occurred at Hilly in Norfolk in 1945 when a man heard, but did not see, what he thought was Black Shuck. He became aware of a faint howling which slowly became louder, until it was 'ear-splitting.' It was accompanied by the sound of a chain being dragged along the road. The man, now quite frightened, broke into a run, slowing down as the howling died away. The witness later wrote: 'I later realized that this was the first time I had been afraid of a dog, my hair was standing on end, but why I could not understand . . . . I love dogs and have never been afraid of the fiercest in my life.'"

"...the airman saw a huge black beast..."

"Probably the most terrifying wartime encounter with Black Shuck," says Downes, "is this tantalizingly brief account from Nigel Blundell who wrote: 'Maybe it was Black Shuck who terrified a young American airman and his wife in the early years of the last war. They were staying in a flat-topped hut on the edge of Walberswick Marsh, Suffolk. One stormy evening they heard a pounding on the door. Looking out of the window, the airman saw a huge black beast battering itself against their temporary home. The couple pushed furniture against the door and cowered in terror as the assault went on, the beast hammering against each wall in turn, then leaping on to the roof. After some hours, the noise died away, but the couple could not sleep. At first light, they ventured cautiously outside to inspect the damage. But there was no sign of the attack, and no paw or claw marks in the mud. A similar black dog - the Mauthe or Moddey Dhoo - used to haunt Peel Castle on the Isle of Man. Soldiers on guard duty refused to patrol the ramparts alone. One boastful sentry who did so was found gibbering insanely and died three days later.'"

DOWNES' THOUGHTS ON THE BLACK DOG

Summing up, Jon Downes offers the following, thought-provoking words on the specific nature of the beast under our monstrous microscope:

"One peculiar thing about quasi-fortean phenomena is that they appear to happen in cycles. For example, during the eighteenth and nineteenth centuries there were a large number of reports of living frogs and toads found apparently entombed in solid rock. These phenomena seem to have died out during more recent times, and have been replaced within the pantheon of contemporary forteana by such phenomena as crop circles and sightings of the infamous, black, flying triangles.

"Black Dog sightings have followed a similar pattern. Whereas they have been reported intermittently throughout history, sightings began to tail off in the late nineteenth century. In the interests of brevity, we have only recounted a few of the accounts from the period that are on our files; but the fact that, as we have seen, there was a minor resurgence of them during the years when Europe was at war, is, we feel, somewhat interesting."

Downes closes as follows: "It is also interesting to note that whilst there have been postwar Black Dog sightings across Britain, these have been very few and far between, and it does seem as if our forefathers, who drew an arcane parallel between sightings of `The Wild Hunt` and imminent war and catastrophe, knew more about the nature of reality than we do."

Mark North, black dog authority.
Copyright Nick Redfern.

A CANADIAN CONNECTION

In 2007 the British Center for Fortean Zoology published an updated and revised edition of Mark North's acclaimed book, *Dark Dorset*, which detailed the many and varied mysteries of his home-county of Dorset, England. Around the time of the book's publication, I flew over to England and spoke with Mark about his thoughts on the black dog conundrum, and he told me:

"There are a lot of stories in there about the phantom black dogs. I've done a lot of investigations into the stories and myths around black dog tales. If you go back to the older tradition of black dogs, I think a lot of it could have been invented. On the Dorset coast, for example, there was a very big smuggling trade going on centuries ago. I think a lot of the stories of these animals were invented to frighten people and keep them away from the smuggling areas.

"What was also happening around this time is that Dorset had a lot of connections with Newfoundland and they used to do a lot of trading with the fishermen there. It was around this time that the Newfoundland dogs were brought over here, to this country.

"So, you have a new type of dog being brought over here, which was very large and that no one had ever seen before, and then you have these tales of large black dogs roaming around, and smugglers inventing these black dog tales. So, I think it could be that part of the story at least is that the Black Dog legends have their origins in these large, working black dogs brought over from Newfoundland."

Was it possible that Britain's entire mythology of ghostly black dogs was based solely upon the tall-tales of smugglers? Both Mark and I considered such an all-encompassing possibility to be highly unlikely, given the fact that sightings of such nightmarish beasts had been made all across the British Isles, and long before the smugglers of Dorset were up to their tricks.

In all likelihood, we concluded, those same smugglers had merely modified for their own ends already-existing black dog legends – something which worked even better for them with the introduction to the British Isles of the gigantic Newfoundland hound, which is indeed a formidable-looking animal. Ironically, however, the Newfoundland is actually a gentle animal noted particularly for its love of people.

And as Mark also told me: "Back in the 1600s and 1700s, when many of these stories started, people were very superstitious. Back then, it was a completely different world. And that's what I like about it: it was very innocent in some ways. You've got this superstition of these black dogs there that turn everything around and it made it a completely different world. You could go into some of the old woods, and on the moors, and it would have been like being in a different world, where anything might have happened."

Thus, in Mark's view, there is a very real black dog mystery, but it was one that had been ingeniously exploited by smugglers to scare people away from their plundered hoards – no wonder, then, that the mystery is steeped in both confusion and controversy!

NEWFOUNDLAND OR NIGHTMARE

On June 9, 2007, Martin Whitley, a professional falconer, born and bred in the county of Devon, contacted the research organization *Big Cats in Britain* with the following story: "I was flying a hawk on Dartmoor with some American clients, when one of them pointed out this creature. It was walking along a path about 200 yards away from us. It was black and gray and comparable in size to a miniature pony.

"It had very thick shoulders, a long, thick tail with a blunt end, and small round ears. Its movement appeared feline; then 'bear-like' sprang to mind. There was a party climbing on the Tor opposite, making a racket, but this it ignored completely."

Big-cat researcher Merrily Harpur noted: "Martin's American clients took a series of photos. They show the Dartmoor landscape, the school party on the Tor, and in the middle distance an animal which seems to change shape in each frame, from cat, to bear, to pony, to boar, to various breeds of dog."

Martin was adamant that the animal was no dog: "I have worked with dogs all my life and it was definitely not canine. I have also seen a collie-sized black cat in the area, about ten years ago, and it was not that – this was a lot bigger."

Not everyone was in agreement, however. Shortly after the photographs were provided to *Big Cats in Britain*, copies were also sent to Jon Downes – the Director of the Devonshire-based Center for Fortean Zoology - who confided in me by telephone late one night that, despite the admittedly odd fact that the creature in the pictures did appear to change in shape from shot to shot, he was convinced that it was nothing stranger than a large dog of physical, rather than paranormal, origins; and suggested that the "morphing" effects were merely a by-product of the camera's technical limitations.

Jon was not alone in his opinion. Perhaps inevitably, Britain's media soon latched onto the story. And they soon claimed the answer to the puzzle, too. The *Daily Mail*, in an article titled *That's not the Beast of Dartmoor...it's my pet dog*, revealed that they had spoken with a woman named Lucinda Reid, who lived close to the area, and who was convinced that the photos provided by Martin Whitley actually showed her two-year-old, 168-pound Newfoundland dog, Troy! Certainly, Newfoundlands are huge beasts and can look both imposing and terrifying to the untrained eye. Lucinda told the newspaper:

"I was in stitches when I read that someone thought Troy was the Beast of Dartmoor. I spotted that it was him right away – you can tell by the shape and the way he is walking. We go up to that spot on Dartmoor all the time. It is only ten minutes away from our home and Troy loves to run about there. A lot of people don't have a clue what he is, because he's so big."

Lucinda continued: "Troy frightens the life out of everyone because of his size and he doesn't look like a dog from a distance. He sometimes disappears off round the rocks on his own, and that's when he must have been photographed. But Troy is certainly nothing to be afraid of, he's a big softie. So, if anyone else sees him on the moor – there's no need to panic."

But, given that the locale was none other than definitive black dog territory – namely, Dartmoor - was the hunting ground of the devilish black hounds of centuries-past, the theory persisted that Troy was not the culprit, after all. The legend, almost inevitably, lived on.

Now, with the cases addressed, let's take a look at the theories that have been advanced to explain the presence of these unearthly creatures in our midst.

"...the guardians of the road to hell..."

In his definitive book on the subject *Explore Phantom Black Dogs*, author and researcher Bob Trubshaw wrote thus:

"The folklore of phantom black dogs is known throughout the British Isles. From the Black Shuck of East Anglia to the Mauthe Dhoog of the Isle of Man, there are tales of huge spectral hounds 'darker than the night sky' with eyes 'glowing red as burning coals.' The phantom black dog of British and Irish folklore, which often forewarns of death, is part of a worldwide belief that dogs are sensitive to spirits and the approach of death, and keep watch over the dead and dying. North European and Scandinavian myths dating back to the Iron Age depict dogs as corpse eaters and the guardians of the roads to hell. Medieval folklore includes a variety of 'Devil dogs' and spectral hounds."

FROM MAN TO BEAST

Dr. Dave Clarke, a long-time Fortean, who has a PhD in folklore, says: "One enduring folk belief is that human beings, as well as devils, witches and fairies, could shapeshift and appear in animal form. This type of story appears in trial records, pamphlets and folklore throughout the middle ages where animal familiars are identified with the devil. Earlier accounts lack the preoccupation with demonic creatures. An early list of shape-shifting apparitions was prepared by a Cistercian monk in North Yorkshire around 1400. It contains accounts of ghosts changing forms from human to crow, dog, goat, horse and even a haystack. These are described as human souls trapped in purgatory, appealing for help from the living to escape their predicament."

"...their spirits take permanently the form of animals..."

Elliott O'Donnell was the author of numerous classic titles on all manner of mysteries, but it is his 1912 book, *Werewolves*, that has a bearing upon the very matters under the microscope – namely, the black dogs of Britain.

O'Donnell presented a fascinating body of data in his near-legendary book, which is essential reading for anyone wishing to acquaint themselves with hard-to-find data on all manner of strange beast, including black dogs, and not solely the werewolves of the book's title. Nevertheless, O'Donnell's words are deeply applicable to this particular debate concerning the real nature of the British black dog.

He wrote: "It is an old belief that the souls of cataleptic and epileptic people, during the body's unconsciousness, adjourned temporarily to animals, and it is therefore only in keeping with such a view to suggest that on the deaths of such people their spirits take permanently the form of animals. This would account for the fact that places where cataleptics and idiots have died are often haunted by semi and by wholly animal types of phantasms."

O'Donnell's words relative to "idiots" and "such people" might not be perceived by the tedious politically-correct brigade of today as being particularly heart-warming, but they do, without doubt, offer a theory that is fascinating to muse upon. And, there are other parallels, too, that can be found in folklore. They also deal with the matter of man becoming terrible animal when physical life ends, and at which point a new life - and a highly strange life, I might add - duly begins.

THE DOGMEN OF NEWGATE

Bob Trubshaw notes: "Newgate Gaol was the scene of a haunting by 'a walking spirit in the likeness of a black dog.'" So the story went, says Bob, "Luke Hutton, a criminal executed at York in the late 1590s, left behind an account of the phantom hound. Published as a pamphlet in 1612, *The Discovery of a London Monster, called the black dog of Newgate* suggested the dog was the ghost of a scholar imprisoned in Newgate who had been killed and eaten by starving inmates."

A BROTHERLY BLACK DOG

Then there is the very weird tale of William and David Sutor. The dark saga all began late one night in December 1728, when William, a Scottish farmer, was hard at work in his fields and heard an unearthly shriek that was accompanied by the briefest of glimpses of a large, horrific-looking, dark-coloured dog. And on several more occasions in both 1729 and 1730, the dog returned, always seemingly intent on plaguing the Sutor family.

It was in late November of 1730, however, that the affair ultimately reached its apex. Once again the mysterious hound manifested before the farmer, but this time, incredibly, it was supposedly heard to speak in English, and uttered the following, concise words: "Come to the spot of ground within half an hour."

The shocked William did so; and there waiting for him was the spectral animal.

"In the name of God and Jesus Christ, what are you that troubles me?" pleaded the terrified William. The hound answered that he was none other than David Sutor – William's brother - and that he had killed a man at that very spot some thirty-five years earlier.

William cried: "David Sutor was a man and you appear as a dog."

To which the hound replied: "I killed him with a dog; therefore I am made to appear as a dog, and I tell you to go bury these bones."

Finally on December 3, and after much frantic searching and digging, the bones of the murdered man *were* finally found at the spot in question, and were duly given a respectful, Christian burial within the confines of the old Blair Churchyard. The dog – David Sutor in animalistic, spectral form, legend maintains – vanished, and was reportedly never seen again.

"...man has in him two spirits – an animal spirit and a human spirit..."

The last missive on this admittedly highly controversial aspect of the British Bigfoot controversy goes to Elliott O'Donnell:

"According to Paracelsus, Man has in him two spirits – an animal spirit and a human spirit – and that in after life he appears in the shape of whichever of these two spirits he has allowed to dominate him. If, for example, he has obeyed the spirit that prompts him to be sober and temperate, then his phantasm resembles a man; but on the other hand, if he has given way to his carnal and bestial cravings, then his phantasm is earthbound, in the guise of some terrifying and repellent animal."

While O'Donnell's words were meant as a collective warning to his many and faithful readers, frankly, the latter sounds far more appealing and adventurous than does coming back as some chain-rattling spectre of human proportions. Give me terrifying and repellent, rather than sober and temperate, any day of the week!

OVERSEAS PARALLELS

And now we turn our attentions to the work of Simon Burchell, the author of *Phantom Black Dogs in Latin America*. Running at 38 pages, it is obviously very much a booklet rather than a full-length book. But that doesn't detract from the most important thing of all: its pages are packed with case after case, each offering the reader little-known and seldom-seen information on the definitive Latin American cousin to Britain's more famous counterpart.

And the reason I reference Burchell's title is because his observations on the beast may very possibly offer us more than a few answers to our questions concerning its British cousin.

What impresses and intrigues me most of all about Burchell's publication is the truly startling wealth of similarities between those creatures seen centuries ago in England, and those reported throughout Latin America in the last 100 years: namely:

- the diabolical, glowing eyes;
- the association that the phantom hound has with life after death;
- how seeing the beast may be a precursor to doom and tragedy;
- its occasional helpful and guiding qualities;

-     the fact that the animal is usually witnessed in the vicinity of bridges, cross-roads, and cemeteries – which are classic locales where paranormal activity occurs time and time again; its ability to shape-shift and change in size;

-     and not forgetting the most important thing, of course: namely, its perceived paranormal origins.

Burchell also reveals how the legends of the phantom black dog of some Latin American nations – such as Guatemala – have been exploited by those with draconian and outdated morals. For example, there are widespread tales of people that enjoy having a drink or several incurring the dire wrath of the phantom black dog – which, as Burchell says: "…was certainly popularized by the Catholic Church which used this legend and others as moralizing tales."

Winged hounds – whose appearances and activities smack strongly of the modern day Chupacabras of Puerto Rico and UFO lore – are discussed; as are copious amounts of data that make a link with tales of a truly dark and satanic nature.

Burchell also reveals intriguing data suggesting that at least some tales of the black dog might be based upon cultural memories and stories of very real, large and ferocious hounds brought to the New World by the Conquistadors centuries ago – "savage and ferocious dogs to kill and tear apart the Indians."

That said, however, it is clear that the overwhelming majority of reports of the phantom black dog in Latin America parallel those of Britain to a truly striking, eerie and extraordinary degree – in the sense that they appear to be something other than flesh-and-blood entities.

A Brit, Burchell lived in the highlands of western Guatemala for three years, and knows his stuff. And his is a great little publication written by someone with a passion not just for his subject matter, but for the cultures and countries that appear within its pages.

As Burchell states:

"Although the Black Dog may appear at first glance to be a British or north European phenomenon, it exists in essentially the same form across the entire length and breadth of the Americas. Much has been written upon the presumed Germanic, Celtic or Indio-European origin of the legend but such an origin would not explain how a highland Maya girl can meet a shape-shifting Black Dog at a Guatemalan crossroads. It appears that the Black Dog, much like the poltergeist, is a global phenomenon."

CONCLUSIONS

And there we have it: a tale of a monstrous entity – the fiery eyed black dog - that is equal parts macabre, mystifying, bizarre, terrifying, supernatural, paranormal, eerie and even devilish. As for its origins: well, it seems that the beast – in some fashion, at least – is linked to death, looming death, tragedy, disaster and negativity.

In other words, it's a not a creature with which you particularly want to cross paths. And those origins are clearly most ancient in nature, dating back to the Middle-Ages and possibly even much earlier than that. And that sightings of the hounds of horror extend to the present day and are even celebrated - such as by the people of Bungay, Suffolk – demonstrates the sheer, overwhelming power and allure that the black dog still holds over the people of Britain.

And, as a result of a very curious set of circumstances, theories, sightings, tales and more, the very existence and legend of Britain's black dog directly set in motion the wheels that led Sir Arthur Conan Doyle to write one of the most famous and loved novels of all time: *The Hound of the Baskervilles.*

Regardless of the precise nature and intent of the legendary beast, I say: long-live the spectral black-dog of the British Isles. And long-live *The Hound of the Baskervilles*, which, without its real-life counterpart, would never, ever, have seen the light of day.

Thus, in a very strange and decidedly roundabout fashion, each and every one of us who love Sir Arthur Conan Doyle's adventures of Sherlock Holmes and Dr. Watson have a monstrous beast to thank for one of the world's most famous literary classics! It doesn't get much stranger than that!

REFERENCES:

- *Explore Phantom Black Dogs*, Bob Trubshaw (Editor), Heart of Albion Press, 2005.
- *Dartmoor Mystery Beast*, Merrily Harpur, www.forteantimes.com, August 6, 2007.
- *That's not the Beast of Dartmoor...it's my Pet Dog*, Daily Mail, August 3, 2007.
- *The Hunter with the Stony Visage*, www.bbc.co.uk, October 27, 2005.
- *The Dark Huntsman* and *Wistman's Wood*, www.legendarydartmoor.co.uk.
- *The Hound of the Baskervilles: Hunting the Dartmoor Legend*, Philip Weller, Halsgrove, 2001.
- *Dark Dorset*, Mark J. North & Robert J. Newland, CFZ Press 2007.
- *There's something in the Woods*, Nick Redfern, Anomalist Books, 2008.
- *Monster Hunter*, Jonathan Downes, CFZ Press, 2004.
- *Wildman*, Nick Redfern, CFZ Press, 2012.
- *The Mystery Animals of the British Isles: Staffordshire*, Nick Redfern, CFZ Press, 2012.
- *The Mystery Animals of the British Isles: London*, Neil Arnold, CFZ Press, 2011.
- *The Mystery Animals of the British Isles: Kent*, Neil Arnold, CFZ Press, 2009.
- *Phantom Black Dogs in Latin America*, Simon Burchell, Heart of Albion Press, ??
- *Animal Ghosts: Or Animal Hauntings and the Hereafter*, Elliott O'Donnell, Kessinger Publishing, 2003.

- *Mystery Animals of Britain and Ireland*, Graham McEwan, Robert Hale Ltd., London 1987.
- *Werewolves*, Elliott O'Donnell, Kessinger Publishing, 2003.
- *Strange Staffs*, Tim Prevett, *Paranormal Magazine*, February 2009.
- *In Search of Herne the Hunter*, Eric L. Fitch, Capall Bann Publishing, 1994.
- *The World's Greatest Ghosts*, Roger Boar and Nigel Blundell, Reed International Books, Ltd., 1994.

BIG BLACK DOGS AND PHANTOM HOUNDS IN AMERICA
By Andrew Gable

PART ONE: MARYLAND AND DELAWARE

Legends of black dogs and phantom hounds are widespread throughout the Chesapeake Bay region, which was one of the earliest areas settled by the English. The tales of British black dogs were combined with werewolf traditions and typical ghost stories, as well as possibly with cryptozoological sightings of weird creatures, to create traditions that are like the British ones, and yet unlike them at the same time.

BLACK DOGS OF WARFIELDSBURG

The tiny village of Warfieldsburg in Carroll County is haunted by a black dog. Recounted by Maryland folklorists Annie W. Whitney and Caroline C. Bullock is the story of two men who were riding along near the Ore Mine Bridge at dusk around 1887. They saw a large black dog which passed through a fence, crossed the road, and passed through another fence. Whitney and Bullock also recount the tale of a man who stood under a tree near a bridge, possibly the Ore Mine Bridge, because he was told a phantom black dog would come by. The dog appeared, and according to him the dog followed him for a brief time before vanishing. Yet another instance was of a man who saw a black dog dragging a length of chain. This black dog can apparently never appear more than once to the same person, and it is said that the crack of a whip near it will cause it to vanish. In some variants of the story, the dog is the phantom of Leigh Masters, a notorious Carroll County landowner who was supposedly quite cruel. Masters is also associated with the haunting of Avondale, his manor house.

There was a case in 1975 in which a group of motorists supposedly struck a large black dog standing on a road near Warfieldsburg. They felt the impact of the strike and felt the animal under the wheels, but when the car passed by the black dog was standing in the road, baring its teeth at them before vanishing.

BLUE DOG OF ROSE HILL

Perhaps the oldest ghost story of Maryland is that of the Blue Dog of Rose Hill. Near the town of Port Tobacco (Charles County) is a rock covered in reddish discolorations. Called the "Peddler's Rock," it supposedly marks the spot where a trader was killed at some point in the latter part of the 1700s. In true ghost story fashion, there are many variants of the tale. Some have it that the body was found lying on the rock, some that the body was buried. Some have it that the victim was not a trader, but a returning Civil War soldier. In any case, the man's money was left behind, and his dog - a great blue-tinged mastiff, almost black - was killed during the murder. After the crime, the men returned to seize the treasure and were warded off by howling and then charged by a large, luminous dog.

During the Civil War, men under the command of General Joseph Hooker supposedly tried to retrieve the peddler's treasure but were, like the murderers, frightened away by howling and the approach of a large hound. I don't know of any confirmation of this story, but in the early 1860s General Hooker was, indeed, engaged in maneuvers around Washington, D.C. (The number of camp followers attached to Hooker's army, by the way, were the source of hooker, a common slang term for prostitute). As recently as February of 1971, locals claimed to hear the howling of the dog coming from the vicinity of the Rock.

It could be just another variant of an urban legend or a wholly separate story, but the city Frederick (Frederick County) has its own Blue Dog of Rose Hill. The grounds of Rose Hill Manor off Route 355 in the northern part of the city are also haunted by a phantom blue dog. This blue dog was the pet of a previous owner of the manor. The owner had buried treasure "six feet from the old oak tree" on the property. The ghostly dog appears at midnight, wanders the grounds, and vanishes as mysteriously as it appeared. Now-deceased Maryland researcher Mark Chorvinsky of "Strange Magazine" investigated the tales of the Frederick Blue Dog.

The tales of Snarly Yow were enough to scare the daylights out of any believer.

SNARLY YOW

"Snarly Yow" is the name given to a phantom hound which haunted a section of the National Pike near Turner's Gap (Frederick County). The hound was first mentioned by Madeleine V. Dahlgren in 1882. Her book, "South Mountain Magic," details no less than a dozen sightings of the beast. One account is from a Daniel Mesick, whose father kicked at a huge dog near Dame's Quarter. His foot passed directly through it. Sticks, rocks and even bullets were recorded as having passed through the beast in Dahlgren's accounts. Other accounts have stated that the dog left physical traces and frightened horses to the extent that they threw their riders. The dog was seen numerous times by a minister at a small church in Glendale. A staple of Frederick County legendry for years, the Yow was seen in 1962 near Zittlestown. In this instance, it was headless, white, and dragged a chain along behind it.

The South Mountain area is also the traditional home of a number of werewolves.

FENCE RAIL DOG

The Fence Rail Dog is an enormous hound, nearly ten feet in length, which haunts a stretch of Route 12 near Frederica in Delaware. Mentioned by Charles J. Adams III, a Pennsylvania-based author on paranormal topics, the dog appears in the wake of automobile accidents on the road. Not much information is at hand, but as folklore from around the globe speaks of dogs as a sort of psychopomp – or spirits which guide the dead to the afterlife – its appearance in the wake of death may be an example of this.

RED DOG FOX

The Brandywine Creek State Park in northern Delaware near Wilmington is home to appearances of a large dog or fox which is often seen to rise up into the apparition of Gil Thoreau, an outdoorsman. Once again, not much information is known on this creature.

BULLBEGGER CREEK

It isn't technically in Maryland or Delaware, but in the northern portion of the small finger of Virginia on the Delmarva Peninsula is a feature called Bullbegger Creek. There is also a nearby village called Bullbegger. British readers will be familiar with the term, which refers to a phantom or goblin that haunted several regions across the isle. Traditions do exist in Virginia of free-roaming humanoid phantoms which change into black dogs, but I can't place those traditions geographically and can't say definitively whether this accounts for Bullbegger Creek's name. It is certainly an odd name, however! I wouldn't doubt there are some sorts of traditions are around there.

Many of the dog-beasts were said to be able to stand erect and rip the throats out of human victims.

As can be seen from the above cases, the phantom hounds found in this region of the eastern United States are both similar to, and different from, the British cases. Chain-dragging seems to be a fairly common feature of the accounts, as it is in the cases of the Gytrash and other English hounds. Only the dog haunting Warfieldsburg is reputed to follow individuals as is common in the British lore. Another common feature of the stories (also common to Pennsylvania lore, as will be discussed later) is a clearly phantasmal nature, and in several of the instances the dog is clearly defined as the phantom of a specific individual.

An interesting facet of the case is that the dog traditions seemed to, for the most part, die off in the 1970s, the late 1960s and 1970s being the timeframe that Bigfoot sightings began in earnest in Maryland. Also interesting is that some sightings, particularly of Frederick County's "Dwayyo" in 1973, do have a rather canine cast to their features. One wonders whether some of what are reported as Bigfoot sightings are actually sightings of black dogs

PART TWO: PENNSYLVANIA

ADAMSTOWN BLACK DOG

In the northern corner of Lancaster County lies the small burg of Adamstown. The town is haunted by no less than four separate phantoms – two female ghosts called the White Lady and the Black Lady, a headless swine, and, most relevant to this volume, a small black dog which appears seemingly at random. The dog follows pedestrians and then vanishes as mysteriously as it appeared.

HANS GRAF CEMETERY

A prominent urban legend in Lancaster County circles around a cemetery on the outskirts of Marietta, near the tiny village of Rowenna. Properly called the Shock Cemetery (a name infamous in black dog circles in its own right), and also known at times as the Wildcat Cemetery, the burying ground is called the Hans Graf Cemetery in most parlance. While the graveyard doesn't hold the grave of Hans Graf, one of the earliest settlers of Lancaster County (a popular misconception), the name is inspired by a plaque on the surrounding wall which states that "Within this God's acre rest the descendants of Hans Graf." The cemetery is actually far from an "acre" - it's barely as big as my living room. Bizarrely, the cemetery has no gate or other entry - it is bounded by an unbroken stone wall roughly three feet high.

This tale has been a particular passion of mine for some years. Stories I've heard associated with the cemetery include mysterious lights within its bounds, winds with little to no apparent origin, that walking the walls seven times by the light of a full moon will cause death, and that walking the walls backwards thirteen times summons some manner of ghoul. The most common tales, however, are those of a phantasmal white dog which haunts its grounds. Many are the tales of people who've heard a barking dog as they approach or enter the cemetery. The spot is a favorite one for local paranormal investigators, and several have received EVP voices from the cemetery. One investigator has seen a white dog or wolf appear and vanish within the grounds.

On the trip I made to the cemetery, I noted that though the cemetery as a whole was disgustingly overgrown, there was a roughly man-sized spot in the corner bare of vegetation. The spot was also present on several subsequent trips I made. I vaguely seem to recall something about a spot where nothing would grow in the version of the tale I heard - but as that was years ago, I can't swear to it. As I first approached the walls, I did indeed hear a dog barking. Although my dog was in the car, I'm certain that's not what this was. I found some graffiti on the back wall which may have been simply that, but which appeared to be some runic lettering in the Futhark language as well. I personally saw or experienced nothing, but back in the car my dog was apparently reacting to something, frantically jumping back and forth and finally cowering in the back seat.

MR. ETLINGER AND MR. ELLINGER

In 1909, Pennsylvania folklorist Henry W. Shoemaker penned "The Black Wolf of Oak Valley." In this story, an outlaw by the name of Silas Werninger was cornered in his home, but committed suicide rather than be captured by his pursuers. He was buried in the forest near his home, and after his death a large black wolf emerged from the grove and menaced townspeople. A witch advised the people to dig up Werninger's remains and bury them in consecrated ground in order to dispel the phantasmal wolf.

This tale was a thinly-veiled reference to real events which took place in Centre County, Pennsylvania, in 1896. The true name of the outlaw was William Etlinger, and he was indeed cornered in his cabin near the town of Woodward after taking his wife and children hostage. Etlinger committed suicide amidst the wreckage of his home, which was burnt by authorities in an effort to flush him out. He was, indeed, buried in the mountain forests near his burnt cabin as nobody would claim the body for burial; and his body has, indeed, been removed from its wooded grave to the town cemetery.

Although there are ghostly legends associated with the Etlinger debacle, they seem to involve the appearance of a phantasmal cabin on the burnt foundations where his once stood. So how did the black dog become associated with the legend? For one thing, northern Pennsylvania and more specifically the exact region where these events happened has historically had a population of troublesome black wolves. It isn't inconceivable that a black wolf loitered around Etlinger's grave in order to get itself a free meal and that this was the reason the body was moved.

A more intriguing possibility is provided by no less than the governor of Pennsylvania in the early years of the 20th Century, Samuel Pennypacker. Pennypacker was a tireless researcher into the folklore of the area where he resided - near Schwenksville in Montgomery County. Writing in 1907, the governor uncovered tales of the local ne'er-do-wells, the Ellingers. The Ellingers, he discovered, were originally blacksmiths (William Etlinger was also a blacksmith, according to some contemporary news accounts), but went on to operate a tavern along the Skippack Pike where they robbed and murdered a number of travelers. The creek-side forests near the Ellinger tavern were the haunt of many a phantom for years afterward, ranging from headless horses and calves to ghostly fireballs and skeletal shepherds.

There were also tales of white demonic dogs associated with the Ellinger ruins. Around 1890, a man named Frank Ziegler was riding on the road near the ruins of the tavern when his horse froze in fear. From out of the ruins came a massive white dog which gradually dissolved into shadow. In 1896 Henry Wireman encountered a monstrous phantom "with eyes as large as plates" near the ruins - although it isn't specified whether this was caniform, the dinner-plate eyes are certainly a feature of many black dog reports.

Another man - Henry Landis, a principal at a Philadelphia school - recounted how his horse froze near the tavern immediately before the appearance of another white dog, which on this occasion reared onto its hind legs and snapped at the horse. As Landis frantically rode off, he glanced back to see the still-bipedal dog gradually fade away as it did on the previous occasion.

As both a folklorist and a contemporary, it seems highly likely that Pennypacker and Shoemaker would have communicated. I find myself wondering whether Pennypacker mentioned these legends to Shoemaker - and whether he, in turn, vaguely remembered the stories of blacksmiths named Ellinger as he wrote the tale and remembered it as stories about a blacksmith named Etlinger.

DEATH RODE A PALE...WOLF?

In his "*American Myths & Legends*," folklorist Charles Skinner recounted a tale from Warren County (not Venango, as the title of the tale implies). A huge white wolf lived on the Cornplanter Reservation (now

It is not uncommon to hear tales of shapeshifting from demon dog to full-fledged werewolf.

inundated beneath the waters of Lake Kinzua), and was associated in particular with the Jacobs clan of Native American huntsmen. Sightings of the wolf were thought to be a sure sign of misfortune to follow. A group of hunters caught wind of the stories and took to the chase – during this hunt, Jim Jacobs, patriarch of the clan, encountered the white wolf and was killed in an accident a short time later (this detail likely dates the story to the late 1870s, as Jim Jacobs – who definitely was a real figure – was killed by a train in 1880). At the conclusion of this hunt, however, the white wolf plunged over a gorge to elude capture and vanished in mid-air. A record-sized wolf was, indeed, killed on the Cornplanter Reservation in the late 1870s; also, a popular tale associated with Jim Jacobs claims that he killed a huge wolf in a snowstorm when only a child – the white wolf could have been the phantom of that one.

THE DOGS OF LOCK HAVEN

An urban legend circulating among the students of Lock Haven University and the townsfolk concerns a large hilltop cemetery near the grounds of the college. Said to be used for Satanic rites (but then, according to legend, what cemetery isn't?) and also in the vicinity of several Indian burial grounds, according to a 2009 "*Lock Haven Express*" article, the cemetery is reputedly haunted by a number of black canine forms, which are usually concentrated near a certain mausoleum in a back corner. Sloan Hall, the section of the university nearest the haunted cemetery, is in turn haunted by several phantoms. One of these is an eerie and mobile black mist, which may have some sort of connection to the dogs.

THE HELL HOUND TOLD YOU NOT TO!

In his pioneering book *Lo!* (1931), Charles Fort mentioned the tale of a talking dog. The actual tale, mentioned in a Pittsburgh newspaper, was far more sinister than Fort's humorous recounting made it seem: a small dog walked in front of two men and greeted them with a rather cheerful "Good morning!" But then the dog made a second utterance, "I speak for myself," and walked on. One of the men lunged to grab the dog, which moved out of his way and said, "Don't touch me." The man didn't listen, and severely scorched his hand when it made contact with the conversant canine.

THE WEREWOLF AND MS. PAUL

May Paul, who lived on her family's farm along the Schwaben Creek in Northumberland County, gradually befriended an old hermit. The old man often came and sat on a log, watching her herd her family's sheep. The other wolves in the area were frightened off by the mere sight of the old man. One night (in the 1850s or thereabouts) a local farmer shot a huge gray wolf, which he then tracked to a hut where he discovered said hermit dying of a gunshot wound. The Pauls later claimed that in subsequent years, their sheep were never the targets of wolf attacks, even though neighbors lost their livestock to the carnivores. Was the spirit of the werewolf protecting the flock even after his death? The area of the Paul's farm is now called *Wolfmannsgrob* – "the wolfman's grave."

THE WHITE WOLF OF SUGAR VALLEY

Henry W. Shoemaker recounts the story of a huge white wolf seen in this region of Clinton County near Loganton. First encountered by Philip Shreckengast, the white wolf killed livestock and generally made itself a nuisance. The people of Sugar Valley sought the aid of Granny McGill, a witch, who suggested that a black lamb, born under a new moon in the autumn, be tied near a trap. The plan worked and the wolf was captured. John Schrack of Carroll had the pelt, which had shaggy hair like a sheep or goat rather than the short hair of a wolf (I am endeavoring to determine whether this pelt is still in existence). The head of the wolf was reputed to keep wolves away from Jacob Rishel's sheep paddock, to flash green light from its eyes at night and to move its jaws.

WAYNE SPOOK WOLF

In his 1920s book on the lore of the wolf in Pennsylvania, Henry W. Shoemaker recounts the tale of George Wilson of Wayne Township, Clinton County, who long believed a neighbor of his was a werewolf. He shot a large brownish wolf in the foreleg with a silver bullet one night, and soon afterwards the suspected witch was found to have a broken arm. Then, a few years later, Wilson again shot a werewolf when a three-legged wolf was found on his property. I'm personally uncertain whether Shoemaker meant that it was completely missing a leg (three-legged animals in general were held to be portents of evil among the forests of Pennsylvania), or whether a lame animal was meant, thereby implying it was the same wolf previously shot.

The weird world of the strange has a contented home at the Albany Rural Cemetary.

CHARLES FORT LIES BURIED NEARBY – THE RED-EYED HOUNDS OF ALBANY'S RURAL CEMETERY

By Claudia Cunningham – The "MIB Lady"

One cannot help but get the feeling that the spirit of Charles Fort is keeping close tabs on the paranormal events taking place in the Albany Rural Cemetary. (Photo by Penny Lane)

Tim Beckley must have figured that my favorite Sherlock Holmes tale is "The Hound of the Baskervilles," which I have on an old VHS video tape and have played many times. It's a great story and it parallels so much of the information we have on the sightings of phantom hounds and devil dogs. I am not surprised to learn that in some ways it is based on historical cases of these specters that Sir Arthur Conan Doyle obviously knew about.

I have been friends with Tim now for several years. He calls me "the MIB Lady" because I have collected quite a number of stories about the notorious men-in-black, especially those encounters that have taken place near where I live in upstate New York. We have done several radio talk shows together discussing the matter, including Coast to Coast AM and The Para Cast.

Initially, I told the editor of "The Conspiracy Journal" that I knew of a haunted cemetery where Charles Fort, the great researcher and writer, is buried, along with one of our lesser known presidents, Chester Arthur. It's the Albany Rural Cemetery just outside of the state capitol of New York and as far as I am concerned it's rather spooky.

* * * * *

And perhaps the site where Fort and his entire family are entombed is a fitting locale for dastardly black hounds and phantom dogs from hell to be seen. Fort collected such beastly stories throughout his writing career and placed them in the volumes that make up "The Complete Works Of Charles Fort" (available in a 1000-plus page, 4 volume, large print set available directly from the publisher of this current work).

Often the hounds were found to be hideous killers of farm animals and even household pets that had wandered out upon the moors. As a case in point, let us take these typical examples that have been culled from Fort's intensive studies. Are these refer-

While no black phantom dogs with glowing red eyes or MIB were seen, researchers Tim Beckley and Claudia Cunningham scope out the area around the gravemarker of Charles Fort searching for anything unusual.

ences to a phantom hound, or just some annoying "large dog," or something too thorny to contemplate?

In the month of May, 1810, something appeared at Ennerdale, near the border of England and Scotland, and killed sheep, without devouring them, sometimes slaughtering seven or eight of them in a night by biting into the jugular vein and sucking the blood. That's the story. The only mammal that I know of that does something like this is the vampire bat. It has to be accepted that stories of the vampire bat are not myths. Something was ravaging near Ennerdale, and the losses by sheep farmers were so serious that the whole region was aroused. It became a religious duty to hunt this marauder. Once, when hunters rode past a church, out rushed the whole congregation to join them, the vicar throwing off his surplice on his way to a horse. Milking, the cutting of hay, and the feeding of livestock was neglected. For more details, see "*Chambers' Journal*," 81-470. On the 12th of September, someone saw a dog in a cornfield and shot it. It is said that this dog was the marauder, and that with its death the killing of sheep stopped.

For about four months, in the year 1874, beginning on January 8th, a killer was abroad in Ireland. In "*Land and Water*," March 7, 1874, a correspondent writes that he had heard of depredations by a wolf in Ireland, where the last native wolf had been killed in the year 1712. According to him, a killer was running wild in Cavan, slaying as many as 30 sheep in one night. There is another account, in "*Land and Water*," March 28. Here, a correspondent writes that in Cavan sheep had been killed in a way that led to the belief that the marauder was not a dog. This correspondent knew of 42 instances, in three townships, in which sheep had been similarly killed – throats cut and blood sucked, but no flesh eaten. The footprints were like a dog's, but were long and narrow and showed traces of strong claws. Then, in the issue of April 11th of "*Land and Water*," came the news that readers had been expecting. The killer had been shot. It had been shot by Archdeacon Magenniss, at Lismoreville, and was only a large dog.

This announcement ends the coverage in "*Land and Water*." Almost anybody, at least in the distant past, before suspicions regarding conventional journalism had developed to what they are today, who read these accounts down to the final one, would say, "Why, of course! It's the way these stories always end up. Nothing to them."

But it is just the way these stories always end up that has kept me busy. Because of my experiences with the "pseudo-endings" of mysteries, or the mysterious shearing and bobbing and clipping of mysteries, I delved more into this story that was said to be no longer mysterious. The large dog that was shot by the Archdeacon was sacrificed not in vain, if its story shut up the minds of readers of "*Land and Water*," and if it be desirable somewhere to shut up minds upon this earth.

See the "*Clare Journal*," issues up to April 27th: the shooting of the large dog, with no effect upon the depredations; another dog shot; and the relief of the farmers, who believed that this one was the killer; still another dog shot, that again was supposed to be the killer; then the killing of sheep continuing. The depredations were so great as to be described as "terrible losses for poor people." It is not definitively said that something was killing sheep vampirishly, but that "only a piece was bitten off, and no flesh sufficient for a dog ever eaten."

The scene of the killings shifted.

"*Cavan Weekly News*," April 17, reported that near Limerick, more than 100 miles from Cavan, "a wolf or something like it" was killing sheep. The writer says that several persons, alleged to have been bitten by this animal, had been taken to the Ennis Insane Asylum, "laboring under strange symptoms of insanity."

It seems that some of the killings were simultaneous near Cavan and near Limerick. At both places, it was not reported that any animal known to be the killer was shot or identified. Given that these things may or may not be dogs, their disappearances are as mysterious as their appearances.

There was a marauding animal in England toward the end of the year 1905. London's "*Daily Mail*," Nov. 1, 1905, reported "the sheep-slaying mystery of Badminton." It is said that, in the neighborhood of Badminton, on the border between Gloucestershire and Wiltshire, sheep had been killed. Sergeant Carter, of the Gloucestershire Police, is quoted as saying, "I have seen two of the carcasses myself, and can say definitely that it is impossible for it to be the work of a dog. Dogs are not vampires, and do not suck the blood of a sheep, and leave the flesh almost untouched."

And, going over the newspapers, just as we're wondering what's delaying it, here it is:

London's "*Daily Mail*," December 19: "Marauder shot near Hinton." It was a large, black dog.

So then, if in London any interest had been aroused, this announcement stopped it.

We go to newspapers published nearer the scene of the sheep-slaughtering. "*Bristol Mercury*," November 25, reported that the killer was a jackal which had escaped from a menagerie in Gloucester. And that stopped mystification and inquiry, in the minds of readers of the "*Bristol Mercury*."

Suspecting that there had been no such escape of a jackal, we go to Gloucester newspapers. In the "*Gloucester Journal*," November 4, in a long account of the depredations, there is no mention of the escape of any animal in Gloucester, nor anywhere else. In following issues, nothing is said of the escape of a jackal, nor of any other animal. So many reports were sent to the editor of this newspaper that he doubted that only one slaughtering thing was abroad. "Some even go so far as to call up the traditions of the werewolf, and superstitious people are inclined to this theory."

We learn that the large, black dog had been shot on December 16th, but that in its region there had been no reported killing of sheep, from about November 25th. The appearance of the data leads to another scene-shifting. Near Gravesend, an unknown animal had, up to December 16th, killed about 30 sheep (London's "*Daily Mail*," December 19). "Small armies" of men went hunting, but the killing stopped, and the unknown animal remained unknown.

I go on with my yarns. I no more believe them than I believe that twice two are four.

* * * * *

I have a friend, Linda, who initially told me all about the Albany Rural Cemetery and the creepy, eerie stories associated with this massive city of the dead. And believe me, there are quite a few of them!

One day Linda was driving along its many twisting and turning roads, passing by large mausoleums and musty crypts. There are a number of historical figures, like mayors and governors, not to mention the man who spent his entire life investigating the strange and unknown.

It was a rather nice day, as Linda spins her account. It was warm and sunny, but there were several shadowy patches she could drive through that emitted a cool breeze of a sort in contrast to the brilliant glare that encompassed her car, blinding her at times.

She went up a hill and around a curve and pulled over to stop. She felt someone was following her. Suddenly, she was astounded to see a massive black SUV, almost military-like, so close behind her it could have parked in her rear seat. The vehicle looked like it had just pulled out of the showroom,￼ it was so neat and polished – just like in the tales "Mothman Prophecies" author John Keel wrote about the vehicles the men-in-black were known to arrive in as they went about their task of silencing UFO witnesses.

Most astonishing of all is the fact that while the roads were paved with gravel she never heard a sound as the strange vehicle pulled up close and eventually passed her. As the SUV crept along, she noticed the windows were completely black and – most fear-provoking of all – it turned down one of the side roads that would take you back to the main entrance to the cemetery . . . only when Linda tried to follow in close pursuit the road ended onto a chain fence which it would have been impossible to drive through.

Later, as she drove by the main office to leave the cemetery, she saw the car parked in the middle of the road as if it were waiting for her. One moment there was a "person" standing next to the vehicle only to vanish – blink out – in her rearview mirror.

Eventually, I did some checking around and found that others had encountered vanishing black cars, more men-in-black and a couple who fly over the headstones at dusk in their pajamas.

This is in addition to the legends of the big black dog that wanders about at night with its blazing red eyes. One couple claims to have heard the clumpity, clump, clump of some heavy animal paws right along the road where my friend Linda says the SUV vanished through a chained off area. They were apparently walking their own dog, possibly a poodle, when they were overcome with fear and concerned for the safety of themselves and their pet and decided to pick up the pace. When they got under what they thought was the safety of some street lights, they turned around and looked into the face of a huge black dog with red eyes – at least they thought it was a dog – and the funny thing is that their own dog merely walked on without reacting to this "monster"-looking beast.

The phantom creature walked really fast, keeping up with the couple as they ran near the gates. As they watched, the dog simply blinked out as if it had never existed. This is a very common urban legend around these parts, but where there is smoke there is usually fire.

PROFESSOR JAVA'S AND MY OTHER DUSTY DOG STORIES

Not too far away is Professor Java's, located in Albany on Wolf Road (is it a coincidence that it is so justifiably located?) where it is said that an Indian woman has been seen floating in through the back door, but quickly disappearing. Bottles have been known to fly off the shelves behind the bar and people have heard a ghost baby crying as well as the sound of a howling dog who seems troubled by something. To confirm these rumors, I went to the restaurant and had dinner there with a girlfriend once and we DID hear a dog barking faintly. I talked with a barmaid to confirm this, and she said the week before the situation was really bad. On one particular night bottles would shatter and fall off the shelves as if being pulled down by an invisible hand.

I have two mysterious ghostly dog stories of my own to contribute to the strange canine legacy. They may not seem so scary, but I can vouch that they are true.

Our dog Napoleon – a mix of Doberman and Lab – died while my grandmother was living with us. My grandmother was very attached to the dog, as we all were. He lived to be 15 years old, but we were still very unhappy about losing him. About a week or so after he passed on, my grandmother had just gotten into bed and had turned the light off. In the dark, she heard Nappy's little chain that he wore around his neck rattling and actually felt the thump-thump-thump-thump of his tail hitting the side of the bed, like he used to do when he was happy to see someone. My grandmother had a history of such paranormal experiences. She said she saw my uncle who died in World War II standing directly in front of her, and even had a sighting of my deceased father shortly after his passing. Naturally, because of her familiarity with the afterlife, I wasn't too surprised to hear that Nappy had paid Gram one last visit.

Also, my mother had a little Yorkie, Jack. I had given her Jack after her little dog Tiffany died. Jack was quite a character, a sprightly and lively Yorkshire Terrier. Everyone was in love with him. My grandmother had died, as did little Tiffany, so I thought Jack would be just the kind of dog to cheer mom up. He was all personality and charm . . . if you can describe a dog that way. My mother was devoted to him. Sadly, he developed diabetes and his last years were spent in agony. He had to be put to sleep. I thought I would lose her because she cried night and day. So I moved mom into my place in Delmar for two years before we moved together back to her home in Glenmont.

My mother was in my guest room asleep one night and she told me the next morning she awoke to see a big black butterfly gently fly across the room. The wings were very lacey looking, and it floated into her bathroom and disappeared. She was amazed and wondered if she dreamed it.

Then a month later I knew I had to replace Jack because my mother wasn't any better, so my friend who runs the Greene County Humane Society recommended I come and fetch a charming Pekingese named Stella to replace Jack. Once I saw her I fell in love with her and, being a quiet lap dog, she would be perfect for my mother, who is in her 90s. I drove down to Hudson to have a look at her, and promised I'd be back in a couple of weeks to bring her home. My mother was still grieving and I wanted to give her time to pull herself together before bringing Stella home, as I thought she wasn't ready for another dog.

One Saturday, before getting Stella, we went to a thrift store and my mother said,

"You know, I think the black butterfly was Jack telling me he was in Heaven." A sentimental and charming thought. Then she asked me to look around for a figurine with a butterfly on it. I said, "Look at what you're leaning on!" and there was this big gold butterfly with lacey wings! There are no coincidences in life. It is still on her dresser next to Jack's picture.

The night before I brought Stella home, mom saw the butterfly again, and we think this was Jack saying, "It's OK to replace me . . ."

It's funny, but I bought a book on animals in the afterlife and the first paragraph said that animals have a way of telling us they are OK after they pass, and they will send you butterflies, which stand for eternal life. And he did. Funny, but that first year after losing him all we saw was butterflies in the yard . . . even into November!

Tim Beckley notes that Harry Houdini may have also appeared as a butterfly as proof of life after death because apparently he wasn't able to come through a medium utilizing direct voice communications or physical materialization. Beckley says that another immensely popular celebrity he met is said to have "come back" to Earth in a similar manner, but for "delicate" privacy reasons he cannot name this well known personality, though he once had a TV show that was enormously popular and made him a household name to this day.

I am sure Charles Fort would have had a comment or two on these personal tales as well as the ones he was able to document on his own. Black dogs and phantom canines are the thrust of this work and obviously had a deep impact on Sir Arthur Conan Doyle and the writing of one of my favorite works, "The Hound of the Baskervilles."

The Man Who Fell From A Clear Blue Sky

by

William Kern

All Rights Reserved 2012

William Clifford Kern
6460-65 Convoy Court
San Diego, California 92117
May 21st, 2012

I have often wondered if "changelings," especially human/ wolf changelings (hulfs) have not gotten a bad rap in the pages of contemporary literature. Certainly, there is ample anecdotal evidence to indicate that "werewolves" have existed and that they may have been responsible for gruesome crimes. But what if the hulfs were innocent of the crimes and have only been the scapegoats to cover up the crimes of other humans? This brief story examines such a possibility.

How Dark The Blaze of Noon
O dark, dark, dark, amid the blaze of noon,
Irrevocably dark, total eclipse...
Total eclipse! no sun, no moon!
All dark amidst the blaze of noon!

THE MAN WHO FELL FROM A CLEAR BLUE SKY
by
William Kern

At The End Of The Universe Lies The Beginning Of Life

Because it occurs in Time, there is no beginning to this adventure and, therefore, it will have no ending; at least no ending that the reader might recognize as an ending. It is a tale about people and the world they inhabit, about the world and the various people in it, about how people view and struggle with the world that often seems to thwart their every move, and how the world (and the cosmos for that matter) uses and consumes the creatures that dwell in it.

There is no great, earth-shattering moral to the story, unless the reader finds something his or her mind is listening to as they read, and connects those unspoken unthoughts to this tale. If there is an underlying thought, it will be to question whether or not humans and other creatures have any control over their existence while they are dwellers on this strange and often hostile world.

Since the story has no chronological beginning, it might as well begin today; this morning as I was strolling down the street on my way to the market to purchase food for my evening meal. I had twice seen an old man (or a man who appeared old, but who may have been middle-aged). He had the look and demeanor of a wretched homeless person and, yet, he walked with a stride and purpose that told me he was going somewhere important to him and that to get there was important. A most purposeful stride that was taking him to a meaningful destination, a dreadful mission. I was determined, out of curiosity, if nothing else, to follow him and find out what he was up to. I probably should have minded my own business.

*****

The old man looked like an oily rag someone had thrown into a pond; he just kind of floated through the world all sloshy and raggedy and older than the scaly serpent itself. No one paid much attention to him; first he was there then he wasn't and few noticed either way. He was gutter rain and trash blowing across the street. Everyone knew he was there but no one cared. He was in the corner of your eye, the corner of your mind; he was sneeze or clear your throat or scratch an itch. He happened to the world automatically like he was invisible most of the time and probably that was the way he wanted it. The only reason the old man came to my attention at all was because I spotted him twice in the same day almost the same hour all wrinkly and brown dirty mail pouch to-

57

bacco barn siding skin, tattered clothes, dull brown eyes, dull brown greasy hair, streaks of gray, dull brown lips that looked like they hadn't cracked a smile in a thousand years walking in front of me the same way I was going with his gnarled dull brown hands permanently semi-clenched like dead chicken feet, sculling himself along the sidewalk with a stick he had found somewhere and I wondered where he lived and how he managed to survive in a world that cared little or nothing for homeless things.

I recalled someone mentioned that they had heard the old man had fallen from the sky and no one bothered him because the brassface police and the street thugs were scared to death of him saying he was immortal and invincible powerful filled with magic.

Everyone thought he was a magician from another world and who was to say otherwise?

It took some doing just to catch up with him and I thought maybe he even slowed down some so I could get up beside him without running and I said hi but he just kept rowing himself down the sidewalk like he either didn't see or hear me or did but didn't give a damn so I said hi again and he said go away or I'll hit you with this stick you nosy damned kid stop bothering me or I'll bust your head like a rotten punkin so I sidestepped a little but kept on walking with him and pretty soon he just stopped dead without warning and I took two steps before I could stop and he swung the stick like swoosh an inch from my face and I put up my arm and caught a mighty whack on the palm of my hand goddamn I hollered and he grinned like that was about the funniest thing he had seen in a long time.

Okay he says come along and I'll tell you the story of how I happened to fall from the sky to land on this here miserable piece of real estate. How did you know I asked and he said that's what everyone who follows me wants to know so why would you be any different and I rubbed my hand with my other hand and walked with him into a dark gloomy alley between two old derelict buildings the city hadn't got around to tearing down and through a kind of doorway that seemed to appear from the darkness and into a black room with a couple of small boxes next to a bigger box like your old basic table and chairs and he lit a candle on the big box using a match from a folder that I couldn't even see until the light came up and I could see that the old man and me and the three boxes and the candle and the folder of matches were the only things in the room about sixty feet square, a room so large the candle light barely reached the graffiti walls, the peeling scarred gray dull concrete windowless walls ciphered with lifetimes of chalk and spray-paint, sad memories and forlorn wisdom.

The raggedy man seemed to waver in the flickering candle glow, staring at his hands, flexing and unflexing his fingers and marveling at the motion as if he had never really seen such wonders before that very moment.

We sat and he rested his chin in the palms of his upturned hands, staring into the flickering candlelight. He seemed to have died as soon as he sat for he did not move did not blink and I thought he did not even breathe for almost a minute.

The mirror people, he said of a sudden, cast me here when I least expected it to happen. I'd known for some weeks, couple of months really, that the people in the mirror were real, were alive, were watching me, every move I made, even when I wasn't in front of a mirror. They knew what I was doing, knew what I was thinking because they were doing and thinking the same thing. I began to fear sleeping, thinking the dopplegangers would come to get me in the darkness while I was dreaming of pretty girls and sweet cherry blossoms falling like pink snow.

Not certain what made me think of it the first time. I wasn't even in front of a mirror. I began to wonder if the image—the mirror image—extended beyond what could be seen in the glass. Look here, if you step slightly to one side of the mirror you can see the door to the bedroom. If you step the other way you can see the shower or the wardrobe. And a little more you can see down the hallway leading into the living room. You can't see the living room because it is around corners and behind walls but isn't the living room there all the same? Everything in your house or apartment is there, in the mirror. Even the world beyond your front door, the very cosmos itself, is in the mirror; you just have to be able to figure out how to see around the corners and through the walls.

You get so interested in the image in the mirror that it becomes you, and you forget who you were, who you are, who you could become. You become the person in the mirror.

I had everything I wanted. I envied no one, wanted no one else's life. Having survived the experience of living on Earth for a full forty years, I felt I was unique, unlike anyone else. I began to imagine that I had discovered some great universal secret, this new world in the mirror. It was the place where ghosts live, where spooks and haunts and creatures of the night reside until we think them into existence. I was reborn into a completely new reality and, having realized that, I had just begun to live.

The images in the mirror were from a parallel universe just waiting to be explored, just waiting there in the silvered glass, drawing me closer with every glance.

I began to obsess on this idea, wondering before I slept or soon after waking, if there was another being, a doppleganger, reclining on a bed identical to mine, only mirror-image, who was thinking about me lying in bed thinking about him. I began to fear that one day, when I least expected it, one of those beings in the mirror world would come and snatch me away.

I worried that I was mad and hoped that I was prepared for it but I knew I wasn't.

They didn't come for me at all. I went to them as easily as if I walked through a doorway into another room, just slipped right into the mirror one early Fall morning as if I'd been sucked up by a vacuum and landed in a backwards world. Everything seemed perfectly normal but in the back of my head I knew my world, what I thought of as the real world, was on the other side of the mirror. I wanted to go back but didn't know how. Going back was not as easy as crossing over.

I jumped from my world of 1851 to the first reflected world of 1951, a full one hundred years into their future. But the mirror world of 1951 was, I believe now, unlike the world that would have existed in 1951 where I originated. Perhaps it was or wasn't. I don't know anymore. I thought I had died and that I was in the world of death. I was certain God had forsaken me as punishment for my sins, which at that time were legion. I was afraid, scared stupid for a long time, but soon I accepted my life as the real life and began to suspect that the life I'd had on the other side of the mirror was an illusion.

As soon as I grabbed a hold of the mirror world, strange new things began to happen. I would wake up and be in a different world every morning, go to sleep in a different world every night. I almost couldn't keep up with it at first. But it was not long before I couldn't remember my life before I fell into the mirror.

Things happened slowly at the beginning like I was being prepared for my new world carefully, but soon came one adventure after another, a carousel whirling past me so quickly everything was a blur. I can't remember the first hundred years clearly but I do remember a couple of things that happened before I fell back through the mirror to land here. Now all I can think about is going back to find the people I knew there, in the last world into which I had fallen, the people I loved, the people I long for.

"You said 'the first hundred years,' " said I. "Were you there that long?"

"Twice as long, perhaps thrice as long. It is not in me to remember so many years, so many adventures. Sometimes I think I am dreaming it all, even now here with you. But I was going to tell you about the people I cared for, wasn't I?"

"Yes, tell me," I said, and he pursed his dull gray lips and nodded sagely. Presently he spoke and when he did his voice was thin and dark and ancient.

* * * * *.

Gold and frankincense and myrrh. The earth exploded beneath a new star. I walked under the vast electric midnight sky. Wise men arrived at last but they did not stop to ask for directions; they knew where they were going. The oak tree, naked in the shadow, was not interested in cherry blossoms or dancing cranes in far away Japan. An imprisoned monk sipped warm tea before a dusty window while he peered at the four strangers, barely visible on the road below. It was quiet except for the faint white voices of geese winging southward in the high and lonely sky.

The sea darkened; the tall cliffs, newly washed by crashing high tide, stood as mute guardians against the invincible intruding waves.

How cold it was.

The gray pink fog, never far behind, accompanied the winter wind, pushed, stirred up the loose, torn off bits of seagrass, ready or not, and dragged them into the relentless surf, carried them to where, scattered all about, remained the rumpled souvenirs of heaven's flame, all one pile.

Unarmed but for faith I walked across the dying embers of the universe, holy golden funeral pyre, low and crackling, where the bleating wind swirled the ashes as they rose to the nameless hill in the mist.

Rain, falling like hard, rusted nails, a sudden late autumn shower. I was newly baptized. I reached out and touched the rook's impulsive call, a massive melody agonizing downward from the greening shade. The planets hesitated. Martyrs with ashen faces looked up briefly from the temple, sputtering madness, incredulous, then withdrew into their lairs, heads bowed beneath uncombed hair.

All was still once more.

A green frog, its form freshly painted by the clinging mist, sprang into an old pool, plopping into the sound of water. My footsteps alarmed the rooks and they flew madly just above the withered reeds, protesting my approach. Soon will come the first soft snow, enough to bend the leaves of the fragile jonquil and in the frog's cry was a portent of the winter death to come.

Still shivering, I longed for cherry blossoms and butterflies, for brightly colored Maples and sun-filled skies. Last days of autumn, first days of winter. No one traveled the road now but I, steeped in thoughts and loneliness as dawn ascended. Far down the stream I could see the rough wooden bridge that joined the path leading to the stone house on the cliff. The ammonia-colored moon was hidden now and then by angry dark clouds; the stars were gone. Around the harvest pool more frogs leaped away as I longed for the warmth of home. I thought I would not like to die here in this place behind the mirror, in this dream, in this gloom where there was no joy, no sky, no moon, no stars, no flowers.

How cold it was, how cold. No familiar sky, no familiar earth, but still the snow will fall.

In the pale light I stared into the stream and saw my father's face. The clouds parted for a moment and I could see the Milky Way Galaxy at the bottom of the dark water. When I looked up it was already gone. I was naked in the darkness. I stirred the water with my hand, remembering the vision of the stars but only a slight muddiness appeared.

The imprisoned monk, having finished his warm tea, was playing his flute all out of tune. The horizon was glowing lighter in the east. Soon the sun would rise, still lost to my sight above the black clouds. In the half light I longed for love and the cold wind turned to rain again, smudging the clouds that snaked through the stream. The bridge was not far but I leaped across the narrow stream and struggled up the far bank in the mud, too eager for the shelter and warmth of the hearth.

A lightning flash in the faraway sky. Between the forest trees I saw the shape of a creature watching as I approached. When the lightning flashed again, it was gone. It saw all it needed to see.

In that morning's mad world, visions of the hulf.

I was cold and now I was smeared with mud to my knees. I mounted the trail to the stone house above on the windswept cliff. The footpath was slick and the going was slow.

Dreams in my head like wet heavy rain, like soot on a broken window, like a soft and terrible machine, like a skulking young hulf and when she growled I could hear under the purling little girl voice the dark, lean, terrible animal living in the heat of her throat.

This hulf had been stalking me for at least an hour, from the moment I left the safety of the village where she wished not to show herself, and I could tell from the sound of her panting it was a female. I never saw her clearly, but I knew she was there in the underbrush trying to keep pace with me and I wondered if she was hungry, if she would pounce upon me and kill me.

But it had been an hour and still she had only followed and I pondered to what purpose.

I stopped and peered into the dense brush then upward at the house above me on the headland, longing all the more for its safety and comfort.

"Hulf," said I with a gentle voice, "Why do you not come out to the path where the ground is firmer, where we may walk together to the house yonder?"

Silence in the bush, then a low purling, then a stirring and parting of the green, and she crept into view first on all fours—I started at the sight of her— then she stood with amazing agility, smiling a little smile, her eyes keen upon me, her hands curled as if to attack but her back straight and strong. When she spoke her voice was remarkably masculine and deep, a counterpoint to the siren female whisper above it as if she spoke with two voices at once.

"I am not good at tracking," she intoned through her white wolf teeth and dark red hunger, wondering aloud if we humans had to sleep with the fear of waking someday to find we, too, were changing into the hulf, part human and part wolf, sometimes more of one than the other and I just smiled back at her with deliberate silence, eyes narrowed and piercing, until she turned away to gaze with feral curiosity at the stone house above us on the rocky promontory.

"And are you going there?" she asked presently.

"I am."

"May I go with you?"

"If you wish it." And I wondered if she had children and if they, too, were hulfs living in the dystopian world of terror and blackness beneath the city streets, beneath the darkness, beneath the thin line between self and the unspeakable world of monsters and murder.

"My forerunners were human like you," she said. "It was only after the disease accident that we became the hulf living on the swiftness of our limbs. I was only thirteen years alive when I began to change. Now I am twenty years alive and I have had no children." She thrust out her ample bare human breasts and laughed gaily, almost a puppylike yelp. "Not yet."

"Did you think perhaps to kill me and have me for breakfast back there?" I asked.

"Briefly," said she, "but I suppose I am too much human and too little wolf to do it."

And nothing else.

And so we walked to the house together without further conversation.

I felt, for a moment, that she wanted to reach out and take my hand, to walk swinging it gaily back and forth like a child at a circus with her father. But, perhaps, it was I who wanted to hold the hulf's hand so that both she and I would feel more at ease.

I did and she did not draw away.

When we reached the house I began to search for the key in my kit while she gazed about at the mist-covered trees and brush, the spider webs bejeweled with glistening droplets of crystal rain, and she soon spied an enormous rook perched upon a barren limb, preening and combing its feathers fastidiously.

Here the hulf mustered up some urge to commune with nature. Perhaps she wished to see some design among the fallen leaves and receive some backtalk from the mute sky or the frantic rook, open to any gesture on the part of nature to grant a brief respite from fear of what she had become. The hope of such a moment of transcendent beauty and communion seemed worth the wait for that which she interpreted as that rare, random granting of a miracle.

The rook, arranging and rearranging its feathers, seemed like a fastidious spinster in comparison with the strange form of the sad hulf. It was an object set out on the landscape for no particular purpose, because her real desire was some backtalk from the recalcitrant human. Neither rook nor sky nor human spoke, but the hulf herself was very wordy, full of parenthetical phrases, uttered half whispers, concerned not with the actual landscape but with her own thoughts. She finally reattached these thoughts to the landscape by declaring that the rook might be a tasty morsel, a repast enjoyed in the company of bejewelled columbines.

She was aglow, was the hulf, in the notion that she might have been the first of her pack to travel this high mountain trail, delighted by a rook on a bare branch autumn morning, and last summer's berry canes and vines binding the sagging fence, and the stone house of a human who had actually taken her hand and urged her upward to the lonely headland.

I left most of my wet and muddy garments on the screened porch, then fetched towels. The she hulf had no idea what to do with a towel, so I showed her by first drying her and then myself. She allowed me to touch her without the least bit of shame.

Her hair was long and unkempt although it seemed not to be dirty. Her upper torso was as human as any human girl I had ever seen but her lower torso was covered with a soft, light colored downy fur. Except that her face appeared to protrude a bit more than normal at the jaw, she was quite a striking looking girl. The most unusual features were her legs and feet. The heel was high, exactly like a canine's and she walked on toes which terminated in canine claws. She had slightly pronounced canine teeth.

A month earlier creatures such as that she hulf filled me with disgust and revulsion; now I watched her with admiration and, perhaps, something more; adoration, or if not adoration, then empathy.

I struck a fire on the hearth which at first filled her with temerity. I sat before the flames to show that the fire would only harm her if she fell into it or got too near. She crept toward it, cautious and inquisitive, soon sat with her legs beneath her haunches and gazed at the hypnotic curling.

In the light I could see that she was beautiful, almost diaphanous, both in form and in features. Her dark wolf eyes turned toward me and caught me stealing her beauty. She smiled softly and I blushed.

"Have you a name?" I asked.

"Name?"

"Yes, a name. What do the others call you?"

"They call me to them by saying 'hulf'."

"And the others," I asked, "are they also addressed as 'hulf'?"

She nodded to affirm it.

I could not refer to her as 'hulf'; it was not in me to do it. "May I call you by a human name?"

"Yes," said she absently, still mesmerized by the dancing fire.

"I'll call you Cybele, then. Is that alright?"

"See-bee-lee," she repeated and nodded her head slightly.

"My human name is Guillaume," I said. "Close friends call me Gill."

"Gill." She nodded again as she repeated the name and her old stones and mossy voice made it sound like thunder echoing from faraway mountains.

Hulf and human, Cybele and Gill, we took breakfast of hot chocolate and honeyed biscuits under one roof together, moon in a field of clover and among all the moon gazers at the ancient temple grounds below, there was not one nearly so beautiful as the hulf. I was enchanted and she was the enchantress.

Later I dozed in my chair before the hearth, wrapped in a soft comforter, and she lay upon a cushion at my feet, refusing my invitation to sit in the facing chair, saying the position of sitting as a human was too difficult for her, too uncomfortable, too foreign. By mid morning, we slept soundly and the fire burned down to cold ash.

When I awoke, she was gone, the door closed securely behind her and I felt strangely and sadly alone, longing for her to return, cold and empty inside.

She had taken the towel and I wondered why.

The wise men, ever erudite and pedantic, had told us that we might all change eventually into the hulf and laws were passed after that forbidding anyone to kill them.

64

Generally speaking, the hulfs presented no danger to those of us who had not changed. Even so, most people shunned them and tried to drive them away. As long as there was adequate food, the hulfs stayed to themselves, formed their own communities as packs and were civil to each other and to humans.

But when food was not plentiful, or when the populations of hulfs outgrew the food supply (they were prolific breeders), there would in some towns occur an occasional kill and human bones would be found in the ditches and fields. Then the humans would put their guns by their doors and sit by the fires all night, alert for sounds of skulking creatures outside in the darkness, some of the men looking for any excuse to reduce the populations of the changelings, never thinking that the victims might have been killed by other humans.

* * * * *

I dreamed of a man of power standing at a podium with his hand raised to heaven, invoking the wisdom of God. The man of power said God told him the hulfs were evil and should all be killed. Next morning he was found torn to shreds on his living room floor.

All in my dream.

A week later one of the pundits who advocated the deaths of the hulfs was found torn to shreds on his living room floor. I think it was a coincidence that it happened the way I dreamed it.

* * * * *

Winter drew closer with each passing hour and I grew keen to close the house and go to my apartment in the village below. I put it off day after day hoping the she-hulf would return. I did not want her to find the house locked and empty.

Strange that I should have been so concerned for her. The thought of her living in the dystopian world of terror and blackness beneath the city streets, beneath the darkness, beneath the thin line between self and the unspeakable world of monsters and murder filled every hour of every day of my life.

A linnet sang, and through a thicket of barren larches the late moon shone. That cool morning was swept away into the sea. All along the road to the village not a single soul, only the autumn dawn came, seen but not heard; the branches of the forlorn trees poured rainwater into puddles when they leaned, then, with the solitaire for a soul, they slept peacefully, awaiting the first snows already lurking above the peaks to the north.

Dark autumn old age settled down on me like heavy clouds or dying birds and dead morning glory vines secured the gate in the old fence; the hand of death strangling the life from the world. Crossing half the sky, as I stared at the raging gray ocean below, massive clouds promised snow and, later, a sudden winter shower sent the noisy rooks diving into the shelter of the eaves.

Day and night. Night and day. Even those long and dreary days and nights were not long enough to empty my mind of the she hulf Cybele. No words can express how sad I was, propped unceremoniously against the great window frame staring dumbly at the darkening seasons outside.

I wished she were there to listen to my words. The world is wearisome when there is no one to share it. I stalked from room to room through that house of dreadful night.

Raindrops spiraled down from unknown universes, carrying their precious cargoes of microscopic life. The seas darkened and the wild geese had all gone to their breeding grounds far to the south. I wished I had gone with them. From every direction winter approached. The house had become a trap; I yearned to close it and go to the village.

But I determined to wait one more day for Cybele.

When I awoke the next morning (late, for I slept fitfully), there was a light covering of fresh snow upon the ground. Thin, it would melt by noon. A foot from the bottom step of the porch was a yellow patch where something had pissed in the snow. I began to look from window to window, front and back, side to side, for signs of Cybele, hoping she had returned, hoping she was waiting, worrying that she would be cold and wet. At first nothing, then, near the shed behind the house I saw her crouching to examine something in the tall, brown grass. When she stood, she was holding a tiny rabbit. She pulled the towel from her shoulders and wrapped the bunny in it and held it close to her breasts.

I opened the back door and she turned toward me and came in, just like that, without a word, and went in to sit before the fire newly built upon the hearth.

"Something for this tiny?" she asked, and I brought some greens from the refrigerator, watched amazed as she caressed it and fed it until it slept in the warm towel.

I wondered aloud, unfortunately, if she was saving it for a meal and she glared at me with accusing eyes. "That is offensive. This is an orphan who has survived the first snow of winter here on this high place. To think that I would kill it is a knife in my heart. Never ask such things of me again."

I apologized sincerely and she turned away with a nod to begin caressing once more the orphaned survivor of the first snow of winter. I felt terrible to have misjudged her so.

"When you were here before," I began to ask.

"Yes?"

"Why did you take the towel?"

"I needed it for this tiny," she answered and the occult wisdom of the response slammed into my brain like a hammer. Had she really foreseen the discovery of the cold little orphan? I suspected she had.

* * * * *

"Can you imagine it?" he asked me, still staring into the candle flame.

"I can. But did you close the house and go to the village as you had planned?"

"No. After Cybele returned I never even thought of it again. We spent the first months of winter there, a mild winter as it turned out, and I was often able to go into the village for provisions. I bought girl clothes for her, warm things because it seemed to me she was often uncomfortable with the cold. She was rarely without a towel for a shawl, although it may have been a security blanket rather than a hedge against the cold. It pleased her to receive the gifts and I must admit it pleased me to give them."

"Did you fall in love with her?" I asked.

"Oh, yes, of course, from the very beginning, despite knowing it was an impossible thing for both of us."

"Did you...ah...sleep with her?" I asked as delicately as possible.

He smiled wryly and looked away into the darkness at the edge of the light. "Always that imprudent question. The answer is no, I did not; something I often thought of and more often regretted having not done. She was an innocent child and I was two hundred years old. I thought to protect her and she thought of me as her guardian. To kiss her, to caress her would have been the same as to destroy her innocence for no purpose. You see that it was... not possible. But you are wondering why I am here and she is not. A long story and a sad one."

"Why do you say you were two hundred years old?" I asked.

"Quite simply because I was at least that old. I am even older now that I am here. When I fell into the mirror, or to be more precise, when my image and I exchanged places in the mirror, the year was 1851. I landed in an alternate world of the hulfs where it was, by my time reckoning, 1951, and now I am here where, if I reckon aright, it is the year 2054. I have been here for two years and each day of that I have been trying to figure out how I can return to the world of the hulfs. I am beginning to fear that it is not possible."

"You do not look like a two hundred years old man," said I, appraising him with a sideways glance and thinking he might be more than a little bit mad.

"I have not aged a day since I fell into this strange world. I am still forty years old although I have lived nearly two hundred and fifty years."

"Is that, do you think, a paradox of the parallel universe?

"I imagine, although I have not really given it much thought. But, probably, it is."

"But you are safe here and secure. No one has any thought to harm you. Why do you feel you must return?" I asked.

He was quite for a time, rocking gently back and forth on the creaky wooden box chair.

"Because I had promised to lead them to safety, to a sanctuary, where they could live without fear of the humans but I was unable to complete the journey. We began our dangerous journey without much planning in the last days of winter, escaping from men who would murder us.

"It was terrible. We were constantly hungry and thirsty. I was always cold and wet and I feared that if the humans did not find and kill me, I would perish from disease or exposure to the elements.

"Sometimes we walked; sometimes we ran, always hiding during the day and making our way through unfamiliar lands at night. We had fled for hundreds of miles in those months of late winter and early spring and I began to think that we might reach our destination safely within just a few more days.

"And, then, one morning, I awoke to find myself here in this abandoned building, with not a clue as to what might have happened to the others. I believe, or I want to believe, that my mirror self continued with them and completed that mad journey to freedom.

"But I must know the truth. If I do not return, I fear they may all perish. Time may not be the same for them as it is for me. A hundred years or a thousand may have passed for them. They may have already reached their haven safely, or they may have perished, but I must find out.

"It is I who is now living in the dystopian world of terror and blackness upon the land, beneath the darkness, beneath the thin line between self and the unspeakable world of monsters and murder.

"My dear God, I am at an age now and at a time where life stops giving and begins to take. What a mockery our bodies make of us when they are finished with us. It would be better if we simply evaporated when we grow too old and weary to go on living; a puff of smoke drifting skyward and that would be the end of us."

* * * * *

It was cold enough to make the devil swear on the evening the others came, the other hulfs, two dozen to be sure, slipping into the yard under cover of darkness and asking entrance to the house. I struggled to understand the meaning of their visit until Cybele explained that a vaccine had been formulated that would protect humans against the disease that had affected the hulfs. The hulfs, living in their dystopian world of terror and blackness beneath the thin line between self and the unspeakable world of monsters and murder, could not be protected; they would continue to change until they perished from the disease or were killed by humans.

And I came to understand that evening the true reason Cybele had taken the towel. It bore my scent and that scent had led the pack around the village, through the forest and up the steep incline to my doorstep, the beginning of their hazardous and fearful escape from certain death.

The world I had thought secure now changed into something new and foreboding. The hulfs, all of the pack to which Cybele belonged, were asking that I lead them away to a place of safety in the South; a place they were told about by others who had journeyed there and returned to spread the word that a haven existed for any hulf brave enough to chance it. They could no longer travel safely in the world of humans now that a preventive had been found. Hulfs were hunted and killed without mercy. They had become expendable, a sacrifice to science. Six from their pack had already been slain.

I was filled with dread for the hulfs, but most especially for Cybele and the pups, and, at the end, I agreed to lead them to the unknown sanctuary in the South. I had no idea where to begin. In wiser days, when I was younger and stronger, I might have made a plan for salvation before the night was over but that evening I was stymied and loathe to dice with death. And, oh, I could see in their eyes, their shining eyes, their hopeful eyes, the growing fear that I might abandon them to the mad guns cursing in the village below, and some began to decry their hope in knowing tones.

Picture it; we fools, I and they, now all with the dying and the dead, standing mute around the fading hearth and wondering, all of us, we miserable fools, they and I, how we might tend toward this task. Darkness never seemed so dark; dread never seemed quite so dreadful as on that smothering night.

Now here I am, sleeping on a bed of nails with one foot in the fire. Some days when you wake up, you think you are the same person who went to sleep in your bed the night before.

Believe me, you aren't.

In wiser days, in days before I first fell into the mirror (oh, how I wish I knew how it happened,) I had no thoughts of heroic adventures. I worked and enjoyed my life as most ninteenth century forty-year-old men did, giving little or no thoughts to the lives and wants of others, even of those I thought I loved. Live and let live, you see.

Now, here in this place where I am imprisoned, I can think of little else save Cybele and the others and trying to find a way to get back to them. Yes, I know the mirror me must have taken them to their sanctuary, but I dearly want to know if they made it or not.

"Perhaps," said I, "you don't want to know. What if you learn they didn't safely reach their destination? What if you find they and you—the mirror you—perished before you reached the sanctuary?"

"Perished? How perished?"

"Accident or at the hands of others," I said.

"The humans, you mean?" the raggedy man asked.

"Or perhaps other hulfs who saw you as a threat...or see you as a threat, as the case may be or may have been."

"I think they would not ever have done that, and yet..." he let the thought slip away as his mind drifted back to that time moments ago or hundreds of ages past when he had promised to lead the hulfs to safety in the south of whatever world he had found himself in.

"No," he said at last, "If my double had been killed or even injured there, I could not have come here, or I would have come here injured, and I did not".

"Are you certain that's how it works?"

"Yes."

"Always?"

His piercing grey eyes bored into me. "For me, at least, up to this point."

He stood slowly and languidly, stretching his lean frame wearily. "You should go now," he said at length. "I want to continue my experiments with the transference, to see if I can discover what beam or current existed on the occasions that I fell into these alternate worlds."

"But have you a mirror?" I asked.

"Pieces that I have salvaged from the trash bins. They are not adequate, I think, since I have been unable to effect a transfer. Perhaps you might fetch one for me and bring it tomorrow."

"Several, perhaps. Large or small?"

"Small," he said. "About this size." He made a circle with his arms, fingertips touching.

"Then I shall bring two when I take my lunch hour."

"Oh, of course," he said quietly. "I forget people here must work for...things."

He promised to continue with his story the following day and, after getting a list of things he could use—not the least of which was a boxful of food and toiletries, bottles of drinking water and clean clothes—I bid him farewell.

I turned and looked back at him as I left the building and saw that he was again sitting on the hard wooden box with his mouth working chants and silent, unspoken dreams that seemed to fall away from him like smoke and summer rain. He made little gestures with his thin, gnarled fingers, pointing and waving, brushing his thoughts away and inventing others from the still, dark air.

*****

I did not go to work the following day. I called in for a vacation day and went directly to a hardware store to purchase the two mirrors, then, with the boxes of supplies and the mirrors, I drove to the abandoned building where I expected to find the traveler waiting for me. He was not there. I lighted the candle to dispel the darkness and sat to wait for him. It was nearly ten o'clock before he rowed himself through the open doorway holding in his right hand a small book.

"Library," he said, by way of explaining where he had been. "I have no library card, so I had to steal it." He held the book toward me so I could read the title. Currents From The Void, was imprinted on the spine. His eyes gleamed with some sort of ethereal light, almost glowing with electric fire, and for a moment I was frightened that I was in the presence of a demon. I started backward but he pointed to some debris beyond the ring of light; wooden stands that I had not seen. He placed the book upon the box he used as a table.

"You'll return it for me, won't you?" he asked.

"What?"

"The book. You'll return it?"

"Oh, of course."

He began arranging the wooden stands near the table. "If you want to see ghosts," he said, "just look into the mirror. Or, better still, have the two mirrors look at each other." As he spoke, he went busily about placing the two mirrors in a way that they directly faced one another, each reflection creating an infinite passageway into and out of the other.

"According to the book, by placing these two mirrors facing one another, the light energy reflected back and forth between them might create a vortex, an energy beam or current, that might create a transfer of my mirror double from his world to this one."

"And you to his," I said.

"Precisely, exactly, yes."

Light might be coaxed out of empty space, he explained, when in the presence of reflective surfaces. It was, he said, a process known as the "Casimir Effect" where two metallic plates or mirrors placed in close proximity to one another can result in an attraction between the two, despite there being no charge running into the plates to create an electromagnetic force. The reflecting coatings of mirrors is silver, an excellent conductor of electricity.

"The attraction seems to come from the fact that virtual photons—that is, particles of light energy that only exist for a limited time and space—exist in greater numbers outside the two plates, rather than between them. The resulting force, though miniscule, is still strong enough to be measured." He wagged a finger at the book. "I read it there."

He motioned me to the table and sat, then began sorting through the food and clothes I had brought. He constructed a large sandwich and ate parts of it while he examined the clothing and toiletries, humming and nodding, nodding and humming, until he had selected a shirt and trousers, shoes and stockings that suited him.

"These will do nicely. Thank you."

I nodded and managed a smile. "Sturdy togs for traveling," said I. "In case you are thinking of traveling, I mean."

"Yes. Now or tomorrow or next week, if I can transfer."

"And if you cannot?

"I will keep trying."

He ate slowly, deliberately, as he explained his arrangement of the mirrors. In all the years of thinking of mirrors, it had never occurred to him, he said, to place two of them facing each other, precisely aligned so that one reflected the other and nothing else, either to the sides or to the top or bottom. Mirrors so placed should be able to collect and store virtual photons, if even for a fraction of a second, and be reflected as light, vibrating back and forth, reflected back and forth endlessly, infinitely, billions of times per second, creating a magnetic field, a beam, a current exactly like a river, a physical bond between the mirrors upon which one might travel to the far fields of space and time.

"And, according to this fellow in the book, the virtual photons do not merely create light where none exists; ethereal light, it also retains the images of everything that passed before it and all that passed in one's life. Images, sound, sensations and actual memories. That is why I experienced so many adventures when I exchanged worlds the first time. I was living and reliving the lives of every mirror double with whom I was reacting. When I at last slipped into that one life of the gent who lived in the stone house upon the headland, all the others faded away."

"So you think that you can step into this virtual energy and be whisked away back to the world of the hulfs?" I asked. "What makes you think you can go back to the world you left? This is like a time machine of some sort. Aren't you afraid you will appear on another world in the middle of a war, or in the middle of a plague, or some other mass extinction?"

He shook his head with dark, brooding eyes. Clearly he was not afraid of any of those possibilities. Or he simply refused to acknowledge them. He was focused upon returning to Cybele; intent upon saving her from the guns of the madmen who wanted only to kill the hulfs.

"The mirrors create light and memories from empty space where none actually exists," he cried, hands above his head, sweeping the air as if to clear it of debris and call down blazing shards of fire and brimstone. "If I step into the current, the dopplegangers will also step into the current of their mirrors at the same time because we are always doing exactly the same things with the mirrors, and we should transfer; I there and he, here. Or I to some other world and he to another, rather than I to his and he to mine. That is the chance one takes when posing before the mirror. The world to which I transfer will be like this one in nearly all respects. See, I had never thought of using two mirrors before. I always tried to use a single mirror. But in my home in the year 1851 there were two mirrors in the room, facing each other. And in the home upon the headland, there was but a single mirror in the great room. In none of the rooms were there two mirrors facing each other. It did not occur to me that the mirrors would actually produce the current of virtual energy that could project me into another existence, a parallel universe, a mirror cosmos."

"How, then, did you transfer here?" I asked.

He finished eating the sandwich and wiped his mouth upon the sleeve of his ragged coat. His eyes grew empty and he drew down a somber face. "Ah," he said at last, "that is the story, isn't it? That is the error. That is the flaw I could not see."

The raggedy man fell into a deep silence, still and hardly breathing. "What if I fail?" he said at last. "What if I cannot transfer? Perhaps my plan for the mirrors is a fantasy and all that happened before was simply some kind of mad coincidence. What if I cannot return to lead them to safety?" He sagged, with his neck drawn down into his shoulders, and he shook his head forlornly.

"Then one day, when this world had ended, she will join you. Cybele, I mean. You will be together somewhere, somewhen," I said and touched his arm reassuringly.

He drew away and stared at me incredulously. "Do you really imagine the cosmos is so tender, so gracious, so kind? How came I here before I completed my task if that is so?"

I told him I didn't know the answer to that but that I felt certain if his love for the she-hulf was strong enough, they might meet again in another life.

"Strangely enough," he said with narrowed eyes, "I have some memories of such things, although I cannot be certain they are not memories of dreams or nightmares or hallucinations. I remember living briefly and dying on the planet Mars." He looked up quickly, fixing me with his fierce, mad gaze, assured himself I did not think him possessed, and looked away into the shadows at the edges of the room. "Perhaps it is a sort of madness brought about by the mirror world in which I dwelled for some many years. And it is all of them who share my concern equally."

"What?"

"I want to return to save all the hulfs; not just Cybele, although she does concern me most, I confess."

I cleared my throat of the tight dryness I felt there. "Perhaps, when their world has ended, they will appear here to be with you," I said.

"Their world has already ended. It is no longer their world. They were driven out, brutalized, and to appear here would be the worst of all situations! Can you imagine what would happen to them in this world if they suddenly appeared as hulfs, as I left them? They would be murdered just as quickly here as there and perhaps even more brutally. Are they dead now? Were they ever alive? Am I alive or dead? I don't even know anymore. But I shall surely die if I cannot return to learn if they were saved. I can feel myself growing older and closer to the fate that awaits all humans since I fell to this place."

"You can try," I said softly. "Only try."

"Yes." He nodded gravely. "Only try."

"Perhaps, if you are successful with the mirrors, you will find them again," I said as I watched him arrange and rearrange the mirrors. "Perhaps you will find Cybele again."

"One must be lost in order to be found. They are not lost; it is I who has gone missing." He stared at the grafitti-covered walls with empty eyes. "Why do you test me?" he growled. "Have I not been tested enough these last two-hundred years?"

He was clearly challenging whatever god he thought might be listening at that moment, shamelessly, as if he had no shame at all.

"Oh, dear Cybele! Jack! Pups! Apollo! Naomi! Why, Shiatan, do you test me so?" He breathed a long, quivering sigh and turned back to me. "I must complete my arrangements here to learn if I can create the vortex or energy field that will carry me on to the next world, or back to that world which I so long to see again."

* * * * *

We do not know what we do not know. And we fools; all of us, could not know what awaited us when we planned so carefully our perilous escape. Had I known the dangers, the sadness, the treachery we would encounter, I might have told the hulfs that we could not go. But, we planned through the winter, often huddling around the blazing fire late into the evenings, that we should begin soon after the first promising warm days of spring.

We heard no fearful reports from the village of more killings and we sank into a kind of trusting denial, thinking that everything would be alright, believing that the villagers had decided to try to live with the hulfs; even if in an uneasy peaceful coexistence. These were naive, foolish dreams. The reason we heard no gunshots or further reports of death was because nearly all the hulfs had been killed by mid-winter, and only a few had managed to flee to the south, to safety, or the promise of it.

But we did not know these things for we remained secluded in the stone house on the headland, rarely venturing out for fear of being seen, and only I, at that, and only to go into the village for provisions that we needed to survive. The plan had been to always keep a small store of supplies to take with us, food and water we could not buy or find as we moved southward, and to live off the land as much as possible.

It was easy to plan but, as we were to discover, nearly impossible to accomplish. In late winter and early Spring, there is little growing from the cold earth to sustain man or beast. Seeds and berries and herbs still lay dormant beneath patches of lingering snow. It is a wonder any of us managed to survive at all.

Cybele came to me early one late winter morning, wrapped in the blanket she had become accustomed to carrying with her, still sleepy-eyed from her warm pallet in the cellar.

"We have been talking and thinking," she said.

"Yes?"

"Some are thinking of leaving in a few days even if you choose not to lead us."

I was astonished. "But, why?" I asked.

"They... some of them... are afraid. They say they can smell death in the village.

They say they cannot hear the voices of the other hulfs. They are afraid."

"And you?"

"Yes," she responded softly. "I, too, am afraid. Not of staying until warmer days, but of their fear and what it might drive them to do. They do not trust the humans; some are beginning wonder if even you might betray them. I worry that some harm may come to you."

Do you care for me that much? I wondered, and saw in her eyes that she did.

"Did they send you to speak with me?" I asked.

"I told them I would do it because I trust you. I know you will not deceive us."

I turned away from her and held my hands toward the fire, rubbing warmth into my fingers and arms. At length I faced her. "We shall leave in two days. Tell them that. No, I shall tell them myself after all are awakened and have eaten."

And, so, for two days we packed our provisions—scant few that we had—wrapped our bedding and selected clothing so that all would appear at a distance to be humans, placed as much as we could into two small carts and enjoyed, on that last afternoon in the stone house, a substantial meal.

After sunset at middle March, the hulfs all dressed as humans dress and we ventured into the night. I did not even bother to lock the house, knowing even then that I should never return. It was still quite cold.

There was no moon that night.

* * * * *

One of the problems with being the last of your kind is that, if things do not work out, if your plans for the future fail and your dreams go awry, then you and your blood line shall soon cease to exist. Nothing will remain of you to remind future generations that you were even here, except, perhaps, some myths and legends whispered around an evening hearth. It was likely that the two dozen hulfs who had stayed with me through the winter and a few dozen more from the village were the only ones who had managed to escape the guns and axes of the humans. How many others had already fled to the sanctuary in the south and found safety we could only guess.

I had done all I could to encourage the hulfs, to convince them we could reach the unknown sanctuary had we but the courage, stamina and perseverance to accomplish it. Secretly, I hoped my promises would not be revealed to be the hollow mutterings of a fool.

The arrow of time moves forward only. Things done can never be undone but, perhaps, they can be repeated or duplicated or reenacted differently, or dreamed again on a new night with less terrifying conclusions. Perhaps. Perhaps.

*****

Sometimes we walked; sometimes we ran, always hiding during the day and making our way through unfamiliar lands at night. It was dreadful. We were constantly hungry and thirsty. I was always cold and wet and I feared that if the humans did not find and kill me, I would perish from disease or exposure to the elements. In moments of fevered madness I even imagined that the hulfs would kill me as I slept and eat me.

We had fled for hundreds of miles in those months of late winter and early spring and I began to think that we might reach our destination safely within just a few more days. We began to see signs, trails and pathways, hulf prints, bits of hair clinging to the brush, that indicated we were on or near the road leading to the sanctuary. We fell into a kind of complacency, thinking that beyond the next turn or over the next hill we would find our salvation.

It did not occur to me that if we could see and follow the signs, the human hunters could follow them as well. And, so, we were caught in their trap.

I plodded beside one of the carts keeping my eyes fixed on the top of a tree which showed against the sky above the pines. The trees might mean that a stream or lake was near. I was a good foot taller than the largest of the male hulfs and had been walking with my shoulders hunched forward under my heavy tattered and dirty shirt so I would not present a noticable target in case we were observed by humans who might be lurking in the forests.

My height made walking difficult, for I had to cut down my normal stride to accommodate my speed to the progress of those pulling the carts. After months of stumbling along behind them my back and shoulders ached unmercifully.

We had been twenty-six in number when we left the headland in March and we had moved slowly but unfaltering, sometimes covering as much as twenty miles in a night. Now there were only twenty-two of us. Four had sickened and died within the first month, and those of us who remained had weakened from hunger and exposure.

As our provisions dwindled, we transferred as much as we could to the largest of the carts and abandoned the smaller in a copse beside a stream where we had stayed for two days and nights.

The single cart and its load had become a living thing, a determined, nearly unmovable object, everlastingly pitting its weight against our strength.

I shifted the two pistols hidden under my coat and shivered a little. I had hoped to find warmth and sunshine as we trekked southward, gentle breezes that might restore strength to all of us. The hope had become a jest. Bitter cold had followed implacably from the moment we had left the great stone house on the headland above the village.

It would settle down with deathly frostiness as soon as the sun was gone, numbing us into mindless zombies and shivering the uncomplaining pups, lying so still in the bottom of the cart.

I lost all track of time. Not until we crossed a broad, winding ice-free river whose banks were lined with crocus and Queen Anne's Lace did I realize we had journeyed into Spring. It was the twenty-fourth of June! Three long, miserable months since we had begun our escape from certain death. In that time, not one of us had been injured or killed by the humans, although we often saw them in the distance watching us as we passed and once we were pursured by hunters on horses. They gave up the chase when their mounts were unable to follow us through the dense forests.

But it was there, in the forest, that we found the abandoned homes and farms, the abandoned hopes and dreams, of the humans who had succumbed to the disease of the hulfs. Empty houses stared back at us with sightless eyes, the dreams of their owners dead and forgotten, leaving populous, prosperous villages to be overrun by encroaching forests.

In the wagon, I heard one of the she-hulfs moan. I halted the company and walked to the back, lowering the heavy tailboard. A she-hulf lay in one corner, the piled-up provisions towering above her, a lovely girl barely in her mid-teens, scarcely heavy enough to depress the thick pallet beneath her. At the sight of me she smiled, but her lips were colorless and pinched, and her golden eyes were bright with fever.

"What is it?" I asked.

"She is pregnant, Gill," Cybele said behind me. "The pup will come soon. Are we near any place where we can stop?"

"There must be something soon." I placed a hand on her forehead, felt the heat and smoothed back her golden hair. It was damp beneath my fingers. Cybele took out a cupful of water, then raised her with an arm beneath her shoulders and let the girl drink.

She took but a swallow. Cybele found a cloth, moistened it from the cup, and gently bathed her forehead and temples.

She moaned again. For an instant we stood staring down at her swollen belly, rounding the folds of the long cloak which covered her. Her lean face was tight with despair.

"How did this happen?" I asked.

Cybele's eyebrows went up a half inch. "How? Do you not understand the mating?"

"Yes, of course," I stammered. "But I mean when did this happen, how without my seeing or knowing?"

"The males are stealthy and filled with cunning, Gill. Wherever we're going, we'd better hurry, or we'll have a pup before we get there."

I straightened and pulled the covers over the she-hulf, then swept back my long unshorn hair. The company plodded on through the early morning toward a sagging house across a meadow of knee-high grass.

The sun glowed bronze through a haze, and was already riding above the towering tops of the trees. The temperature was slowly rising and the mist swept from the meadow on a light breeze.

We did not see the humans, coiled like a panther, waiting at the edge of the trees, waiting to shoot and hack with their terrible guns and axes, waiting to kill us all, hulfs and human alike, as if we were all so much garbage to be disposed of at the command of madmen.

Within minutes after reaching the house, I had a fire going and a kettle filled with vegetables hanging on a tripod.

The heat repelled the coldness. Squatting down beside the flames, for a time we could almost believe that we had reached the end of the journey. The woods around us seemed friendly, like the windrow of some quiet farm. The cart was as secure as a small fortress. The girl on the bed inside it was young and healthy and happy, and seemed safe from any harm. I lifted her gently and carried her into the old house while Cybele carried in the padded pallet. When she was comfortable, I went outside to sit by the fire.

The stew began to simmer. I rose and went to talk to the other hulfs, who had all gathered to sleep at the edge of the woods, to get a feel for their hopes, and to give them encouragement for the journey ahead of us.

I stopped in the half-darkness of the trees. Behind me the clearing showed bright, giving me the sensation of standing outside a window and looking into a lighted room. I lowered my hands to close about the coolness of the pistols and stood frozen, looking at the sandy ground marked with human boot-prints.

I moved a few steps forward, bent over as if in a dream, and touched a piece of rope circling one of the trees. From there I moved on quietly to touch three others. All were covered with blood. I could see that from the flickering rays of the rising sun which danced through the trees, bringing light from the clearing.

I knelt and pulled one of the pistols from my belt, scanning the brightening forest for signs of humans or hulfs. At a distance, I could see the form of a man behind one of the trees, his fat belly and face silhouetted against the light from the clearing.

I leveled the pistol and cocked the hammer. Suddenly, someone grabbed me about the neck and pulled me backward, snatching the pistol from my hand at the same time.

"They have taken four of us," a voice rasped in my ear. It was Jack, the Alpha male.

"Taken? Where are they taking them?" I croaked.

"To death with their knives."

"Oh, God, oh, God."

"Your god cannot help them now," Jack said as he released me from his powerful grip.

"How many are they?" I asked.

"I counted nine with knives and guns. They knew we were coming, Gill. I think they have been following us for days."

"Why could you not smell them?"

"They have covered their clothing and skin with a lotion that masks their scent. But I have smelled that scent since the day we were at the river."

We sat in silence for some time, waiting for the assault that we knew must surely come. Jack leaned back against the base of a tree and raised his snout to the sky, his nostrils flaring.

"They are still here," he said.

"Where are the other hulfs?"

"They have gone by ones and twos back to house. There is some safety there."

"I'm sorry, Jack," I said weakly, close to tears.

"For what?"

"For the hulfs. For the deaths of the hulfs."

"It was not your fault. Come."

We went back and stood leaning against the cart. Steam came up from the kettle of water and hovered above the simmering stew.

My back grew cold, and I draped a blanket about my shoulders, reaching again for the pistols in my belt, to assure myself they were still there, ready and deadly. Many times I heard a rustle, but it was only wind in the treetops.

The fire had died and twice been replenished when we heard the young she-hulf scream. Hours later, she gave birth to a son. Some of the females bathed the tiny, squalling pup, wrapped it in clean old linen, and laid it beside its mother.

Her lips moved feebly. "I'm very tired."

"You have a son," someone said in the shadows.

She closed her eyes. After a while, Cybele put her hand on the girl's ashen face and found it cold.

Across the clearing a shot flashed out from the trees, then, closer, another one. I ran out to crouch behind the shelter of the cart, pistols out and ready.

"Come inside, fool," Jack growled. "The air will not stop their bullets but perhaps the timbers of the house will."

He grabbed my arm and dragged me inside where most of the survivors were clustered together for protection.

Hideous and demonic figures broke from the trees, yelling and screaming. I held my fire, then coolly picked out the nearest hunter and shot him. He fell, his arms sprawled wide. Another was killed seconds later.

"Seven more," I thought. "And I have but ten more rounds."

It didn't seem to matter, for the thought of the dead she-hulf, herself no more than a child, lying in the next room had crept deep into my soul.

There was a noise outside. Hurried steps bounded up on the porch, and someone knocked at the door. I flung it open.

A hulf I did not recognize stood outside in a long leather coat. "There's firing!"

"Where?"

"Just south of here. Not very far."

"Where were you?"

"In the forest, following the nine humans who took the four hulfs. I turned from the trail and heard firing as I was coming in."

At a soft command, water was dumped on the flaming logs, raising a cloud of ruby-colored steam. More water came, and the fire died.

I stood by the half-opened door waiting for the humans to attack in force. Jack and some of the other hulfs watched at the windows.

Cybele stood, and was trembling. "Be careful, Gill."

"I'm always careful, girl. I've been careful all my life. Too careful, perhaps. Now is the time for madness and action or we shall all perish." I pulled her close and kissed her. "Nothing living shall kill me tonight."

"Nothing but another human's gun," she whispered, pressing her fingers to her lips as if to seal the kiss there forever. "Be careful."

I motioned for Jack and two of the other hulfs to go with me into the forest to get behind the hunters. Together we went down from the porch and crept around to the back of the house.

Cybele watched without speaking. My eyes swept the camp, darkened now except for the sputtering fire.

When we had reached the edge of the forest, I turned to Jack and indicated that he and one hulf should go to the left while I would take the other hulf to the right. The idea was to get behind the humans and kill them one at a time.

"We'll circle to meet and home in on the noise of any firing. Watch for an ambush."

I had no worries about Jack. He could travel the woods in daylight or darkness with the speed and silence of a spectre.

When I was certain we were behind the humans, I stopped and listened. There was no sound of firing, but somewhat northward I heard a soft whistle. An instant later, to the left, it was answered by another. The hulf touched my shoulder.

"Not humans," he said quietly.

I nodded and we moved forward toward the sound.

"Let's push on. There'll be no more firing. Whatever it is, their work is done. The two dead humans have spooked them. They're probably wondering how hulfs could have killed their comrades."

We approached a clearing and pulled up short. There was smoke in the air, and the smell of burned powder. To our right were the last few embers of a dying fire in the camp where the humans had waited.

Jack, with the other hulf in tow loomed from the shadows, ghost-like, to stand beside us.

"We've circled the clearing," Jack said grimly. "We found the bodies of the four taken earlier. They were skinned and their paws cut off. They took the heads of the two females."

"Come away from the fire," I said, "in case they are watching. We'll make easy targets in the glow of this smoke."

"The seven hunters are over there," Jack said, pointing toward the south. "They are all together, hiding, afraid. No one is watching for us."

"In that case," I said, "they will be easy pickings for my pistols."

"Are you certain you want to do that?" Jack asked. "You are human; they are humans. Is it not murder in the eyes of your laws?"

"Self-defense is not murder."

"It is if one is a hulf."

I had no answer for that. I checked the pistols to make certain I had ten rounds. I silently wished I had more. "The Lord provideth, and equally taketh away."

"Nonsense," Jack growled. "But do what you must. I will take these hulfs back to the house to protect the others. Be careful; someone or something besides the hunters is in this forest tonight."

They moved silently, drifting away like the smoke from the dying campfire.

Tomorrow you'll christen the baby and bury his mother with a few words from the Scriptures, I thought, as I made my way into the forest toward the hunters. I tried to think of words of Scripture I could say and found I could not remember any. They were lost two hundred years behind me.

It was strangely silent as I crept forward into the greening forest. There were no animal sounds, no bird calls, no human voices from the camp now only yards away. Smoke from their fire curled upward and was borne away on the breeze. The sun was now already above the trees and I could see the hunters slumped around the meager fire as if asleep.

I stopped at the edge of the small clearing. No one was on watch. I looked for the bags holding the hulf skins and heads, but could not see them anywhere. From my left came a single soft whistle and from the right, moments later, came an answer.

"Not human," the hulf had told me.

I eased forward until I was less than ten feet from the nearest sleeping hunter. There was a pungent smell of death in the camp. I searched again for the bags of hulf skins and realized with a start that the hunters were not sleeping at all—they were dead; killed where they sat by some unseen and unheard creature.

Horrified, I stood and backed away from the goulish scene, then turned and began to run as fast as I could through the tangled brush. I had not gone ten yards when two large male hulfs stepped into view before me. I tried to stop, tried to turn away, but one grabbed me around the neck and flung me to the ground, mouth open wide to crush my throat.

"Hold!" came a harsh command from the shadows.

I looked beyond the hulf to see a large, muscular male appear from behind a tree. He waved his arm and the hulf holding me down sprang away, leaving me breathless and choking.

The great hulf stepped to my side and bent near me, sniffing and snorting. I feared then that he would kill me himself.

He straightened and relaxed a bit. "You have the scent of a she-hulf on you," he said. "The young one with the newborn pup in the house yonder. And another, perhaps, as well."

I could not answer, only nod affirmatively.

"Do you lead them to the sanctuary?"

Nodding again.

"We have been watching you for some time, wondering where you are going, what you are doing. This morning we thought you had led them here into the trap to be killed by the humans."

I shook my head no.

"I see that. If you seek the sanctuary, you are leading them in the wrong direction. You took the wrong trail at the river two days ago and you are moving away from the sanctuary. It is a trap the humans have devised by leaving bits of fur and paw prints to make it appear as though hulfs have gone down the one path while they swept away the tracks from the other."

I swallowed away the dryness in my throat and managed to sit upright. I looked back toward the hunter's camp. "Did you... ?"

"Of course we did. We cannot leave this baggage alive to kill our brothers and sisters. Some of the hulfs are already cleaning the campsite of the refuse so other hunters will never know what happened there. More are back at the river to make sure the trap signs are removed. It is something we try to do every day. It is why we are here."

"How many are you?" I asked.

He raised his head suspiciously and eyed me askance. "We are many," he said simply. "But you are now only nineteen, counting the newborn pup."

"The mother died," I said quietly.

He grimaced and looked away into the forest, growling deep in the heat of his throat. Presently, he turned back to me. "Eighteen, then. Do you have lactating females to care for the pup? If you do not, we will take him and our camp will raise him."

"I don't know. I'll ask when I return."

"Come." He extended his hand—still human but lengthened and distorted and clawed and covered with dark fur—and snatched me from the ground as easily as he might lift an infant. "We have much to do this day."

I wanted to ask his name but knew he would only say, 'hulf,' if he answered at all.

*****

"I would spend days in those intercrossing mirror worlds which ran into one another, trembled, vanished, only to reappeared again," the raggedy man said softly.

"I gave my mind, my body, my soul to those fathomless distances, those echoing vistas, those separate universes cutting across my own and existing, despite my consciousness of them, in the same place at the same time. That extended reality, separated from me by the smooth surface of silvered glass, drew me towards itself by a kind of unknowable, intangible touch, dragging me into the gleaming surface, as if into a mysterious abyss.

"I was drawn towards the apparition which posed before me when I came near the mirror and which strangely doubled my being. I tried to imagine how this other was different from me, how it was possible that my right hand should be his left, and that all the fingers of my hands should change places.

"My thoughts were confused when I attempted to probe that enigma, to solve it. In this world, where everything could be touched, where voices were heard I lived, actually, and in that reflected world, which it was only possible to imagine, was he, the phantom, the ghost. He was almost myself and yet not really myself; he repeated all my movements, but not a single one of those movements exactly matched my own.

"He, that other, that phantom, knew something I could not divine, he held a secret hidden from my understanding; a secret that would soon come crashing down upon me to fill me with terror and wonder.

"But I noticed that each mirror had its own separate and special world. Put two mirrors in the very same place, one after the other, and there will arise two different universes. And in different mirrors before which I posed, there would rise before me

83

different apparitions, all of them similar to me but never exactly like me and never exactly like the others.

"According to the strange conditions of their worlds they take the form of the person who poses before the glass but under this borrowed image they each preserved their own personal characteristics.

"There were some worlds of mirrors which I loved; others which I hated. I did not love all my doubles. I felt most were hostile toward me, if only because they were forced to drape themselves in my likeness.

"There were some whom I despised. There were others, on the other hand, whom I feared, who were too strong for me and who dared in their turn to mock me to do as they demanded.

"I smashed the mirrors where these hostile doubles lived. I would not look into them. I hid them, gave them away, even broke them into pieces.

"But every time I destroyed a mirror I wept for hours, knowing that I had broken to pieces a distinct, distant universe. And hateful, terrible faces stared up at me from the broken fragments of the worlds I had scattered upon the floor."

*****

I returned to the abandoned house, accompanied by twelve guardian hulfs, eight of them adult males, four of them adult females, but they were certainly not all who were in the forest that night.

Our frightened company were huddled in one corner of the room sharing the vegetable stew. They were elated when they saw the guardians and and began enthusiatic conversations. Some of them knew a few of the guardian hulfs as being from the village from which they, themselves, had recently fled.

The alpha male guardian hulf asked about the newborn pup and learned we had no lactating females. He told one of his females to take the pup and, because she was lactating, she began nursing it. He let us know that they would take the pup to their camp and raise it as their own.

I named the alpha male Apollo and the nursing female Naomi, although I never addressed them by those names because I feared it might offend them to be called by human names.

Cybele brought me a cup of still warm stew. "Are you okay?" she asked. "You look strange and you are so quiet."

"I'm okay now that I am back here with you. It was a cruel morning and a sad one."

"It is not your fault that the hulfs were taken. Don't punish yourself for something you cannot or could not prevent." She looked at the cup of stew I held in my trembling hands. "Drink now," she said tenderly.

I lifted the cup and drank a bit of the broth. "The hulfs have told me we are going in the wrong direction," I said. "We will have to go back to the river where the trails diverged, or cut across from here if there is a trail which will take us to the sanctuary."

"Yes, there is a secret way, but it leads to a large lake where we may take a ferry across. It is but two days through the forest. If the ferry is not there, or if the captain will not or cannot take us, we will have to go around. It will be a month or more if we go around; only four days if we can cross."

"Then let us hope we can cross," I said as I finished the cup of stew. "Did anyone say how far the sanctuary is from the lake?"

"Two more days." Cybele said. "They said we would be safe from harm once we cross the lake."

"Or journey around it."

"Yes." She looked away briefly and shifted awkwardly. "You kissed me, Gill," she said so softly that I had to lean forward to hear.

"Yes, I did. Should I not have done it? I didn't mean anything wanton by it. It is a human gesture toward someone they care about. It is meant to reassure the other that everything will be okay."

"For someone you love?"

"Well, yes, I suppose that's the way to say it."

"And do you love me?"

"Dear Cybele, I have loved you from the first day when we met on the path to the stone house."

"You never told me."

"Because it is not possible for us to be together. We live in different worlds. You have the world of the hulfs and I ... ."

She touched my lips with a finger. "I, too, have loved you and no other since that first day. But I know we cannot be together. Our different worlds will not allow it. Still, we can be companions for many years."

I did not have the heart or the courage to tell her how different our worlds really were, that I might one day simply vanish, fall into a mirror and simply vanish. I could not screw up the courage to explain it, to tell her that I was two hundred years old and that if I did not vanish into a mirror, I might just drop dead. I wanted so badly to say it, but I could not. And so the traitor in me said, "Yes."

*****

The raggedy man began to weep. Not aloud, not pitifully, but silently. Tears crept down his brown, wrinkled cheeks to fall into his lap.

"I'm sorry," he said after a time. His lips tembled. He shook his head from side to side. "I'm sorry. I loved her so."

"And she loved you."

"And I deserted her at her hour of need…at their hour of greatest need… by doing that which I feared so much. I fell into this world where I have lived as a pauper, longing only to return to my most beloved Cybele."

*****

In the days when the hulf disease began, there was little trouble between the hulfs and men. They lived apart— the men in the villages and farms and the hulfs in the swamps and thickets and on the wide grassy meadows between the villages.

Sometimes a horse or cow would stray into the marshes or meadows to become a meal, and sometimes the hulfs would find one already dead, and drive off the vultures and feral cats, and feast well to their heart's content for days.

The hulfs of the old time were clumsy of foot and dull-coloured, with rough fur and large heads, many of them misshapen and ugly. They came every spring north into the villages, after the willows turned green and before the fruit trees flowered, when the grass on the wide meadows grew long. They came only in small groups then, each pack an alpha male and two or three females with a pup or two, having their own hunting territory, and they went again to hunt in the foothills when the Harlequin Maples were red and the antelope came down from the mountains.

But, as the disease evolved, the hulfs became sleek and swift, brave and cunning; the males strong and handsome, the females lithe and lovely. The pups were simply beautiful to behold by the time I had fallen into their world.

It was their custom to hunt in the open, going into cover only in the heat of the day. They avoided the long stretches of tangled forest, preferring the openness of meadows and farms near the edges of the villages where they often found portions of food thrown out by humans.

It was difficult, if not impossible, to come upon them unawares. They were not fighters; their teeth were only for prey, but if they were provoked or threatened, once they began, no living thing came near them; no other living creature could withstand their power and ferocity.

And in those early days when men seemed to be trying to account for the disease and to find a cure, humans, by and large, seemed harmless; indeed, many wanted to do all they could to help the sad and hopeless hulfs.

But no utterance of prophecy warned the hulfs of the terrible savagery that was to come, of the clubs and guns and axes to be wielded to drive the packs from the villages into the dystopian world of terror and blackness beneath the city streets, beneath the darkness, beneath the thin line between self and the unspeakable world of monsters and murder that was to replace the wide meadows and the freedom of the earth.

*****

Season changes had compensations. The bitter cold, which lasted for intense, shivering periods that winter and sent us sometimes from our beds to shiver about the edge of a roaring fire, equally rid the encampment of the pesky insects and brought great flocks of wild ducks and geese into the nearby rivers and lakes.

Relief from the cold came with spring, but the insects returned, and a new caution was necessary against the deadly snakes and panthers and bears which had come out from hibernation to bask in the sun.

But it was worth trudging through the thin, lingering snow and ankle-deep icy marshes just to smell again the sweetness of blossoming trees and flowers, and to know that the fish of the lakes and streams would soon begin to rise again to be snatched by a quick, clawed hand.

*****

Most humans, and especially their children, had never seen hulfs closely, but soon they saw them every day as they began to raid out from their lairs on the edges of the villages, joining and raiding together in search of food. The hulfs in the countryside came together in larger and stronger packs, forming communities around many of the abandoned farms that dotted the countryside.

The bears and panthers had become afraid of them, and when they caught wind of a hulf they turned aside. When the humans saw this, they, too, became afraid of the hulf living on the swiftness of their limbs and the deep, dark, red heat of their throats.

And many humans began to keep guns and axes beside their doors to drive away or kill any hulf who might stray too close. They surrounded themselves with fear and loathing, never suspecting they might, one day, also become a creature of the darkness to be loathed and feared by those who loved them but a day before.

*****

Apollo and Naomi came to me in the evening to say that they would lead us to the secret trail to the lake, would take us as far as they could before turning back to guard and protect any others who might seek the sanctuary by the same path we had traveled.

Naomi was nursing the pup and I watched unabashed the tender scene, knowing that the pup would be safe and loved, growing someday to a strong adult, running free and hunting the marshes and meadows of the sanctuary.

"Sanctuary is but eight days away if you are fortunate enough to cross the lake. But the ferry is not always at the lake," said Apollo. "If it is taking others across, and if it left only a day before, or the morning before you arrive, it will be eight days before it returns. It is not safe on this side of the lake. Human bounty hunters have discovered the pier and they lurk nearby, waiting for some luckless straggler to arrive... ."

"Then they kill!" Naomi growled, slashing the air with her fingers. "And they take their skins and the feet of the males and the heads of the females back to the villages to prove they have killed those who make the pups so they can claim their bounties."

"They are paid small fees for males," Apollo said. "Larger fees for the females because when they kill a female, they are killing the future of the packs. Fewer pups means we soon will be gone forever."

*****

"I am weary," said the raggedy man. "I should find a place to bathe and change into these clothes you have brought me. Then I must arrange my mirrors and try to return to Cybele."

I looked at my watch and realized that it was evening. Outside, the sun was already on the horizon and it would soon be dark.

"Is there anything I can do to help?" I asked.

"Not really. If the mirrors are arranged properly, I will vanish and some other man or creature will appear in my place. If not, then we will continue our conversation tomorrow."

"If you go—fall into the mirror, I mean—will the man who replaces you know what happened in the world where you left the hulfs?"

"If he is from that world, yes, I suppose he will. But it has been two years. How many adventures will he have survived in so long a time?"

"Yes," I said softly. "How many adventures?"

"And he might not be from the world of the hulfs. He might be from the past, or from a future so distant that he would not recognize this world at all. It might not even be a human."

"I see," I said, standing to go. I reached out and took the raggedy man's wrinkled brown hand in my own. "If I do not see you again, then I wish you a safe journey and hope you find those you left behind and loved so much."

The raggedy man said nothing, stood with lips pursed and eyes bright with tears. He took the book from the large box and gave it to me.

I walked away, then, without looking back.

And, so, the raggedy man's story ends. When I returned the next morning, everything was gone. The boxes, the mirrors, the food and clothing, the easels, even the folder of matches and the candle had vanished as if they had never existed at all.

No man or creature was lurking in the dark building to explain what had transpired the previous night. I want to believe that the transfer occured and that the newcomer, eager to escape the filthy delelict building, had thrown everything into the trash bin to hide any evidence of his arrival and had then gone into the outside world to live another fantastic adventure.

I want to believe that the raggedy man returned to the world of the hulfs, returned to Cybele, and lived with her in the sanctuary until the end of his days.

But I would never know.

Only the paw prints of a large canine were lightly visible upon the dusty concrete floor. But the pattern was of two paws only, as if the creature walked upon its hind legs in the manner of a human.

I had one more task to do. I took the book to the library on my way to work, dropping it unnoticed into the night return slot.

I never saw the raggedy man again and realized he had never told me his name and had never explained why or how he had fallen into this world.

The following pages contain an unabridged, fully illustrated, version of Sir Arthur Conan Doyle's Hound of the Baskervilles. Originally published in 1889, it soon became among the most popular books in the Sherlock Holmes detective series. Its popularity has only increased over the years, spawning numerous motion picture adaptations.

Born: May 22, 1859, Edinburgh
Died: July 7, 1930, Crowborough
Children: Adrian Conan Doyle
Spouse: Jean Leckie (m. 1907–1930), Louisa Hawkins (m. 1885–1906)

HOUND of the Baskervilles

by Sir Arthur Conan Doyle

CHAPTER I. MR. SHERLOCK HOLMES

Mr. Sherlock Holmes, who was usually very late in the mornings, save upon those not infrequent occasions when he was up all night, was seated at the breakfast table. I stood upon the hearth-rug and picked up the stick which our visitor had left behind him the night before. It was a fine, thick piece of wood, bulbous-headed, of the sort which is known as a "Penang lawyer." Just under the head was a broad silver band nearly an inch across. "To James Mortimer, M.R.C.S., from his friends of the C.C.H.," was engraved upon it, with the date "1884." It was just such a stick as the old-fashioned family practitioner used to carry—dignified, solid, and reassuring.

"Well, Watson, what do you make of it?"

Holmes was sitting with his back to me, and I had given him no sign of my occupation.

"How did you know what I was doing? I believe you have eyes in the back of your head."

"I have, at least, a well-polished, silver-plated coffee-pot in front of me," said he. "But, tell me, Watson, what do you make of our visitor's stick? Since we have been so unfortunate as to miss him and have no notion of his errand, this accidental souvenir becomes of importance. Let me hear you reconstruct the man by an examination of it."

"I think," said I, following as far as I could the methods of my companion, "that Dr. Mortimer is a successful, elderly medical man, well-esteemed since those who know him give him this mark of their appreciation."

"Good!" said Holmes. "Excellent!"

"I think also that the probability is in favour of his being a country practitioner who does a great deal of his visiting on foot."

"Why so?"

"Because this stick, though originally a very handsome one has been so knocked about that I can hardly imagine a town practitioner carrying it. The thick-iron ferrule is worn down, so it is evident that he has done a great amount of walking with it."

"Perfectly sound!" said Holmes.

"And then again, there is the 'friends of the C.C.H.' I should guess that to be the Something Hunt, the local hunt to whose members he has possibly given some surgical assistance, and which has made him a small presentation in return."

"Really, Watson, you excel yourself," said Holmes, pushing back his chair and lighting a cigarette. "I am bound to say that in all the accounts which you have been so good as to give of my own small achievements you have habitually underrated your own abilities. It may be that you are not yourself luminous, but you are a conductor of light. Some people without possessing genius have a remarkable power of stimulating it. I confess, my dear fellow, that I am very much in your debt."

He had never said as much before, and I must admit that his words gave me keen pleasure, for I had often been piqued by his indifference to my admiration and to the attempts which I had made to give publicity to his methods. I was proud, too, to think that I had so far mastered his system as to apply it in a way which earned his approval. He now took the stick from my hands and examined it for a few minutes with his naked eyes. Then with an expression of interest he laid down his cigarette, and carrying the cane to the window, he looked over it again with a convex lens.

"Interesting, though elementary," said he as he returned to his favourite corner of the settee. "There are certainly one or two indications upon the stick. It gives us the basis for several deductions."

"Has anything escaped me?" I asked with some self-importance. "I trust that there is nothing of consequence which I have overlooked?"

"I am afraid, my dear Watson, that most of your conclusions were erroneous. When I said that you stimulated me I meant, to be frank, that in noting your fallacies I was occasionally guided towards the truth. Not that you are entirely wrong in this instance. The man is certainly a country practitioner. And he walks a good deal."

"Then I was right."

"To that extent."

"But that was all."

"No, no, my dear Watson, not all—by no means all. I would suggest, for example, that a presentation to a doctor is more likely to come from a hospital than from a hunt, and that when the initials 'C.C.' are placed before that hospital the words' Charing Cross' very naturally suggest themselves."

"You may be right."

"The probability lies in that direction. And if we take this as a working hypothesis we have a fresh basis from which to start our construction of this unknown visitor."

"Well, then, supposing that 'C.C.H.' does stand for 'Charing Cross Hospital,' what further inferences may we draw?"

"Do none suggest themselves? You know my methods. Apply them!"

"I can only think of the obvious conclusion that the man has practised in town before going to the country."

"I think that we might venture a little farther than this. Look at it in this light. On what occasion would it be most probable that such a presentation would be made? When would his friends unite to give him a pledge of their good will? Obviously at the moment when Dr. Mortimer withdrew from the service of the hospital in order to start in practice for himself. We know there has been a presentation. We believe there has been a change from a town hospital to a country practice. Is it, then, stretching our inference too far to say that the presentation was on the occasion of the change?"

"It certainly seems probable."

"Now, you will observe that he could not have been on the staff of the hospital, since only a man well-established in a London practice could hold such a position, and such a one would not drift into the country. What was he, then? If he was in the hospital and yet not on the staff he could only have been a house-surgeon or a house-physician—little more than a senior student. And he left five years ago—the date is on the stick. So your grave, middle-aged family practitioner vanishes into thin air, my dear Watson, and there emerges a young fellow under thirty, amiable, unambitious, absent-minded, and the possessor of a favourite dog, which I should describe roughly as being larger than a terrier and smaller than a mastiff."

I laughed incredulously as Sherlock Holmes leaned back in his settee and blew little wavering rings of smoke up to the ceiling.

"As to the latter part, I have no means of checking you," said I, "but at least it is not difficult to find out a few particulars about the man's age and professional career." From my small medical shelf I took down the Medical Directory and turned up the name. There were several Mortimers, but only one who could be our visitor. I read his record aloud.

"Mortimer, James, M.R.C.S., 1882, Grimpen, Dartmoor, Devon. House-surgeon, from 1882 to 1884, at Charing Cross Hospital. Winner of the Jackson prize for Comparative Pathology, with essay entitled 'Is Disease a Reversion?' Corresponding member of the Swedish Pathological Society. Author of 'Some Freaks of Atavism' (Lancet 1882). 'Do We Progress?' (Journal of Psychology, March, 1883). Medical Officer for the parishes of Grimpen, Thorsley, and High Barrow."

"No mention of that local hunt, Watson," said Holmes with a mischievous smile, "but a country doctor, as you very astutely observed. I think that I am fairly justified in my inferences. As to the adjectives, I said, if I remember right, amiable, unambitious, and absent-minded. It is my experience that it is only an amiable man in this world who receives testimonials, only an unambitious one who abandons a London career for the country, and only an absent-minded one who leaves his stick and not his visiting-card after waiting an hour in your room."

"And the dog?"

"Has been in the habit of carrying this stick behind his master. Being a heavy stick the dog has held it tightly by the middle, and the marks of his teeth are very plainly visible. The dog's jaw, as shown in the space between these marks, is too broad in my opinion for a terrier and not broad enough for a mastiff. It may have been—yes, by Jove, it is a curly-haired spaniel."

He had risen and paced the room as he spoke. Now he halted in the recess of the window. There was such a ring of conviction in his voice that I glanced up in surprise.

"My dear fellow, how can you possibly be so sure of that?"

"For the very simple reason that I see the dog himself on our very doorstep, and there is the ring of its owner. Don't move, I beg you, Watson. He is a professional brother of yours, and your presence may be of assistance to me. Now is the dramatic moment of fate, Watson, when you hear a step upon the stair which is walking into your life, and you know not whether for good or ill. What does Dr. James Mortimer, the man of science, ask of Sherlock Holmes, the specialist in crime? Come in!"

The appearance of our visitor was a surprise to me, since I had expected a typical country practitioner. He was a very tall, thin man, with a long nose like a beak, which jutted out between two keen, gray eyes, set closely together and sparkling brightly from behind a pair of gold-rimmed glasses. He was clad in a professional but rather slovenly fashion, for his frock-coat was dingy and his trousers frayed. Though young, his long back was already bowed, and he walked with a forward thrust of his head and a general air of peering benevolence. As he entered his eyes fell upon the stick in Holmes's hand, and he ran towards it with an exclamation of joy. "I am so very glad," said he. "I was not sure whether I had left it here or in the Shipping Office. I would not lose that stick for the world."

"A presentation, I see," said Holmes.

"Yes, sir."

"From Charing Cross Hospital?"

"From one or two friends there on the occasion of my marriage."

"Dear, dear, that's bad!" said Holmes, shaking his head.

Dr. Mortimer blinked through his glasses in mild astonishment.

"Why was it bad?"

"Only that you have disarranged our little deductions. Your marriage, you say?"

"Yes, sir. I married, and so left the hospital, and with it all hopes of a consulting practice. It was necessary to make a home of my own."

"Come, come, we are not so far wrong, after all," said Holmes. "And now, Dr. James Mortimer ———"

"Mister, sir, Mister—a humble M.R.C.S."

"And a man of precise mind, evidently."

"A dabbler in science, Mr. Holmes, a picker up of shells on the shores of the great unknown ocean. I presume that it is Mr. Sherlock Holmes whom I am addressing and not ———"

"No, this is my friend Dr. Watson."

"Glad to meet you, sir. I have heard your name mentioned in connection with that of your friend. You interest me very much, Mr. Holmes. I had hardly expected so dolichocephalic a skull or such well-marked supra-orbital development. Would you have any objection to my running my finger along your parietal fissure? A cast of your skull, sir, until the original is available, would be an ornament to any anthropological museum. It is not my intention to be fulsome, but I confess that I covet your skull."

Sherlock Holmes waved our strange visitor into a chair. "You are an enthusiast in your line of thought, I perceive, sir, as I am in mine," said he. "I observe from your forefinger that you make your own cigarettes. Have no hesitation in lighting one."

The man drew out paper and tobacco and twirled the one up in the other

with surprising dexterity. He had long, quivering fingers as agile and rest-
less as the antennae of an insect.

Holmes was silent, but his little darting glances showed me the interest
which he took in our curious companion.

"I presume, sir," said he at last, "that it was not merely for the purpose of
examining my skull that you have done me the honour to call here last night
and again to-day?"

"No, sir, no; though I am happy to have had the opportunity of doing that
as well. I came to you, Mr. Holmes, because I recognized that I am myself an
unpractical man and because I am suddenly confronted with a most serious
and extraordinary problem. Recognizing, as I do, that you are the second
highest expert in Europe ———"

"Indeed, sir! May I inquire who has the honour to be the first?" asked
Holmes with some asperity.

"To the man of precisely scientific mind the work of Monsieur Bertillon
must always appeal strongly."

"Then had you not better consult him?"

"I said, sir, to the precisely scientific mind. But as a practical man of affairs
it is acknowledged that you stand alone. I trust, sir, that I have not inadvert-
ently ———"

"Just a little," said Holmes. "I think, Dr. Mortimer, you would do wisely if
without more ado you would kindly tell me plainly what the exact nature of
the problem is in which you demand my assistance."

CHAPTER II. THE CURSE OF THE BASKERVILLES

"I have in my pocket a manuscript," said Dr. James Mortimer.

"I observed it as you entered the room," said Holmes.

"It is an old manuscript."

"Early eighteenth century, unless it is a forgery."

"How can you say that, sir?"

"You have presented an inch or two of it to my examination all the time that you have been talking. It would be a poor expert who could not give the date of a document within a decade or so. You may possibly have read my little monograph upon the subject. I put that at 1730."

"The exact date is 1742." Dr. Mortimer drew it from his breast-pocket. "This family paper was committed to my care by Sir Charles Baskerville, whose sudden and tragic death some three months ago created so much excitement in Devonshire. I may say that I was his personal friend as well as his medical attendant. He was a strong-minded man, sir, shrewd, practical, and as unimaginative as I am myself. Yet he took this document very seriously, and his mind was prepared for just such an end as did eventually overtake him."

Holmes stretched out his hand for the manuscript and flattened it upon his knee.

"You will observe, Watson, the alternative use of the long s and the short. It is one of several indications which enabled me to fix the date."

I looked over his shoulder at the yellow paper and the faded script. At the head was written: "Baskerville Hall," and below in large, scrawling figures: "1742."

"It appears to be a statement of some sort."

"Yes, it is a statement of a certain legend which runs in the Baskerville family."

"But I understand that it is something more modern and practical upon which you wish to consult me?"

"Most modern. A most practical, pressing matter, which must be decided within twenty-four hours. But the manuscript is short and is intimately connected with the affair. With your permission I will read it to you."

Holmes leaned back in his chair, placed his finger-tips together, and closed his eyes, with an air of resignation. Dr. Mortimer turned the manuscript to the light and read in a high, cracking voice the following curious, old-world narrative:—

"Of the origin of the Hound of the Baskervilles there have been many statements, yet as I come in a direct line from Hugo Baskerville, and as I had the story from my father, who also had it from his, I have set it down with all belief that it occurred even as is here set forth. And I would have you believe, my sons, that the same Justice which punishes sin may also most graciously forgive it, and that no ban is so heavy but that by prayer and repentance it may be removed. Learn then from this story not to fear the fruits of the past, but rather to be circumspect in the future, that those foul passions whereby our family has suffered so grievously may not again be loosed to our undoing.

"Know then that in the time of the Great Rebellion (the history of which by the learned Lord Clarendon I most earnestly commend to your attention) this Manor of Baskerville was held by Hugo of that name, nor can it be gainsaid that he was a most wild, profane, and godless man. This, in truth, his neighbours might have pardoned, seeing that saints have never flourished in those parts, but there was in him a certain wanton and cruel humour which made his name a byword through the West. It chanced that this Hugo came to love (if, indeed, so dark a passion may be known under so bright a name) the daughter of a yeoman who held lands near the Baskerville estate. But the young maiden, being discreet and of good repute, would ever avoid him, for she feared his evil name. So it came to pass that one Michaelmas this Hugo, with five or six of his idle and wicked companions, stole down upon the farm and carried off the maiden, her father and brothers being from home, as he well knew. When they had brought her to the Hall the maiden was placed in an upper chamber, while Hugo and his friends sat down to a long carouse, as was their nightly custom. Now, the poor lass upstairs was like to have her wits turned at the singing and shouting and terrible oaths which came up to her from below, for they say that the words used by Hugo Baskerville, when he was in wine, were such as might blast the man who said them. At last in the stress of her fear she did that which might have daunted the bravest or most active man, for by the aid of the growth of ivy which covered (and still covers) the south wall she came down from under the eaves, and so homeward across the moor, there being three leagues betwixt the Hall and her father's farm.

"It chanced that some little time later Hugo left his guests to carry food and drink—with other worse things, perchance—to his captive, and so found the cage empty and the bird escaped. Then, as it would seem, he became as one that hath a devil, for, rushing down the stairs into the dining-hall, he sprang upon the great table, flagons and trenchers flying before him, and he cried aloud before all the company that he would that very night render his body and soul to the Powers of Evil if he might but overtake the wench. And while the revellers stood aghast at the fury of the man, one more wicked or, it may be, more drunken than the rest, cried out that they should put the hounds upon her. Whereat Hugo ran from the house, crying to his grooms that they should saddle his mare and unkennel the pack, and giving the hounds a kerchief of the maid's, he swung them to the line, and so off full cry in the moonlight over the moor.

"Now, for some space the revellers stood agape, unable to understand all that had been done in such haste. But anon their bemused wits awoke to the nature of the deed which was like to be done upon the moorlands. Everything was now in an uproar, some calling for their pistols, some for their horses, and some for another flask of wine. But at length some sense came back to their crazed minds, and the whole of them, thirteen in number, took horse and started in pursuit. The moon shone clear above them, and they rode swiftly abreast, taking that course which the maid must needs have taken if she were to reach her own home.

"They had gone a mile or two when they passed one of the night shepherds upon the moorlands, and they cried to him to know if he had seen the hunt. And the man, as the story goes, was so crazed with fear that he could scarce speak, but at last he said that he had indeed seen the unhappy maiden, with the hounds upon her track. 'But I have seen more than that,' said he, 'for Hugo Baskerville passed me upon his black mare, and there ran mute behind him such a hound of hell as God forbid should ever be at my heels.' So the drunken squires cursed the shepherd and rode onward. But soon their skins turned cold, for there came a galloping across the moor, and the black mare, dabbled with white froth, went past with trailing bridle and empty saddle. Then the revellers rode close together, for a great fear was on them, but they still followed over the moor, though each, had he been alone, would have been right glad to have turned his horse's head. Riding slowly in this fashion they came at last upon the hounds. These, though known for their valour and their breed, were whimpering in a cluster at the head of a deep dip or goyal, as we call it, upon the moor, some slinking away and some, with starting hackles and staring eyes, gazing down the narrow valley before them.

"The company had come to a halt, more sober men, as you may guess, than when they started. The most of them would by no means advance, but three of them, the boldest, or it may be the most drunken, rode forward down the goyal. Now, it opened into a broad space in which stood two of those great stones, still to be seen there, which were set by certain forgotten peoples in the days of old. The moon was shining bright upon the clearing, and there in the centre lay the unhappy maid where she had fallen, dead of fear and of fatigue. But it was not the sight of her body, nor yet was it that of the body of Hugo Baskerville lying near her, which raised the hair upon the heads of these three daredevil roysterers, but it was that, standing over Hugo, and plucking at his throat, there stood a foul thing, a great, black beast, shaped like a hound, yet larger than any hound that ever mortal eye has rested upon. And even as they looked the thing tore the throat out of Hugo Baskerville, on which, as it turned its blazing eyes and dripping jaws

upon them, the three shrieked with fear and rode for dear life, still screaming, across the moor. One, it is said, died that very night of what he had seen, and the other twain were but broken men for the rest of their days.

"Such is the tale, my sons, of the coming of the hound which is said to have plagued the family so sorely ever since. If I have set it down it is because that which is clearly known hath less terror than that which is but hinted at and guessed. Nor can it be denied that many of the family have been unhappy in their deaths, which have been sudden, bloody, and mysterious. Yet may we shelter ourselves in the infinite goodness of Providence, which would not forever punish the innocent beyond that third or fourth generation which is threatened in Holy Writ. To that Providence, my sons, I hereby commend you, and I counsel you by way of caution to forbear from crossing the moor in those dark hours when the powers of evil are exalted.

"[This from Hugo Baskerville to his sons Rodger and John, with instructions that they say nothing thereof to their sister Elizabeth.]"

When Dr. Mortimer had finished reading this singular narrative he pushed his spectacles up on his forehead and stared across at Mr. Sherlock Holmes. The latter yawned and tossed the end of his cigarette into the fire.

"Well?" said he.

"Do you not find it interesting?"

"To a collector of fairy tales."

Dr. Mortimer drew a folded newspaper out of his pocket.

"Now, Mr. Holmes, we will give you something a little more recent. This is the Devon County Chronicle of May 14th of this year. It is a short account of the facts elicited at the death of Sir Charles Baskerville which occurred a few days before that date."

My friend leaned a little forward and his expression became intent. Our visitor readjusted his glasses and began:—

"The recent sudden death of Sir Charles Baskerville, whose name has been mentioned as the probable Liberal candidate for Mid-Devon at the next election, has cast a gloom over the county. Though Sir Charles had resided at Baskerville Hall for a comparatively short period his amiability of character and extreme generosity had won the affection and respect of all who had been brought into contact with him. In these days of nouveaux riches it is refreshing to find a case where the scion of an old county family which has fallen upon evil days is able to make his own fortune and to bring it back with him to restore the fallen grandeur of his line. Sir Charles, as is well known, made large sums of money in South African speculation. More wise than those who go on until the wheel turns against them, he realized his gains and returned to England with them. It is only two years since he took up his residence at Baskerville Hall, and it is common talk how large were those schemes of reconstruction and improvement which have been interrupted by his death. Being himself childless, it was his openly expressed desire that the whole countryside should, within his own lifetime, profit by his good fortune, and many will have personal reasons for bewailing his untimely end. His generous donations to local and county charities have been frequently chronicled in these columns.

"The circumstances connected with the death of Sir Charles cannot be said to have been entirely cleared up by the inquest, but at least enough has been done to dispose of those rumours to which local superstition has given rise. There is no reason whatever to suspect foul play, or to imagine that death could be from any but natural causes. Sir Charles was a widower, and a man who may be said to have been in some ways of an eccentric habit of mind. In spite of his considerable wealth he was simple in his personal tastes, and his indoor servants at Baskerville Hall consisted of a married couple named Barrymore, the husband acting as butler and the wife as housekeeper. Their evidence, corroborated by that of several friends, tends to show that Sir Charles's health has for some time been impaired, and points especially to some affection of the heart, manifesting itself in changes of colour, breathlessness, and acute attacks of nervous depression. Dr. James Mortimer, the friend and medical attendant of the deceased, has given evidence to the same effect.

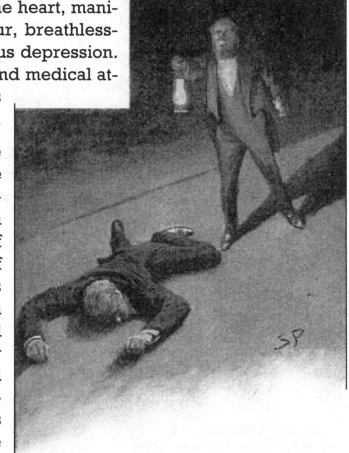

"The facts of the case are simple. Sir Charles Baskerville was in the habit every night before going to bed of walking down the famous Yew Alley of Baskerville Hall. The evidence of the Barrymores shows that this had been his custom. On the 4th of May Sir Charles had declared his intention of starting next day for London, and had ordered Barrymore to prepare his luggage. That night he went out as usual for his nocturnal walk, in the course of which he was in the habit of smoking a cigar. He never returned. At twelve o'clock Barrymore, finding the hall door still open, became alarmed, and, lighting a lantern, went in search of his master. The day had been wet, and Sir Charles's footmarks were easily traced down the Alley. Half-way down this walk there is a gate which leads out on to the moor. There were indications that Sir Charles had stood for some little time here. He then proceeded down the Alley, and it was at the far end of it that his body was discovered. One fact which has not been explained is the statement of Barrymore that his master's footprints altered their character from the time that he passed the moor-gate, and that he appeared from thence onward to have been walking upon his toes. One Murphy, a gipsy horse-dealer, was on the moor at no great distance at the time, but he appears by his own confession to have been the worse for drink. He declares that he heard cries, but is unable to state from what directionthey came. No signs of violence were to be discovered upon Sir Charles's person, and though the doctor's evidence pointed to an almost incredible facial distortion—so great that Dr. Mortimer refused at first to believe that it was indeed his friend and patient who lay before him—it was explained that that is a symptom which is not unusual in cases of dyspnoea and death from cardiac exhaustion. This explanation was borne out by the post-mortem examination, which showed long-standing organic disease, and the coroner's jury returned a verdict in accordance with the medical evidence. It is well that this is so, for it is obviously of the utmost importance that Sir Charles's heir should settle at the Hall and continue the good work which has been so sadly interrupted. Had the prosaic finding of the coroner not finally put an end to the romantic stories which have been whispered in connection with the affair, it might have been difficult to find a tenant for Baskerville Hall. It is understood that the next of kin is Mr. Henry Baskerville, if he be still alive, the son of Sir Charles Baskerville's younger brother. The young man when last heard of was in America, and inquiries are being instituted with a view to informing him of his good fortune."

Dr. Mortimer refolded his paper and replaced it in his pocket.

"Those are the public facts, Mr. Holmes, in connection with the death of Sir Charles Baskerville."

"I must thank you," said Sherlock Holmes, "for calling my attention to a case which certainly presents some features of interest. I had observed some newspaper comment at the time, but I was exceedingly preoccupied by that little affair of the Vatican cameos, and in my anxiety to oblige the Pope I lost touch with several interesting English cases. This article, you say, contains all the public facts?"

"It does."

"Then let me have the private ones." He leaned back, put his finger-tips together, and assumed his most impassive and judicial expression.

"In doing so," said Dr. Mortimer, who had begun to show signs of some strong emotion, "I am telling that which I have not confided to anyone. My motive for withholding it from the coroner's inquiry is that a man of science shrinks from placing himself in the public position of seeming to indorse a popular superstition. I had the further motive that Baskerville Hall, as the paper says, would certainly remain untenanted if anything were done to increase its already rather grim reputation. For both these reasons I thought that I was justified in telling rather less than I knew, since no practical good could result from it, but with you there is no reason why I should not be perfectly frank.

"The moor is very sparsely inhabited, and those who live near each other are thrown very much together. For this reason I saw a good deal of Sir Charles Baskerville. With the exception of Mr. Frankland, of Lafter Hall, and Mr. Stapleton, the naturalist, there are no other men of education within many miles. Sir Charles was a retiring man, but the chance of his illness brought us together, and a community of interests in science kept us so. He had brought back much scientific information from South Africa, and many a charming evening we have spent together discussing the comparative anatomy of the Bushman and the Hottentot.

"Within the last few months it became increasingly plain to me that Sir Charles's nervous system was strained to the breaking point. He had taken this legend which I have read you exceedingly to heart—so much so that, although he would walk in his own grounds, nothing would induce him to go out upon the moor at night. Incredible as it may appear to you, Mr. Holmes, he was honestly convinced that a dreadful fate over hung his family, and certainly the records which he was able to give of his ancestors were not encouraging. The idea of some ghastly presence constantly haunted him, and on more than one occasion he has asked me whether I had on my medical journeys at night ever seen any strange creature or heard the baying of a hound. The latter question he put to me several times, and always with a voice which vibrated with excitement.

"I can well remember driving up to his house in the evening some three weeks before the fatal event. He chanced to be at his hall door. I had descended from my gig and was standing in front of him, when I saw his eyes fix themselves over my shoulder, and stare past me with an expression of the most dreadful horror. I whisked round and had just time to catch a glimpse of something which I took to be a large black calf passing at the head of the drive. So excited and alarmed was he that I was compelled to go down to the spot where the animal had been and look

around for it. It was gone, however, and the incident appeared to make the worst impression upon his mind. I stayed with him all the evening, and it was on that occasion, to explain the emotion which he had shown, that he confided to my keeping that narrative which I read to you when first I came. I mention this small episode because it assumes some importance in view of the tragedy which followed, but I was convinced at the time that the matter was entirely trivial and that his excitement had no justification.

"It was at my advice that Sir Charles was about to go to London. His heart was, I knew, affected, and the constant anxiety in which he lived, however chimerical the cause of it might be, was evidently having a serious effect upon his health. I thought that a few months among the distractions of town would send him back a new man. Mr. Stapleton, a mutual friend who was much concerned at his state of health, was of the same opinion. At the last instant came this terrible catastrophe.

"On the night of Sir Charles's death Barrymore the butler, who made the discovery, sent Perkins the groom on horseback to me, and as I was sitting up late I was able to reach Baskerville Hall within an hour of the event. I checked and corroborated all the facts which were mentioned at the inquest. I followed the footsteps down the Yew Alley, I saw the spot at the moor-gate where he seemed to have waited, I remarked the change in the shape of the prints after that point, I noted that there were no other footsteps save those of Barrymore on the soft gravel, and finally I carefully examined the body, which had not been touched until my arrival. Sir Charles lay on his face, his arms out, his fingers dug into the ground, and his features convulsed with some strong emotion to such an extent that I could hardly have sworn to his identity. There was certainly no physical injury of any kind. But one false statement was made by Barrymore at the inquest. He said that there were no traces upon the ground round the body. He did not observe any. But I did—some little distance off, but fresh and clear."

"Footprints?"

"Footprints."

"A man's or a woman's?"

Dr. Mortimer looked strangely at us for an instant, and his voice sank almost to a whisper as he answered:—

"Mr. Holmes, they were the footprints of a gigantic hound!"

CHAPTER III. THE PROBLEM

I confess at these words a shudder passed through me. There was a thrill in the doctor's voice which showed that he was himself deeply moved by that which he told us. Holmes leaned forward in his excitement and his eyes had the hard, dry glitter which shot from them when he was keenly interested.

"You saw this?"

"As clearly as I see you."

"And you said nothing?"

"What was the use?"

"How was it that no one else saw it?"

"The marks were some twenty yards from the body and no one gave them a thought. I don't suppose I should have done so had I not known this legend."

"There are many sheep-dogs on the moor?"

"No doubt, but this was no sheep-dog."

"You say it was large?"

"Enormous."

"But it had not approached the body?"

"No."

"What sort of night was it?'

"Damp and raw."

"But not actually raining?"

"No."

"What is the Alley like?"

"There are two lines of old yew hedge, twelve feet high and impenetrable. The walk in the centre is about eight feet across."

"Is there anything between the hedges and the walk?"

"Yes, there is a strip of grass about six feet broad on either side."

"I understand that the yew hedge is penetrated at one point by a gate?"

"Yes, the wicket-gate which leads on to the moor."

"Is there any other opening?"

"None."

"So that to reach the Yew Alley one either has to come down it from the house or else to enter it by the moor-gate?"

"There is an exit through a summer-house at the far end."

"Had Sir Charles reached this?"

"No; he lay about fifty yards from it."

"Now, tell me, Dr. Mortimer—and this is important—the

marks which you saw were on the path and not on the grass?"

"No marks could show on the grass."

"Were they on the same side of the path as the moor-gate?"

"Yes; they were on the edge of the path on the same side as the moor-gate."

"You interest me exceedingly. Another point. Was the wicket-gate closed?"

"Closed and padlocked."

"How high was it?"

"About four feet high."

"Then anyone could have got over it?"

"Yes."

"And what marks did you see by the wicket-gate?"

"None in particular."

"Good heaven! Did no one examine?"

"Yes, I examined myself."

"And found nothing?"

"It was all very confused. Sir Charles had evidently stood there for five or ten minutes."

"How do you know that?"

"Because the ash had twice dropped from his cigar."

"Excellent! This is a colleague, Watson, after our own heart. But the marks?"

"He had left his own marks all over that small patch of gravel. I could discern no others."

Sherlock Holmes struck his hand against his knee with an impatient gesture.

"If I had only been there!" he cried. "It is evidently a case of extraordinary interest, and one which presented immense opportunities to the scientific expert. That gravel page upon which I might have read so much has been long ere this smudged by the rain and defaced by the clogs of curious peasants. Oh, Dr. Mortimer, Dr. Mortimer, to think that you should not have called me in! You have indeed much to answer for."

"I could not call you in, Mr. Holmes, without disclosing these facts to the world, and I have already given my reasons for not wishing to do so. Besides, besides —"

"Why do you hesitate?"

"There is a realm in which the most acute and most experienced of detectives is helpless."

"You mean that the thing is supernatural?"

"I did not positively say so."

"No, but you evidently think it."

"Since the tragedy, Mr. Holmes, there have come to my ears several incidents which are hard to reconcile with the settled order of Nature."

"For example?"

"I find that before the terrible event occurred several people had seen a creature upon the moor which corresponds with this Baskerville demon, and which could not possibly be any animal known to science. They all agreed that it was a huge creature, luminous, ghastly, and spectral. I have cross-examined these men, one of them a hard-headed countryman, one a farrier, and one a moorland farmer, who all tell the same story of this dreadful apparition, exactly corresponding to the hell-hound of the legend. I assure you that there is a reign of terror in the district, and that it is a hardy man who will cross the moor at night."

"And you, a trained man of science, believe it to be supernatural?"

"I do not know what to believe."

Holmes shrugged his shoulders.

"I have hitherto confined my investigations to this world," said he. "In a modest way I have combated evil, but to take on the Father of Evil himself would, perhaps, be too ambitious a task. Yet you must admit that the footmark is material."

"The original hound was material enough to tug a man's throat out, and yet he was diabolical as well."

"I see that you have quite gone over to the supernaturalists. But now, Dr. Mortimer, tell me this. If you hold these views, why have you come to consult me at all? You tell me in the same breath that it is useless to investigate Sir Charles's death, and that you desire me to do it."

"I did not say that I desired you to do it."

"Then, how can I assist you?"

"By advising me as to what I should do with Sir Henry Baskerville, who arrives at Waterloo Station"—Dr. Mortimer looked at his watch—"in exactly one hour and a quarter."

"He being the heir?"

"Yes. On the death of Sir Charles we inquired for this young gentleman and found that he had been farming in Canada. From the accounts which have reached us he is an excellent fellow in every way. I speak not as a medical man but as a trustee and executor of Sir Charles's will."

"There is no other claimant, I presume?"

"None. The only other kinsman whom we have been able to trace was Rodger Baskerville, the youngest of three brothers of whom poor Sir Charles was the elder. The second brother, who died young, is the father of this lad Henry. The third, Rodger, was the black sheep of the family. He came of the old masterful Baskerville strain, and was the very image, they tell me, of the family picture of old Hugo. He made England too hot to hold him, fled to Central America, and died there in 1876 of yellow fever. Henry is the last of the Baskervilles. In one hour and five minutes I meet him at Waterloo Station. I have had a wire that he arrived at Southampton this morning. Now, Mr. Holmes, what would you advise me to do with him?"

"Why should he not go to the home of his fathers?"

"It seems natural, does it not? And yet, consider that every Baskerville who goes there meets with an evil fate. I feel sure that if Sir Charles could have spoken with me before his death he would have warned me against bringing this the last of the old race, and the heir to great wealth, to that deadly place. And yet it cannot be denied that the prosperity of the whole poor, bleak country-side depends upon his presence. All the good work which has been done by Sir Charles will crash to the ground if there is no tenant of the Hall. I fear lest I should be swayed too much by my own obvious interest in the matter, and that is why I bring the case before you and ask for your advice."

Holmes considered for a little time.

"Put into plain words, the matter is this," said he. "In your opinion there is a diabolical agency which makes Dartmoor an unsafe abode for a Baskerville—that is your opinion?"

"At least I might go the length of saying that there is some evidence that this may be so."

"Exactly. But surely, if your supernatural theory be correct, it could work the young man evil in London as easily as in Devonshire. A devil with merely local powers like a parish vestry would be too inconceivable a thing."

"You put the matter more flippantly, Mr. Holmes, than you would probably do if you were brought into personal contact with these things. Your advice, then, as I understand it, is that the young man will be as safe in Devonshire as in London. He comes in fifty minutes. What would you recommend?"

"I recommend, sir, that you take a cab, call off your spaniel who is scratching at my front door, and proceed to Waterloo to meet Sir Henry Baskerville."

"And then?"

"And then you will say nothing to him at all until I have made up my mind about the matter."

"How long will it take you to make up your mind?"

"Twenty-four hours. At ten o'clock to-morrow, Dr. Mortimer, I will be much obliged to you if you will call upon me here, and it will be of help to me in my plans for the future if you will bring Sir Henry Baskerville with you."

"I will do so, Mr. Holmes." He scribbled the appointment on his shirtcuff and hurried off in his strange, peering, absent-minded fashion. Holmes stopped him at the head of the stair.

"Only one more question, Dr. Mortimer. You say that before Sir Charles

Baskerville's death several people saw this apparition upon the moor?"

"Three people did."

"Did any see it after?"

"I have not heard of any."

"Thank you. Good morning."

Holmes returned to his seat with that quiet look of inward satisfaction which meant that he had a congenial task before him.

"Going out, Watson?"

"Unless I can help you."

"No, my dear fellow, it is at the hour of action that I turn to you for aid. But this is splendid, really unique from some points of view. When you pass Bradley's would you ask him to send up a pound of the strongest shag tobacco? Thank you. It would be as well if you could make it convenient not to return before evening. Then I should be very glad to compare impressions as to this most interesting problem which has been submitted to us this morning."

I knew that seclusion and solitude were very necessary for my friend in those hours of intense mental concentration during which he weighed every particle of evidence, constructed alternative theories, balanced one against the other, and made up his mind as to which points were essential and which immaterial. I therefore spent the day at my club and did not return to Baker Street until evening. It was nearly nine o'clock when I found myself in the sitting-room once more.

My first impression as I opened the door was that a fire had broken out, for the room was so filled with smoke that the light of the lamp upon the table was blurred by it. As I entered, however, my fears were set at rest, for it was the acrid fumes of strong coarse tobacco which took me by the throat and set me coughing. Through the haze I had a vague vision of Holmes in his dressing-gown coiled up in an armchair with his black clay pipe between his lips. Several rolls of paper lay around him.

"Caught cold, Watson?" said he.

"No, it's this poisonous atmosphere."

"I suppose it is pretty thick, now that you mention it."

"Thick! It is intolerable."

"Open the window, then! You have been at your club all day, I perceive."

"My dear Holmes!"

"Am I right?"

"Certainly, but how?"

He laughed at my bewildered expression.

"There is a delightful freshness about you, Watson, which makes it a pleasure to exercise any small powers which I possess at your expense. A gentleman goes forth on a showery and miry day. He returns immaculate in the evening with the gloss still on his hat and his boots. He has been a fixture therefore all day. He is not a man with intimate friends. Where, then, could he have been? Is it not obvious?"

"Well, it is rather obvious."

"The world is full of obvious things which nobody by any chance ever observes. Where do you think that I have been?"

"A fixture also."

"On the contrary, I have been to Devonshire."

"In spirit?"

"Exactly. My body has remained in this arm-chair and has, I regret to observe, consumed in my absence two large pots of coffee and an incredible amount of tobacco. After you left I sent down to Stamford's for the Ordnance map of this portion of the moor, and my spirit has hovered over it all day. I flatter myself that I could find my way about."

"A large scale map, I presume?"

"Very large." He unrolled one section and held it over his knee. "Here you have the particular district which concerns us. That is Baskerville Hall in the middle."

"With a wood round it?"

"Exactly. I fancy the Yew Alley, though not marked under that name, must stretch along this line, with the moor, as you perceive, upon the right of it. This small clump of buildings here is the hamlet of Grimpen, where our friend

Dr. Mortimer has his headquarters. Within a radius of five miles there are, as you see, only a very few scattered dwellings. Here is Lafter Hall, which was mentioned in the narrative. There is a house indicated here which may be the residence of the naturalist—Stapleton, if I remember right, was his name. Here are two moorland farm-houses, High Tor and Foulmire. Then fourteen miles away the great convict prison of Princetown. Between and around these scattered points extends the desolate, lifeless moor. This, then, is the stage upon which tragedy has been played, and upon which we may help to play it again."

"It must be a wild place."

"Yes, the setting is a worthy one. If the devil did desire to have a hand in the affairs of men ——"

"Then you are yourself inclining to the supernatural explanation."

"The devil's agents may be of flesh and blood, may they not? There are two questions waiting for us at the outset. The one is whether any crime has been committed at all; the second is, what is the crime and how was it committed? Of course, if Dr. Mortimer's surmise should be correct, and we are dealing with forces outside the ordinary laws of Nature, there is an end of our investigation. But we are bound to exhaust all other hypotheses before falling back upon this one. I think we'll shut that window again, if you don't mind. It is a singular thing, but I find that a concentrated atmosphere helps a concentration of thought. I have not pushed it to the length of getting into a box to think, but that is the logical outcome of my convictions. Have you turned the case over in your mind?"

"Yes, I have thought a good deal of it in the course of the day."

"What do you make of it?"

"It is very bewildering."

"It has certainly a character of its own. There are points of distinction about it. That change in the footprints, for example. What do you make of that?"

"Mortimer said that the man had walked on tiptoe down that portion of the alley."

"He only repeated what some fool had said at the inquest. Why should a man walk on tiptoe down the alley?"

"What then?"

"He was running, Watson—running desperately, running for his life, running until he burst his heart and fell dead upon his face."

"Running from what?"

"There lies our problem. There are indications that the man was crazed with fear before ever he began to run."

"How can you say that?"

"I am presuming that the cause of his fears came to him across the moor. If that were so, and it seems most probable, only a man who had lost his wits would have run from the house instead of towards it. If the gipsy's evidence may be taken as true, he ran with cries for help in the direction where help was least likely to be. Then, again, whom was he waiting for that night, and why was he waiting for him in the Yew Alley rather than in his own house?"

"You think that he was waiting for someone?"

"The man was elderly and infirm. We can understand his taking an evening stroll, but the ground was damp and the night inclement. Is it natural that he should stand for five or ten minutes, as Dr. Mortimer, with more practical sense than I should have given him credit for, deduced from the cigar ash?"

"But he went out every evening."

"I think it unlikely that he waited at the moor-gate every evening. On the contrary, the evidence is that he avoided the moor. That night he waited there. It was the night before he made his departure for London. The thing takes shape, Watson. It becomes coherent. Might I ask you to hand me my violin, and we will postpone all further thought upon this business until we have had the advantage of meeting Dr. Mortimer and Sir Henry Baskerville in the morning."

CHAPTER IV. SIR HENRY BASKERVILLE

Our breakfast-table was cleared early, and Holmes waited in his dressing-gown for the promised interview. Our clients were punctual to their appointment, for the clock had just struck ten when Dr. Mortimer was shown up, followed by the young baronet. The latter was a small, alert, dark-eyed man about thirty years of age, very sturdily built, with thick black eyebrows and a strong, pugnacious face. He wore a ruddy-tinted tweed suit and had the weather-beaten appearance of one who has spent most of his time in the open air, and yet there was something in his steady eye and the quiet assurance of his bearing which indicated the gentleman.

"This is Sir Henry Baskerville," said Dr. Mortimer.

"Why, yes," said he, "and the strange thing is, Mr. Sherlock Holmes, that if my friend here had not proposed coming round to you this morning I should have come on my own account. I understand that you think out little puzzles, and I've had one this morning which wants more thinking out than I am able to give it."

"Pray take a seat, Sir Henry. Do I understand you to say that you have yourself had some remarkable experience since you arrived in London?"

"Nothing of much importance, Mr. Holmes. Only a joke, as like as not. It was this letter, if you can call it a letter, which reached me this morning."

He laid an envelope upon the table, and we all bent over it. It was of common quality, grayish in colour. The address, "Sir Henry Baskerville, Northumberland Hotel," was printed in rough characters; the postmark "Charing Cross," and the date of posting the preceding evening.

"Who knew that you were going to the Northumberland Hotel?" asked Holmes, glancing keenly across at our visitor.

"No one could have known. We only decided after I met Dr. Mortimer."

"But Dr. Mortimer was no doubt already stopping there?"

"No, I had been staying with a friend," said the doctor. "There was no possible indication that we intended to go to this hotel."

"Hum! Someone seems to be very deeply interested in your movements." Out of the envelope he took a half-sheet of foolscap paper folded into four. This he opened and spread flat upon the table. Across the middle of it a single sentence had been formed by the expedient of pasting printed words upon it. It ran: "As you value your life or your reason keep away from the moor." The word "moor" only was printed in ink.

"Now," said Sir Henry Baskerville, "perhaps you will tell me, Mr. Holmes, what in thunder is the meaning of that, and who it is that takes so much interest in my affairs?"

"What do you make of it, Dr. Mortimer? You must allow that there is nothing supernatural about this, at any rate?"

"No, sir, but it might very well come from someone who was convinced that the business is supernatural."

"What business?" asked Sir Henry sharply. "It seems to me that all you gentlemen know a great deal more than I do about my own affairs."

"You shall share our knowledge before you leave this room, Sir Henry. I promise you that," said Sherlock Holmes. "We will confine ourselves for the present with your permission to this very interesting document, which must have been put together and posted yesterday evening. Have you yesterday's Times, Watson?"

"It is here in the corner."

"Might I trouble you for it—the inside page, please, with the leading articles?" He glanced swiftly over it, running his eyes up and down the columns. "Capital article this on free trade. Permit me to give you an extract from it. 'You may be cajoled into imagining that your own special trade or your own industry will be encouraged by a protective tariff, but it stands to reason that such legislation must in the long run keep away wealth from the country, diminish the value of our imports, and lower the general conditions of life in this island.' What do you think of that, Watson?" cried Holmes in high glee, rubbing his hands together with satisfaction. "Don't you think that is an admirable sentiment?"

Dr. Mortimer looked at Holmes with an air of professional interest, and Sir Henry Baskerville turned a pair of puzzled dark eyes upon me.

"I don't know much about the tariff and things of that kind," said he; "but it seems to me we've got a bit off the trail so far as that note is concerned."

"On the contrary, I think we are particularly hot upon the trail, Sir Henry. Watson here knows more about my methods than you do, but I fear that even he has not quite grasped the significance of this sentence."

"No, I confess that I see no connection."

"And yet, my dear Watson, there is so very close a connection that the one is extracted out of the other. 'You,' 'your,' 'your,' 'life,' 'reason,' 'value,' 'keep away,' 'from the.' Don't you see now whence these words have been taken?"

"By thunder, you're right! Well, if that isn't smart!" cried Sir Henry.

"If any possible doubt remained it is settled by the fact that 'keep away' and 'from the' are cut out in one piece."

"Well, now—so it is!"

"Really, Mr. Holmes, this exceeds anything which I could have imagined," said Dr. Mortimer, gazing at my friend in amazement. "I could understand anyone saying that the words were from a newspaper; but that you should name which, and add that it came from the leading article, is really one of the most remarkable things which I have ever known. How did you do it?"

"I presume, Doctor, that you could tell the skull of a negro from that of an Esquimau?"

"Most certainly."

"But how?"

"Because that is my special hobby. The differences are obvious. The supra-orbital crest, the facial angle, the maxillary curve, the —"

"But this is my special hobby, and the differences are equally obvious. There is as much difference to my eyes between the leaded bourgeois type of a Times article and the slovenly print of an evening half-penny paper as there could be between your negro and your Esquimau. The detection of types is one of the most elementary branches of knowledge to the special expert in crime, though I confess that once when I was very young I confused the Leeds Mercury with the Western Morning News. But a Times leader is entirely distinctive, and these words could have been taken from nothing else. As it was done yesterday the strong probability was that we should find the words in yesterday's issue."

"So far as I can follow you, then, Mr. Holmes," said Sir Henry Baskerville, "someone cut out this message with a scissors—"

"Nail-scissors," said Holmes. "You can see that it was a very short-bladed scissors, since the cutter had to take two snips over 'keep away.' "

"That is so. Someone, then, cut out the message with a pair of short-bladed scissors, pasted it with paste—"

"Gum," said Holmes.

"With gum on to the paper. But I want to know why the word 'moor' should have been written?"

"Because he could not find it in print. The other words were all simple and might be found in any issue, but 'moor' would be less common."

"Why, of course, that would explain it. Have you read anything else in this message, Mr. Holmes?"

"There are one or two indications, and yet the utmost pains have been taken to remove all clues. The address, you observe is printed in rough characters. But the Times is a paper which is seldom found in any hands but those of the highly educated. We may take it, therefore, that the letter was composed by an educated man who wished to pose as an uneducated one, and his effort to conceal his own writing suggests that that writing might be known, or come to be known, by you. Again, you will observe that the words are not gummed on in an accurate line, but that some are much higher than others. 'Life,' for example is quite out of its proper place. That may point to carelessness or it may point to agitation and hurry upon the part of the cutter. On the whole I incline to the latter view, since the matter was evidently important, and it is unlikely that the composer of such a letter would be careless. If he were in a hurry it opens up the interesting question why he should be in a hurry, since any letter posted up to early morning would reach Sir Henry before he would leave his hotel. Did the composer fear an interruption—and from whom?"

"We are coming now rather into the region of guesswork,"said Dr. Mortimer.

"Say, rather, into the region where we balance probabilities and choose the most likely. It is the scientific use of the imagination, but we have always some material basis on which to start our speculation. Now, you would call it a guess, no doubt, but I am almost certain that this address has been written in a hotel."

"How in the world can you say that?"

"If you examine it carefully you will see that both the pen and the ink have given the writer trouble. The pen has spluttered twice in a single word, and has run dry three times in a short address, showing that there was very little ink in the bottle. Now, a private pen or ink-bottle is seldom allowed to be in such a state, and the combination of the two must be quite rare. But you know the hotel ink and the hotel pen, where it is rare to get anything else. Yes, I have very little hesitation in saying that could we examine the waste-paper baskets of the hotels around Charing Cross until we found the remains of the mutilated Times leader we could lay our hands straight upon the person who sent this singular message. Halloa! Halloa! What's this?"

He was carefully examining the foolscap, upon which the words were pasted, holding it only an inch or two from his eyes.

"Well?"

"Nothing," said he, throwing it down. "It is a blank half-sheet of paper, without even a water-mark upon it. I think we have drawn as much as we can from this curious letter; and now, Sir Henry, has anything else of interest happened to you since you have been in London?"

"Why, no, Mr. Holmes. I think not."

"You have not observed anyone follow or watch you?"

"I seem to have walked right into the thick of a dime novel," said our visitor. "Why in thunder should anyone follow or watch me?"

"We are coming to that. You have nothing else to report to us before we go into this matter?"

"Well, it depends upon what you think worth reporting."

"I think anything out of the ordinary routine of life well worth reporting."

Sir Henry smiled.

"I don't know much of British life yet, for I have spent nearly all my time in the States and in Canada. But I hope that to lose one of your boots is not part of the ordinary routine of life over here."

"You have lost one of your boots?"

"My dear sir," cried Dr. Mortimer, "it is only mislaid. You will find it when you return to the hotel. What is the use of troubling Mr. Holmes with trifles of this kind?"

"Well, he asked me for anything outside the ordinary routine."

"Exactly," said Holmes, "however foolish the incident may seem. You have lost one of your boots, you say?"

"Well, mislaid it, anyhow. I put them both outside my door last night, and there was only one in the morning. I could get no sense out of the chap who cleans them. The worst of it is that I only bought the pair last night in the Strand, and I have never had them on."

"If you have never worn them, why did you put them out to be cleaned?"

"They were tan boots and had never been varnished. That was why I put them out."

"Then I understand that on your arrival in London yesterday you went out at once and bought a pair of boots?"

"I did a good deal of shopping. Dr. Mortimer here went round with me. You see, if I am to be squire down there I must dress the part, and it may be that I have got a little careless in my ways out West. Among other things I bought these brown boots—gave six dollars for them—and had one stolen before ever I had them on my feet."

"It seems a singularly useless thing to steal," said Sherlock Holmes. "I confess that I share Dr. Mortimer's belief that it will not be long before the missing boot is found."

"And, now, gentlemen," said the baronet with decision, "it seems to me that I have spoken quite enough about the little that I know. It is time that you kept your promise and gave me a full account of what we are all driving at."

"Your request is a very reasonable one," Holmes answered. "Dr. Mortimer, I think you could not do better than to tell your story as you told it to us."

Thus encouraged, our scientific friend drew his papers from his pocket, and presented the whole case as he had done upon the morning before. Sir Henry Baskerville listened with the deepest attention, and with an occasional exclamation of surprise.

"Well, I seem to have come into an inheritance with a vengeance," said he when the long narrative was finished. "Of course, I've heard of the hound ever since I was in the nursery. It's the pet story of the family, though I never thought of taking it seriously before. But as to my uncle's death—well, it all seems boiling up in my head, and I can't get it clear yet. You don't seem quite to have made up your mind whether it's a case for a policeman or a clergyman."

"Precisely."

"And now there's this affair of the letter to me at the hotel. I suppose that fits into its place."

"It seems to show that someone knows more than we do about what goes on upon the moor," said Dr. Mortimer.

"And also," said Holmes, "that someone is not ill-disposed towards you, since they warn you of danger."

"Or it may be that they wish, for their own purposes, to scare me away."

"Well, of course, that is possible also. I am very much indebted to you, Dr. Mortimer, for introducing me to a problem which presents several interesting alternatives. But the practical point which we now have to decide, Sir Henry, is whether it is or is not advisable for you to go to Baskerville Hall."

"Why should I not go?"

"There seems to be danger."

"Do you mean danger from this family fiend or do you mean danger from human beings?"

"Well, that is what we have to find out."

"Whichever it is, my answer is fixed. There is no devil in hell, Mr. Holmes, and there is no man upon earth who can prevent me from going to the home of my own people, and you may take that to be my final answer." His dark brows knitted and his face flushed to a dusky red as he spoke. It was evident that the fiery temper of the Baskervilles was not extinct in this their last representative. "Meanwhile," said he, "I have hardly had time to think over all that you have told me. It's a big thing for a man to have to understand and to decide at one sitting. I should like to have a quiet hour by myself to make up my mind. Now, look here, Mr. Holmes, it's half-past eleven now and I am going back right away to my hotel. Suppose you and your friend, Dr. Watson, come round and lunch with us at two. I'll be able to tell you more clearly then how this thing strikes me."

"Is that convenient to you, Watson?"

"Perfectly."

"Then you may expect us. Shall I have a cab called?"

"I'd prefer to walk, for this affair has flurried me rather."

"I'll join you in a walk, with pleasure," said his companion.

"Then we meet again at two o'clock. Au revoir, and good-morning!"

We heard the steps of our visitors descend the stair and the bang of the front door. In an instant Holmes had changed from the languid dreamer to the man of action.

"Your hat and boots, Watson, quick! Not a moment to lose!" He rushed into his room in his dressing-gown and was back again in a few seconds in a frock-coat. We hurried together down the stairs and into the street. Dr. Mortimer and Baskerville were still visible about two hundred yards ahead of us in the direction of Oxford Street.

"Shall I run on and stop them?"

"Not for the world, my dear Watson. I am perfectly satisfied with your company if you will tolerate mine. Our friends are wise, for it is certainly a very fine morning for a walk."

He quickened his pace until we had decreased the distance which divided us by about half. Then, still keeping a hundred yards behind, we followed into Oxford Street and so down Regent Street. Once our friends stopped and stared into a shop window, upon which Holmes did the same. An instant afterwards he gave a little cry of satisfaction, and, following the direction of his eager eyes, I saw that a hansom cab with a man inside which had halted on the other side of the street was now proceeding slowly onward again.

"There's our man, Watson! Come along! We'll have a good look at him, if we can do no more."

At that instant I was aware of a bushy black beard and a pair of piercing eyes turned upon us through the side window of the cab. Instantly the trap-door at the top flew up, something was screamed to the driver, and the cab flew madly off down Regent Street. Holmes looked eagerly round for another, but no empty one was in sight. Then he dashed in wild pursuit amid the stream of the traffic, but the start was too great, and already the cab was out of sight.

"There now!" said Holmes bitterly as he emerged panting and white with vexation from the tide of vehicles. "Was ever such bad luck and such bad management, too? Watson, Watson, if you are an honest man you will record this also and set it against my successes!"

"Who was the man?"

"I have not an idea."

"A spy?"

"Well, it was evident from what we have heard that Baskerville has been very closely shadowed by someone since he has been in town. How else could it be known so quickly that it was the Northumberland Hotel which he had chosen? If they had followed him the first day I argued that they would follow him also the second. You may have observed that I twice strolled over to the window while Dr. Mortimer was reading his legend."

"Yes, I remember."

"I was looking out for loiterers in the street, but I saw none. We are dealing with a clever man, Watson. This matter cuts very deep, and though I have not finally made up my mind whether it is a benevolent or a malevolent agency which is in touch with us, I am conscious always of power and design. When our friends left I at once followed them in the hopes of marking down their invisible attendant. So wily was he that he had not trusted himself upon foot, but he had availed himself of a cab so that he could loiter behind or dash past them and so escape their notice. His method had the additional advantage that if they were to take a cab he was all ready to follow them. It has, however, one obvious disadvantage."

"It puts him in the power of the cabman."

"Exactly."

"What a pity we did not get the number!"

"My dear Watson, clumsy as I have been, you surely do not seriously imagine that I neglected to get the number? No. 2704 is our man. But that is no use to us for the moment."

"I fail to see how you could have done more."

"On observing the cab I should have instantly turned and walked in the other direction. I should then at my leisure have hired a second cab and followed the first at a respectful distance, or, better still, have driven to the Northumberland Hotel and waited there. When our unknown had followed Baskerville home we should have had the opportunity of playing his own game upon himself and seeing where he made for. As it is, by an indiscreet eagerness, which was taken advantage of with extraordinary quickness and energy by our opponent, we have betrayed ourselves and lost our man."

We had been sauntering slowly down Regent Street during this conversation, and Dr. Mortimer, with his companion, had long vanished in front of us.

"There is no object in our following them," said Holmes. "The shadow has departed and will not return. We must see what further cards we have in our hands and play them with decision. Could you swear to that man's face within the cab?"

"I could swear only to the beard."

"And so could I—from which I gather that in all probability it was a false one. A clever man upon so delicate an errand has no use for a beard save to conceal his features. Come in here, Watson!"

He turned into one of the district messenger offices, where he was warmly greeted by the manager.

"Ah, Wilson, I see you have not forgotten the little case in which I had the good fortune to help you?"

"No, sir, indeed I have not. You saved my good name, and perhaps my life."

"My dear fellow, you exaggerate. I have some recollection, Wilson, that you had among your boys a lad named Cartwright, who showed some ability during the investigation."

"Yes, sir, he is still with us."

"Could you ring him up?—thank you! And I should be glad to have change of this five-pound note."

A lad of fourteen, with a bright, keen face, had obeyed the summons of the manager. He stood now gazing with great reverence at the famous detective.

"Let me have the Hotel Directory," said Holmes. "Thank you! Now, Cartwright, there are the names of twenty-three hotels here, all in the immediate neighbourhood of Charing Cross. Do you see?"

"Yes, sir."

"You will visit each of these in turn."

"Yes, sir."

"You will begin in each case by giving the outside porter one shilling. Here are twenty-three shillings."

"Yes, sir."

"You will tell him that you want to see the waste-paper of yesterday. You will say that an important telegram has miscarried and that you are looking for it. You understand?"

"Yes, sir."

"But what you are really looking for is the centre page of the Times with some holes cut in it with scissors. Here is a copy of the Times. It is this page. You could easily recognize it, could you not?"

"Yes, sir."

"In each case the outside porter

will send for the hall porter, to whom also you will give a shilling. Here are twenty-three shillings. You will then learn in possibly twenty cases out of the twenty-three that the waste of the day before has been burned or removed. In the three other cases you will be shown a heap of paper and you will look for this page of the Times among it. The odds are enormously against your finding it. There are ten shillings over in case of emergencies. Let me have a report by wire at Baker Street before evening. And now, Watson, it only remains for us to find out by wire the identity of the cabman, No. 2704, and then we will drop into one of the Bond Street picture galleries and fill in the time until we are due at the hotel."

CHAPTER V. THREE BROKEN THREADS

Sherlock Holmes had, in a very remarkable degree, the power of detaching his mind at will. For two hours the strange business in which we had been involved appeared to be forgotten, and he was entirely absorbed in the pictures of the modern Belgian masters. He would talk of nothing but art, of which he had the crudest ideas, from our leaving the gallery until we found ourselves at the Northumberland Hotel.

"Sir Henry Baskerville is upstairs expecting you," said the clerk. "He asked me to show you up at once when you came."

"Have you any objection to my looking at your register?" said Holmes.

"Not in the least."

The book showed that two names had been added after that of Baskerville. One was Theophilus Johnson and family, of Newcastle; the other Mrs. Oldmore and maid, of High Lodge, Alton.

"Surely that must be the same Johnson whom I used to know," said Holmes to the porter. "A lawyer, is he not, gray-headed, and walks with a limp?"

"No, sir; this is Mr. Johnson, the coal-owner, a very active gentleman, not older than yourself."

"Surely you are mistaken about his trade?"

"No, sir! he has used this hotel for many years, and he is very well known to us."

"Ah, that settles it. Mrs. Oldmore, too; I seem to remember the name. Excuse my curiosity, but often in calling upon one friend one finds another."

"She is an invalid lady, sir. Her husband was once mayor of Gloucester. She always comes to us when she is in town."

"Thank you; I am afraid I cannot claim her acquaintance. We have established a most important fact by these questions, Watson," he continued in a low voice as we went upstairs together. "We know now that the people who are so interested in our friend have not settled down in his own hotel. That means that while they are, as we have seen, very anxious to watch him, they are equally anxious that he should not see them. Now, this is a most suggestive fact."

"What does it suggest?"

"It suggests—halloa, my dear fellow, what on earth is the matter?"

As we came round the top of the stairs we had run up against Sir Henry Baskerville himself. His face was flushed with anger, and he held an old and dusty boot in one of his hands. So furious was he that he was hardly articulate, and when he did speak it was in a much broader and more Western dialect than any which we had heard from him in the morning.

"Seems to me they are playing me for a sucker in this hotel," he cried. "They'll find they've started in to monkey with the wrong man unless they are careful. By thunder, if that chap can't find my missing boot there will be trouble. I can take a joke with the best, Mr. Holmes, but they've got a bit over the mark this time."

"Still looking for your boot?"

"Yes, sir, and mean to find it."

"But, surely, you said that it was a new brown boot?"

"So it was, sir. And now it's an old black one."

"What! you don't mean to say——?"

"That's just what I do mean to say. I only had three pairs in the world—the new brown, the old black, and the patent leathers, which I am wearing. Last night they took one of my brown ones, and today they have sneaked one of the black. Well, have you got it? Speak out, man, and don't stand staring!"

An agitated German waiter had appeared upon the scene.

"No, sir; I have made inquiry all over the hotel, but I can hear no word of it."

"Well, either that boot comes back before sundown or I'll see the manager and tell him that I go right straight out of this hotel."

"It shall be found, sir—I promise you that if you will have a little patience it will be found."

"Mind it is, for it's the last thing of mine that I'll lose in this den of thieves. Well, well, Mr. Holmes, you'll excuse my troubling you about such a trifle——"

"I think it's well worth troubling about."

"Why, you look very serious over it."

"How do you explain it?"

"I just don't attempt to explain it. It seems the very maddest, queerest thing that ever happened to me."

"The queerest perhaps——" said Holmes, thoughtfully.

"What do you make of it yourself?"

"Well, I don't profess to understand it yet. This case of yours is very complex, Sir Henry. When taken in conjunction with your uncle's death I am not sure that of all the five hundred cases of capital importance which I have handled there is one which cuts so deep. But we hold several threads in our hands, and the odds are that one or other of them guides us to the truth. We may waste time in following the wrong one, but sooner or later we must come upon the right."

We had a pleasant luncheon in which little was said of the business which had brought us together. It was in the private sitting-room to which we afterwards repaired that Holmes asked Baskerville what were his intentions.

"To go to Baskerville Hall."

"And when?"

"At the end of the week."

"On the whole," said Holmes, "I think that your decision is a wise one. I have ample evidence that you are being dogged in London, and amid the millions of this great city it is difficult to discover who these people are or what their object can be. If their intentions are evil they might do you a mischief, and we should be powerless to prevent it. You did not know, Dr.Mortimer, that you were followed this morning from my house?"

Dr. Mortimer started violently.

"Followed! By whom?"

"That, unfortunately, is what I cannot tell you. Have you among your neighbours or acquaintances on Daftmoor any man with a black, full beard?"

"No—or, let me see—why, yes. Barrymore, Sir Charles's butler, is a man with a full, black beard."

"Ha! Where is Barrymore?"

"He is in charge of the Hall."

"We had best ascertain if he is really there, or if by any possibility he might be in London."

"How can you do that?"

"Give me a telegraph form. 'Is all ready for Sir Henry?' That will do. Address to Mr. Barrymore, Baskerville Hall. What is the nearest telegraph-office? Grimpen. Very good, we will send a second wire to the postmaster, Grimpen: 'Telegram to Mr. Barrymore to be delivered into his own hand. If absent, please return wire to Sir Henry Baskerville, Northumberland Hotel. 'That should let us know before evening whether Barrymore is at his post in Devonshire or not."

"That's so," said Baskerville. "By the way, Dr. Mortimer, who is this Barrymore, anyhow?"

"He is the son of the old caretaker, who is dead. They have looked after the Hall for four generations now. So far as I know, he and his wife are as respectable a couple as any in the county."

"At the same time," said Baskerville, "it's clear enough that so long as there are none of the family at the Hall these people have a mighty fine home and nothing to do."

"That is true."

"Did Barrymore profit at all by Sir Charles's will?" asked Holmes.

"He and his wife had five hundred pounds each."

"Ha! Did they know that they would receive this?"

"Yes; Sir Charles was very fond of talking about the provisions of his will."

"That is very interesting."

"I hope," said Dr. Mortimer, "that you do not look with suspicious eyes upon everyone who received a legacy from Sir Charles, for I also had a thousand pounds left to me."

"Indeed! And anyone else?"

"There were many insignificant sums to individuals, and a large number of public charities. The residue all went to Sir Henry."

"And how much was the residue?"

"Seven hundred and forty thousand pounds."

Holmes raised his eyebrows in surprise. "I had no idea that so gigantic a sum was involved," said he.

"Sir Charles had the reputation of being rich, but we did not know how very rich he was until we came to examine his securities. The total value of the estate was close on to a million."

"Dear me! It is a stake for which a man might well play a desperate game. And one more question, Dr. Mortimer. Supposing that anything happened to our young friend here—you will forgive the unpleasant hypothesis!—who would inherit the estate?"

"Since Rodger Baskerville, Sir Charles's younger brother died unmarried, the estate would descend to the Desmonds, who are distant cousins. James Desmond is an elderly clergyman in Westmoreland."

"Thank you. These details are all of great interest. Have you met Mr. James

Desmond?"

"Yes; he once came down to visit Sir Charles. He is a man of venerable appearance and of saintly life. I remember that he refused to accept any settlement from Sir Charles, though he pressed it upon him."

"And this man of simple tastes would be the heir to Sir Charles's thousands."

"He would be the heir to the estate because that is entailed. He would also be the heir to the money unless it were willed otherwise by the present owner, who can, of course, do what he likes with it."

"And have you made your will, Sir Henry?"

"No, Mr. Holmes, I have not. I've had no time, for it was only yesterday that I learned how matters stood. But in any case I feel that the money should go with the title and estate. That was my poor uncle's idea. How is the owner going to restore the glories of the Baskervilles if he has not money enough to keep up the property? House, land, and dollars must go together."

"Quite so. Well, Sir Henry, I am of one mind with you as to the advisability of your going down to Devonshire without delay. There is only one provision which I must make. You certainly must not go alone."

"Dr. Mortimer returns with me."

"But Dr. Mortimer has his practice to attend to, and his house is miles away from yours. With all the good will in the world he may be unable to help you. No, Sir Henry, you must take with you someone, a trusty man, who will be always by your side."

"It is possible that you could come yourself, Mr. Holmes?"

"If matters came to a crisis I should endeavour to be present in person; but you can understand that, with my extensive consulting practice and with the constant appeals which reach me from many quarters, it is impossible for me to be absent from London for an indefinite time. At the present instant one of the most revered names in England is being besmirched by a blackmailer, and only I can stop a disastrous scandal. You will see how impossible it is for me to go to Dartmoor."

"Whom would you recommend, then?"

Holmes laid his hand upon my arm.

"If my friend would undertake it there is no man who is better worth having at your side when you are in a tight place. No one can say so more confidently than I."

The proposition took me completely by surprise, but before I had time to answer, Baskerville seized me by the hand and wrung it heartily.

"Well, now, that is real kind of you, Dr. Watson," said he. "You see how it

is with me, and you know just as much about the matter as I do. If you will come down to Baskerville Hall and see me through I'll never forget it."

The promise of adventure had always a fascination for me, and I was complimented by the words of Holmes and by the eagerness with which the baronet hailed me as a companion.

"I will come, with pleasure," said I. "I do not know how I could employ my time better."

"And you will report very carefully to me," said Holmes. "When a crisis comes, as it will do, I will direct how you shall act. I suppose that by Saturday all might be ready?"

"Would that suit Dr. Watson?"

"Perfectly."

"Then on Saturday, unless you hear to the contrary, we shall meet at the 10:30 train from Paddington."

We had risen to depart when Baskerville gave a cry, of triumph and diving into one of the corners of the room he drew a brown boot from under a cabinet.

"My missing boot!" he cried.

"May all our difficulties vanish as easily!" said Sherlock Holmes.

"But it is a very singular thing," Dr. Mortimer remarked. "I searched this room carefully before lunch."

"And so did I," said Baskerville. "Every inch of it."

"There was certainly no boot in it then."

"In that case the waiter must have placed it there while we were lunching."

The German was sent for but professed to know nothing of the matter, nor could any inquiry clear it up. Another item had been added to that constant and apparently purposeless series of small mysteries which had succeeded each other so rapidly. Setting aside the whole grim story of Sir Charles's death, we had a line of inexplicable incidents all within the limits of two days, which included the receipt of the printed letter, the black-bearded spy in the hansom, the loss of the new brown boot, the loss of the old black boot, and now the return of the new brown boot. Holmes sat in silence in the cab as we drove back to Baker Street, and I knew from his drawn brows and keen face that his mind, like my own, was busy in endeavouring to frame some scheme into which all these strange and apparently disconnected episodes could be fitted. All afternoon and late into the evening he sat lost in tobacco and thought.

Just before dinner two telegrams were handed in. The first ran:—

"Have just heard that Barrymore is at the Hall.—BASKERVILLE." The second:—

"Visited twenty-three hotels as directed, but sorry, to report unable to trace cut sheet of Times.—CARTWRIGHT."

"There go two of my threads, Watson. There is nothing more stimulating than a case where everything goes against you. We must cast round for another scent."

"We have still the cabman who drove the spy."

"Exactly. I have wired to get his name and address from the Official Registry. I should not be surprised if this were an answer to my question."

The ring at the bell proved to be something even more satisfactory than an answer, however, for the door opened and a rough-looking fellow entered who was evidently the man himself.

"I got a message from the head office that a gent at this address had been inquiring for 2,704," said he. "I've driven my cab this seven years and never a word of complaint. I came here straight from the Yard to ask you to your face what you had against me."

"I have nothing in the world against you, my good man," said Holmes. "On the contrary, I have half a sovereign for you if you will give me a clear answer to my questions."

"Well, I've had a good day and no mistake," said the cabman, with a grin. "What was it you wanted to ask, sir?"

"First of all your name and address, in case I want you again."

"John Clayton, 3, Turpey Street, the Borough. My cab is out of Shipley's Yard, near Waterloo Station."

Sherlock Holmes made a note of it.

"Now, Clayton, tell me all about the fare who came and watched this house at ten o'clock this morning and afterwards followed the two gentlemen down Regent Street."

The man looked surprised and a little embarrassed. "Why, there's no good my telling you things, for you seem to know as much as I do already," said he. "The truth is that the gentleman told me that he was a detective and that I was to say nothing about him to anyone."

"My good fellow, this is a very serious business, and you may find yourself in a pretty bad position if you try to hide anything from me. You say that your fare told you that he was a detective?"

"Yes, he did."

"When did he say this?"

"When he left me."

"Did he say anything more?"

"He mentioned his name."

Holmes cast a swift glance of triumph at me. "Oh, he mentioned his name, did he? That was imprudent. What was the name that he mentioned?"

"His name," said the cabman, "was Mr. Sherlock Holmes."

Never have I seen my friend more completely taken aback than by the cabman's reply. For an instant he sat in silent amazement. Then he burst into a hearty laugh.

"A touch, Watson—an undeniable touch!" said he. "I feel a foil as quick and supple as my own. He got home upon me very prettily that time. So his name was Sherlock Holmes, was it?"

"Yes, sir, that was the gentleman's name."

"Excellent! Tell me where you picked him up and all that occurred."

"He hailed me at half-past nine in Trafalgar Square. He said that he was a detective, and he offered me two guineas if I would do exactly what he wanted all day and ask no questions. I was glad enough to agree. First we drove down to the Northumberland Hotel and waited there until two gentlemen came out and took a cab from the rank. We followed their cab until it pulled up somewhere near here."

"This very door," said Holmes.

"Well, I couldn't be sure of that, but I dare say my fare knew all about it. We pulled up half-way down the street and waited an hour and a half. Then the two gentlemen passed us, walking, and we followed down Baker Street and along ——"

"I know," said Holmes.

"Until we got three-quarters down Regent Street. Then my gentleman threw up the trap, and he cried that I should drive right away to Waterloo

Station as hard as I could go. I whipped up the mare and we were there under the ten minutes. Then he paid up his two guineas, like a good one, and away he went into the station. Only just as he was leaving he turned round and he said: 'It might interest you to know that you have been driving Mr. Sherlock Holmes.' That's how I come to know the name."

"I see. And you saw no more of him?"

"Not after he went into the station."

"And how would you describe Mr. Sherlock Holmes?"

The cabman scratched his head. "Well, he wasn't altogether such an easy gentleman to describe. I'd put him at forty years of age, and he was of a middle height, two or three inches shorter than you, sir. He was dressed like a toff, and he had a black beard, cut square at the end, and a pale face. I don't know as I could say more than that."

"Colour of his eyes?"

"No, I can't say that."

"Nothing more that you can remember?"

"No, sir; nothing."

"Well, then, here is your half-sovereign. There's another one waiting for you if you can bring any more information. Good night!"

"Good night, sir, and thank you!"

John Clayton departed chuckling, and Holmes turned to me with a shrug of his shoulders and a rueful smile.

"Snap goes our third thread, and we end where we began," said he. "The cunning rascal! He knew our number, knew that Sir Henry Baskerville had consulted me, spotted who I was in Regent Street, conjectured that I had got the number of the cab and would lay my hands on the driver, and so sent back this audacious message. I tell you, Watson, this time we have got a foeman who is worthy of our steel. I've been checkmated in London. I can only wish you better luck in Devonshire. But I'm not easy in my mind about it."

"About what?"

"About sending you. It's an ugly business, Watson, an ugly dangerous business, and the more I see of it the less I like it. Yes, my dear fellow, you may laugh, but I give you my word that I shall be very glad to have you back safe and sound in Baker Street once more."

CHAPTER VI. BASKERVILLE HALL

Sir Henry Baskerville and Dr. Mortimer were ready upon the appointed day, and we started as arranged for Devonshire. Mr. Sherlock Holmes drove with me to the station and gave me his last parting injunctions and advice.

"I will not bias your mind by suggesting theories or suspicions, Watson," said he; "I wish you simply to report facts in the fullest possible manner to me, and you can leave me to do the theorizing."

"What sort of facts?" I asked.

"Anything which may seem to have a bearing however indirect upon the case, and especially the relations between young Baskerville and his neighbours or any fresh particulars concerning the death of Sir Charles. I have made some inquiries myself in the last few days, but the results have, I fear, been negative. One thing only appears to be certain, and that is that Mr. James Desmond, who is the next heir, is an elderly gentleman of a very amiable disposition, so that this persecution does not arise from him. I really think that we may eliminate him entirely from our calculations. There remain the people who will actually surround Sir Henry Baskerville upon the moor."

"Would it not be well in the first place to get rid of this Barrymore couple?"

"By no means. You could not make a greater mistake. If they are innocent it would be a cruel injustice, and if they are guilty we should be giving up all chance of bringing it home to them. No, no, we will preserve them upon our list of suspects. Then there is a groom at the Hall, if I remember right. There are two moorland farmers. There is our friend Dr. Mortimer, whom I believe to be entirely honest, and there is his wife, of whom we know nothing. There is this naturalist, Stapleton, and there is his sister, who is said to be a young lady of attractions. There is Mr. Frankland, of Lafter Hall, who is also an unknown factor, and there are one or two other neighbours. These are the folk who must be your very special study."

"I will do my best."

"You have arms, I suppose?"

"Yes, I thought it as well to take them."

"Most certainly. Keep your revolver near you night and day, and never relax your precautions."

Our friends had already se-cured a first-class carriage and were waiting for us upon the platform.

"No, we have no news of any kind," said Dr. Mortimer in answer to my friend's ques-tions. "I can swear to one thing, and that is that we have not been shadowed during the last two days. We have never gone out without keep-ing a sharp watch, and no one could have escaped our no-tice."

"You have always kept to-gether, I presume?"

"Except yesterday after-noon. I usually give up one day to pure amusement when I come to town, so I spent it at the Museum of the College of Surgeons."

"And I went to look at the folk in the park," said Baskerville. "But we had no trouble of any kind."

"It was imprudent, all the same," said Holmes, shaking his head and looking very grave. "I beg, Sir Henry, that you will not go about alone. Some great misfortune will befall you if you do. Did you get your other boot?"

"No, sir, it is gone forever."

"Indeed. That is very interesting. Well, good-bye," he added as the train began to glide down the platform. "Bear in mind, Sir Henry, one of the phrases in that queer old legend which Dr. Mortimer has read to us, and avoid the moor in those hours of darkness when the powers of evil are exalted."

I looked back at the platform when we had left it far behind, and saw the tall, austere figure of Holmes standing motionless and gazing after us.

The journey was a swift and pleasant one, and I spent it in making the more intimate acquaintance of my two companions and in playing with Dr. Mortimer's spaniel. In a very few hours the brown earth had become ruddy, the brick had changed to granite, and red cows grazed in well-hedged fields where the lush grasses and more luxuriant vegetation spoke of a richer, if a damper, climate. Young Baskerville stared eagerly out of the window, and cried aloud with delight as he recognized the familiar features of the Devon scenery.

"I've been over a good part of the world since I left it, Dr. Watson," said he; "but I have never seen a place to compare with it."

"I never saw a Devonshire man who did not swear by his county," I remarked.

"It depends upon the breed of men quite as much as on the county," said Dr. Mortimer. "A glance at our friend here reveals the rounded head of the Celt, which carries inside it the Celtic enthusiasm and power of attachment. Poor Sir Charles's head was of a very rare type, half Gaelic, half Ivernian in its characteristics. But you were very young when you last saw Baskerville Hall, were you not?"

"I was a boy in my 'teens at the time of my father's death, and had never seen the Hall, for he lived in a little cottage on the South Coast. Thence I went straight to a friend in America. I tell you it is all as new to me as it is to Dr. Watson, and I'm as keen as possible to see the moor."

"Are you? Then your wish is easily granted, for there is your first sight of the moor," said Dr. Mortimer, pointing out of the carriage window.

Over the green squares of the fields and the low curve of a wood there rose in the distance a grey, melancholy hill, with a strange jagged summit, dim and vague in the distance, like some fantastic landscape in a dream. Baskerville sat for a long time, his eyes fixed upon it, and I read upon his eager face how much it meant to him, this first sight of that strange spot where the men of his blood had held sway so long and left their mark so deep. There he sat, with his tweed suit and his American accent, in the corner of a prosaic railway-carriage, and yet as I looked at his dark and expressive face I felt more than ever how true a descendant he was of that long line of high-blooded, fiery, and masterful men. There were pride, valour, and strength in his thick brows, his sensitive nostrils, and his large hazel eyes. If on that forbidding moor a difficult and dangerous quest should lie before us, this was at least a comrade for whom one might venture to take a risk with the certainty that he would bravely share it.

The train pulled up at a small wayside station and we all descended. Outside, beyond the low, white fence, a wagonette with a pair of cobs was waiting. Our coming was evidently a great event, for station-master and porters clustered round us to carry out our luggage. It was a sweet, simple country spot, but I was surprised to observe that by the gate there stood two soldierly men in dark uniforms, who leaned upon their short rifles and glanced keenly at us as we passed. The coachman, a hard-faced, gnarled little fellow, saluted Sir Henry Baskerville, and in a few minutes we were flying swiftly down the broad, white road. Rolling pasture lands curved upward on either side of us, and old gabled houses peeped out from amid the thick green foliage, but behind the peaceful and sunlit country-side there rose ever, dark against the evening sky, the long, gloomy curve of the moor, broken by the jagged and sinister hills.

The wagonette swung round into a side road, and we curved upward through deep lanes worn by centuries of wheels, high banks on either side, heavy with dripping moss and fleshy hart's-tongue ferns. Bronzing bracken and mottled bramble gleamed in the light of the sinking sun. Still steadily rising, we passed over a narrow granite bridge, and skirted a noisy stream which gushed swiftly down, foaming and roaring amid the gray boulders. Both road and stream wound up through a valley dense with scrub oak and fir. At every turn Baskerville gave an exclamation of delight, looking eagerly about him and asking countless questions. To his eyes all seemed beautiful, but to me a tinge of melancholy lay upon the country-side, which bore so clearly the mark of the waning year. Yellow leaves carpeted the lanes and fluttered down upon us as we passed. The rattle of our wheels died away as we drove through drifts of rotting vegetation—sad gifts, as it seemed to me, for Nature to throw before the carriage of the returning heir of the Baskervilles.

"Halloa!" cried Dr. Mortimer, "what is this?"

A steep curve of heath-clad land, an outlying spur of the moor, lay in front of us. On the summit, hard and clear like an equestrian statue upon its pedestal, was a mounted soldier, dark and stern, his rifle poised ready over his forearm. He was watching the road along which we travelled.

"What is this, Perkins?" asked Dr. Mortimer.

Our driver half turned in his seat.

"There's a convict escaped from Princetown, sir. He's been out three days now, and the warders watch every road and every station, but they've had no sight of him yet. The farmers about here don't like it, sir, and that's a fact."

"Well, I understand that they get five pounds if they can give information."

"Yes, sir, but the chance of five pounds is but a poor thing compared to the chance of having your throat cut. You see, it isn't like any ordinary convict. This is a man that would stick at nothing."

"Who is he, then?"

"It is Selden, the Notting Hill murderer."

I remembered the case well, for it was one in which Holmes had taken an interest on account of the peculiar ferocity of the crime and the wanton brutality which had marked all the actions of the assassin. The commutation of his death sentence had been due to some doubts as to his complete sanity, so atrocious was his conduct. Our wagonette had topped a rise and in front of us rose the huge expanse of the moor, mottled with gnarled and craggy cairns and tors. A cold wind swept down from it and set us shivering. Somewhere there, on that desolate plain, was lurking this fiendish man, hiding in a burrow like a wild beast, his heart full of malignancy against the whole race which had cast him out. It needed but this to complete the grim suggestiveness of the barren waste, the chilling wind, and the darkling sky.

Even Baskerville fell silent and pulled his overcoat more closely around him.

We had left the fertile country behind and beneath us. We looked back on it now, the slanting rays of a low sun turning the streams to threads of gold and glowing on the red earth new turned by the plough and the broad tangle of the woodlands. The road in front of us grew bleaker and wilder over huge russet and olive slopes, sprinkled with giant boulders. Now and then we passed a moorland cottage, walled and roofed with stone, with no creeper to break its harsh outline. Suddenly we looked down into a cup-like depression, patched with stunted oaks and firs which had been twisted and bent by the fury of years of storm. Two high, narrow towers rose over the trees. The driver pointed with his whip.

"Baskerville Hall," said he.

Its master had risen and was staring with flushed cheeks and shining eyes.

A few minutes later we had reached the lodge-gates, a maze of fantastic tracery in wrought iron, with weather-bitten pillars on either side, blotched with lichens, and surmounted by the boars' heads of the Baskervilles. The lodge was a ruin of black granite and bared ribs of rafters, but facing it was a new building, half constructed, the first fruit of Sir Charles's South African gold.

Through the gateway we passed into the avenue, where the wheels were again hushed amid the leaves, and the old trees shot their branches in a sombre tunnel over our heads. Baskerville shuddered as he looked up the long, dark drive to where the house glimmered like a ghost at the farther end.

"Was it here?" he asked in a low voice.

"No, no, the Yew Alley is on the other side."

The young heir glanced round with a gloomy face.

"It's no wonder my uncle felt as if trouble were coming on him in such a place as this," said he. "It's enough to scare any man. I'll have a row of electric lamps up here inside of six months, and you won't know it again, with a thousand candle-power Swan and Edison right here in front of the hall door."

The avenue opened into a broad expanse of turf, and the house lay before us. In the fading light I could see that the centre was a heavy block of building from which a porch projected. The whole front was draped in ivy, with a patch clipped bare here and there where a window or a coat-of-arms broke through the dark veil. >From this central block rose the twin towers, ancient, crenelated, and pierced with many loopholes. To right and left of the turrets were more modern wings of black granite. A dull light shone through heavy mullioned windows, and from the high chimneys which rose from the steep, high-angled roof there sprang a single black column of smoke.

"Welcome, Sir Henry! Welcome to Baskerville Hall!"

A tall man had stepped from the shadow of the porch to open the door of the wagonette. The figure of a woman was silhouetted against the yellow light of the hall. She came out and helped the man to hand down our bags.

"You don't mind my driving straight home, Sir Henry?" said Dr. Mortimer. "My wife is expecting me."

"Surely you will stay and have some dinner?"

"No, I must go. I shall probably find some work awaiting me. I would stay to show you over the house, but Barrymore will be a better guide than I. Good-bye, and never hesitate night or day to send for me if I can be of service."

The wheels died away down the drive while Sir Henry and I turned into the hall, and the door clanged heavily behind us. It was a fine apartment in which we found ourselves, large, lofty, and heavily raftered with huge balks of age-blackened oak. In the great old-fashioned fireplace behind the high iron dogs a log-fire crackled and snapped. Sir Henry and I held out our hands to it, for we were numb from our long drive. Then we gazed round us at the high, thin window of old stained glass, the oak panelling, the stags' heads, the coats-of-arms upon the walls, all dim and sombre in the subdued light of the central lamp.

"It's just as I imagined it," said Sir Henry. "Is it not the very picture of an old family home? To think that this should be the same hall in which for five hundred years my people have lived. It strikes me solemn to think of it."

I saw his dark face lit up with a boyish enthusiasm as he gazed about him. The light beat upon him where he stood, but long shadows trailed down the walls and hung like a black canopy above him. Barrymore had returned from taking our luggage to our rooms. He stood in front of us now with the subdued manner of a well-trained servant. He was a remarkable-looking man, tall, handsome, with a square black beard and pale, distinguished features.

"Would you wish dinner to be served at once, sir?"

"Is it ready?"

"In a very few minutes, sir. You will find hot water in your rooms. My wife and I will be happy, Sir Henry, to stay with you until you have made your fresh arrangements, but you will understand that under the new conditions this house will require a considerable staff."

"What new conditions?"

"I only meant, sir, that Sir Charles led a very retired life, and we were able to look after his wants. You would, naturally, wish to have more company, and so you will need changes in your household."

"Do you mean that your wife and you wish to leave?"

"Only when it is quite convenient to you, sir."

"But your family have been with us for several generations, have they not? I should be sorry to begin my life here by breaking an old family connection."

I seemed to discern some signs of emotion upon the butler's white face.

"I feel that also, sir, and so does my wife. But to tell the truth, sir, we were both very much attached to Sir Charles, and his death gave us a shock and made these surroundings very painful to us. I fear that we shall never again be easy in our minds at Baskerville Hall."

"But what do you intend to do?"

"I have no doubt, sir, that we shall succeed in establishing ourselves in some business. Sir Charles's generosity has given us the means to do so. And now, sir, perhaps I had best show you to your rooms."

A square balustraded gallery ran round the top of the old hall, approached by a double stair. From this central point two long corridors extended the whole length of the building, from which all the bedrooms opened. My own was in the same wing as Baskerville's and almost next door to it. These rooms

appeared to be much more modern than the central part of the house, and the bright paper and numerous candles did something to remove the sombre impression which our arrival had left upon my mind.

But the dining-room which opened out of the hall was a place of shadow and gloom. It was a long chamber with a step separating the dais where the family sat from the lower portion reserved for their dependents. At one end a minstrel's gallery overlooked it. Black beams shot across above our heads, with a smoke-darkened ceiling beyond them. With rows of flaring torches to light it up, and the colour and rude hilarity of an old-time banquet, it might have softened; but now, when two black-clothed gentlemen sat in the little circle of light thrown by a shaded lamp, one's voice became hushed and one's spirit subdued. A dim line of ancestors, in every variety of dress, from the Elizabethan knight to the buck of the Regency, stared down upon us and daunted us by their silent company. We talked little, and I for one was glad when the meal was over and we were able to retire into the modern billiard-room and smoke a cigarette.

"My word, it isn't a very cheerful place," said Sir Henry. "I suppose one can tone down to it, but I feel a bit out of the picture at present. I don't wonder that my uncle got a little jumpy if he lived all alone in such a house as this. However, if it suits you, we will retire early to-night, and perhaps things may seem more cheerful in the morning."

I drew aside my curtains before I went to bed and looked out from my window. It opened upon the grassy space which lay in front of the hall door. Beyond, two copses of trees moaned and swung in a rising wind. A half moon broke through the rifts of racing clouds. In its cold light I saw beyond the trees a broken fringe of rocks, and the long, low curve of the melancholy moor. I closed the curtain, feeling that my last impression was in keeping with the rest.

And yet it was not quite the last. I found myself weary and yet wakeful, tossing restlessly from side to side, seeking for the sleep which would not come. Far away a chiming clock struck out the quarters of the hours, but otherwise a deathly silence lay upon the old house. And then suddenly, in the very dead of the night, there came a sound to my ears, clear, resonant, and unmistakable. It was the sob of a woman, the muffled, strangling gasp of one who is torn by an uncontrollable sorrow. I sat up in bed and listened intently. The noise could not have been far away and was certainly in the house. For half an hour I waited with every nerve on the alert, but there came no other sound save the chiming clock and the rustle of the ivy on the wall.

CHAPTER VII. THE STAPLETONS OF MERRIPIT HOUSE

The fresh beauty of the following morning did something to efface from our minds the grim and gray impression which had been left upon both of us by our first experience of Baskerville Hall. As Sir Henry and I sat at breakfast the sunlight flooded in through the high mullioned windows, throwing watery patches of colour from the coats of arms which covered them. The dark panelling glowed like bronze in the golden rays, and it was hard to realize that this was indeed the chamber which had struck such a gloom into our souls upon the evening before.

"I guess it is ourselves and not the house that we have to blame!" said the baronet. "We were tired with our journey and chilled by our drive, so we took a gray view of the place. Now we are fresh and well, so it is all cheerful once more."

"And yet it was not entirely a question of imagination," I answered. "Did you, for example, happen to hear someone, a woman I think, sobbing in the night?"

"That is curious, for I did when I was half asleep fancy that I heard something of the sort. I waited quite a time, but there was no more of it, so I concluded that it was all a dream."

"I heard it distinctly, and I am sure that it was really the sob of a woman."

"We must ask about this right away." He rang the bell and asked Barrymore whether he could account for our experience. It seemed to me that the pallid features of the butler turned a shade paler still as he listened to his master's question.

"There are only two women in the house, Sir Henry," he answered. "One is the scullery-maid, who sleeps in the other wing. The other is my wife, and

155

I can answer for it that the sound could not have come from her."

And yet he lied as he said it, for it chanced that after breakfast I met Mrs. Barrymore in the long corridor with the sun full upon her face. She was a large, impassive, heavy-featured woman with a stern set expression of mouth. But her tell-tale eyes were red and glanced at me from between swollen lids. It was she, then, who wept in the night, and if she did so her husband must know it. Yet he had taken the obvious risk of discovery in declaring that it was not so. Why had he done this? And why did she weep so bitterly? Already round this pale-faced, handsome, black-bearded man there was gathering an atmosphere of mystery and of gloom. It was he who had been the first to discover the body of Sir Charles, and we had only his word for all the circumstances which led up to the old man's death. Was it possible that it was Barrymore after all whom we had seen in the cab in Regent Street? The beard might well have been the same. The cabman had described a somewhat shorter man, but such an impression might easily have been erroneous. How could I settle the point forever? Obviously the first thing to do was to see the Grimpen postmaster, and find whether the test telegram had really been placed in Barrymore's own hands. Be the answer what it might, I should at least have something to report to Sherlock Holmes.

Sir Henry had numerous papers to examine after breakfast, so that the time was propitious for my excursion. It was a pleasant walk of four miles along the edge of the moor, leading me at last to a small gray hamlet, in which two larger buildings, which proved to be the inn and the house of Dr. Mortimer, stood high above the rest. The postmaster, who was also the village grocer, had a clear recollection of the telegram.

"Certainly, sir," said he, "I had the telegram delivered to Mr. Barrymore exactly as directed."

"Who delivered it?"

"My boy here. James, you delivered that telegram to Mr. Barrymore at the Hall last week, did you not?"

"Yes, father, I delivered it."

"Into his own hands?" I asked.

"Well, he was up in the loft at the time, so that I could not put it into his own hands, but I gave it into Mrs. Barrymore's hands, and she promised to deliver it at once."

"Did you see Mr. Barrymore?"

"No, sir; I tell you he was in the loft."

"If you didn't see him, how do you know he was in the loft?"

"Well, surely his own wife ought to know where he is," said the postmaster testily. "Didn't he get the telegram? If there is any mistake it is for Mr. Barrymore himself to complain."

It seemed hopeless to pursue the inquiry any farther, but it was clear that in spite of Holmes's ruse we had no proof that Barrymore had not been in London all the time. Suppose that it were so—suppose that the same man had been the last who had seen Sir Charles alive, and the first to dog the new heir when he returned to England. What then? Was he the agent of others or had he some sinister design of his own? What interest could he have in persecuting the Baskerville family? I thought of the strange warning clipped out of the leading article of the Times. Was that his work or was it possibly the doing of someone who was bent upon counteracting his

schemes? The only conceivable motive was that which had been suggested by Sir Henry, that if the family could be scared away a comfortable and permanent home would be secured for the Barrymores. But surely such an explanation as that would be quite inadequate to account for the deep and subtle scheming which seemed to be weaving an invisible net round the young baronet. Holmes himself had said that no more complex case had come to him in all the long series of his sensational investigations. I prayed, as I walked back along the gray, lonely road, that my friend might soon be freed from his preoccupations and able to come down to take this heavy burden of responsibility from my shoulders.

Suddenly my thoughts were interrupted by the sound of running feet behind me and by a voice which called me by name. I turned, expecting to see Dr. Mortimer, but to my surprise it was a stranger who was pursuing me. He was a small, slim, clean-shaven, prim-faced man, flaxen-haired and lean-jawed, between thirty and forty years of age, dressed in a gray suit and wearing a straw hat. A tin box for botanical specimens hung over his shoulder and he carried a green butterfly-net in one of his hands.

"You will, I am sure, excuse my presumption, Dr. Watson," said he, as he came panting up to where I stood. "Here on the moor we are homely folk and do not wait for formal introductions. You may possibly have heard my name from our mutual friend, Mortimer. I am Stapleton, of Merripit House."

"Your net and box would have told me as much," said I, "for I knew that Mr. Stapleton was a naturalist. But how did you know me?"

"I have been calling on Mortimer, and he pointed you out to me from the window of his surgery as you passed. As our road lay the same way I thought that I would overtake you and introduce myself. I trust that Sir Henry is none the worse for his journey?"

"He is very well, thank you."

"We were all rather afraid that after the sad death of Sir Charles the new baronet might refuse to live here. It is asking much of a wealthy man to come down and bury himself in a place of this kind, but I need not tell you that it means a very great deal to the country-side. Sir Henry has, I suppose, no superstitious fears in the matter?"

"I do not think that it is likely."

"Of course you know the legend of the fiend dog which haunts the family?"

"I have heard it."

"It is extraordinary how credulous the peasants are about here! Any number of them are ready to swear that they have seen such a creature upon the moor." He spoke with a smile, but I seemed to read in his eyes that he took the matter more seriously. "The story took a great hold upon the imagination of Sir Charles, and I have no doubt that it led to his tragic end."

"But how?"

"His nerves were so worked up that the appearance of any dog might have had a fatal effect upon his diseased heart. I fancy that he really did see something of the kind upon that last night in the Yew Alley. I feared that some disaster might occur, for I was very fond of the old man, and I knew that his heart was weak."

"How did you know that?"

"My friend Mortimer told me."

"You think, then, that some dog pursued Sir Charles, and that he died of fright in consequence?"

"Have you any better explanation?"

"I have not come to any conclusion."

"Has Mr. Sherlock Holmes?"

The words took away my breath for an instant, but a glance at the placid face and steadfast eyes of my companion showed that no surprise was intended.

"It is useless for us to pretend that we do not know you, Dr. Watson," said he. "The records of your detective have reached us here, and you could not celebrate him without being known yourself. When Mortimer told me your name he could not deny your identity. If you are here, then it follows that Mr. Sherlock Holmes is interesting himself in the matter, and I am naturally curious to know what view he may take."

"I am afraid that I cannot answer that question."

"May I ask if he is going to honour us with a visit himself?"

"He cannot leave town at present. He has other cases which engage his attention."

"What a pity! He might throw some light on that which is so dark to us. But as to your own researches, if there is any possible way in which I can be of service to you I trust that you will command me. If I had any indication of the nature of your suspicions or how you propose to investigate the case, I might perhaps even now give you some aid or advice."

"I assure you that I am simply here upon a visit to my friend, Sir Henry, and that I need no help of any kind."

"Excellent!" said Stapleton. "You are perfectly right to be wary and discreet. I am justly reproved for what I feel was an unjustifiable intrusion, and I promise you that I will not mention the matter again."

We had come to a point where a narrow grassy path struck off from the road and wound away across the moor. A steep, boulder-sprinkled hill lay upon the right which had in bygone days been cut into a granite quarry. The face which was turned towards us formed a dark cliff, with ferns and brambles growing in its niches. From over a distant rise there floated a gray plume of smoke.

"A moderate walk along this moor-path brings us to Merripit House," said he. "Perhaps you will spare an hour that I may have the pleasure of introducing you to my sister."

My first thought was that I should be by Sir Henry's side. But then I remembered the pile of papers and bills with which his study table was littered. It was certain that I could not help with those. And Holmes had expressly said that I should study the neighbours upon the moor. I accepted Stapleton's invitation, and we turned together down the path.

"It is a wonderful place, the moor," said he, looking round over the undulating downs, long green rollers, with crests of jagged granite foaming up into fantastic surges. "You never tire of the moor. You cannot think the wonderful secrets which it contains. It is so vast, and so barren, and so mysterious."

"You know it well, then?"

"I have only been here two years. The residents would call me a new comer. We came shortly after Sir Charles settled. But my tastes led me to explore every part of the country round, and I should think that there are few men who know it better than I do."

"Is it hard to know?"

"Very hard. You see, for example, this great plain to the north here with the queer hills breaking out of it. Do you observe anything remarkable about that?"

"It would be a rare place for a gallop."

"You would naturally think so and the thought has cost several their lives before now. You notice those bright green spots scattered thickly over it?"

"Yes, they seem more fertile than the rest."

Stapleton laughed.

"That is the great Grimpen Mire," said he. "A false step yonder means death to man or beast. Only yesterday I saw one of the moor ponies wander into it. He never came out. I saw his head for quite a long time craning out of the bog-hole, but it sucked him down at last. Even in dry seasons it is a danger to cross it, but after these autumn rains it is an awful place. And yet I can find my way to the very heart of it and return alive. By George, there is another of those miserable ponies!"

Something brown was rolling and tossing among the green sedges. Then a long, agonized, writhing neck shot upward and a dreadful cry echoed over the moor. It turned me cold with horror, but my companion's nerves seemed to be stronger than mine.

"It's gone!" said he. "The mire has him. Two in two days, and many more, perhaps, for they get in the way of going there in the dry weather, and never know the difference until the mire has them in its clutches. It's a bad place, the great Grimpen Mire."

"And you say you can penetrate it?"

"Yes, there are one or two paths which a very active man can take. I have found them out."

"But why should you wish to go into so horrible a place?"

"Well, you see the hills beyond? They are really islands cut off on all sides by the impassable mire, which has crawled round them in the course of years. That is where the rare plants and the butterflies are, if you have the wit to reach them."

"I shall try my luck some day."

He looked at me with a surprised face.

"For God's sake put such an idea out of your mind," said he.

"Your blood would be upon my head. I assure you that there would not be the least chance of your coming back alive. It is only by remembering certain complex landmarks that I am able to do it."

"Halloa!" I cried. "What is that?"

A long, low moan, indescribably sad, swept over the moor. It filled the whole air, and yet it was impossible to say whence it came. From a dull murmur it swelled into a deep roar, and then sank back into a melancholy, throbbing murmur once again. Stapleton looked at me with a curious expression in his face.

"Queer place, the moor!" said he.

"But what is it?"

"The peasants say it is the Hound of the Baskervilles calling for its prey. I've heard it once or twice before, but never quite so loud."

I looked round, with a chill of fear in my heart, at the huge swelling plain, mottled with the green patches of rushes. Nothing stirred over the vast expanse save a pair of ravens, which croaked loudly from a tor behind us.

"You are an educated man. You don't believe such nonsense as that?" said I. "What do you think is the cause of so strange a sound?"

"Bogs make queer noises sometimes. It's the mud settling, or the water rising, or something."

"No, no, that was a living voice."

"Well, perhaps it was. Did you ever hear a bittern booming?"

"No, I never did."

"It's a very rare bird—practically extinct—in England now, but all things are possible upon the moor. Yes, I should not be surprised to learn that what we have heard is the cry of the last of the bitterns."

"It's the weirdest, strangest thing that ever I heard in my life."

"Yes, it's rather an uncanny place altogether. Look at the hillside yonder. What do you make of those?"

The whole steep slope was covered with gray circular rings of stone, a score of them at least.

"What are they? Sheep-pens?"

"No, they are the homes of our worthy ancestors. Prehistoric man lived thickly on the moor, and as no one in particular has lived there since, we find all his little arrangements exactly as he left them. These are his wigwams with the roofs off. You can even see his hearth and his couch if you have the curiosity to go inside.

"But it is quite a town. When was it inhabited?"

"Neolithic man—no date."

"What did he do?"

"He grazed his cattle on these slopes, and he learned to dig for tin when the bronze sword began to supersede the stone axe. Look at the great trench in the opposite hill. That is his mark. Yes, you will find some very singular points about the moor, Dr. Watson. Oh, excuse me an instant! It is surely Cyclopides."

A small fly or moth had fluttered across our path, and in an instant Stapleton was rushing with extraordinary energy and speed in pursuit of it. To my dismay the creature flew straight for the great mire, and my acquaintance never paused for an instant, bounding from tuft to tuft behind it, his green net waving in the air. His gray clothes and jerky, zigzag, irregular progress made him not unlike some huge moth himself. I was standing watching his pursuit with a mixture of admiration for his extraordinary activity and fear lest he should lose his footing in the treacherous mire, when I heard the sound of steps, and turning round found a woman near me upon the path. She had come from the direction in which the plume of smoke indicated the position of Merripit House, but the dip of the moor had hid her until she was quite close.

I could not doubt that this was the Miss Stapleton of whom I had been told, since ladies of any sort must be few upon the moor, and I remembered that I had heard someone describe her as being a beauty. The woman who approached me was certainly that, and of a most uncommon type. There could not have been a greater contrast between brother and sister, for Stapleton was neutral tinted, with light hair and gray eyes, while she was darker than any brunette whom I have seen in England—slim, elegant, and tall. She had a proud, finely cut face, so regular that it might have seemed impassive were it not for the sensitive mouth and the beautiful dark, eager eyes. With her perfect figure and elegant dress she was, indeed, a strange apparition upon a lonely moorland path. Her eyes were on her brother as I turned, and then she quickened her pace towards me. I had raised my hat and was about to make some explanatory remark, when her own words turned all my thoughts into a new channel.

"Go back!" she said. "Go straight back to London, instantly."

I could only stare at her in stupid surprise. Her eyes blazed at me, and she tapped the ground impatiently with her foot.

"Why should I go back?" I asked.

"I cannot explain." She spoke in a low, eager voice, with a curious lisp in her utterance. "But for God's sake do what I ask you. Go back and never set foot upon the moor again."

"But I have only just come."

"Man, man!" she cried.

"Can you not tell when a warning is for your own good? Go back to London! Start to-night! Get away from this place at all costs! Hush, my brother is coming! Not a word of what I have said. Would you mind getting that orchid for me among the mares-tails yonder? We are very rich in orchids on the moor, though, of course, you are rather late to see the beauties of the place."

Stapleton had abandoned the chase and came back to us breathing hard and flushed with his exertions.

"Halloa, Beryl!" said he, and it seemed to me that the tone of his greeting was not altogether a cordial one.

"Well, Jack, you are very hot."

"Yes, I was chasing a Cyclopides. He is very rare and seldom found in the late autumn. What a pity that I should have missed him!" He spoke unconcernedly, but his small light eyes glanced incessantly from the girl to me.

"You have introduced yourselves, I can see."

"Yes. I was telling Sir Henry that it was rather late for him to see the true beauties of the moor."

"Why, who do you think this is?"

"I imagine that it must be Sir Henry Baskerville."

"No, no," said I. "Only a humble commoner, but his friend. My name is Dr. Watson."

A flush of vexation passed over her expressive face. "We have been talking at cross purposes," said she.

"Why, you had not very much time for talk," her brother remarked with the same questioning eyes.

"I talked as if Dr. Watson were a resident instead of being merely a visitor," said she. "It cannot much matter to him whether it is early or late for the orchids. But you will come on, will you not, and see Merripit House?"

A short walk brought us to it, a bleak moorland house, once the farm of some grazier in the old prosperous days, but now put into repair and turned into a modern dwelling. An orchard surrounded it, but the trees, as is usual upon the moor, were stunted and nipped, and the effect of the whole place was mean and melancholy. We were admitted by a strange wizened, rusty-coated old man servant, who seemed in keeping with the house. Inside, however, there were large rooms furnished with an elegance in which I seemed to recognise the taste of the lady. As I looked from their windows at the interminable granite-flecked moor rolling unbroken to the farthest horizon I could not but marvel at what could have brought this highly educated man and this beautiful woman to live in such a place.

"Queer spot to choose, is it not?" said he as if in answer to my thought. "And yet we manage to make ourselves fairly happy, do we not, Beryl?"

"Quite happy," said she, but there was no ring of conviction in her words.

"I had a school," said Stapleton. "It was in the north country. The work to a man of my temperament was mechanical and uninteresting, but the privilege of living with youth, of helping to mould those young minds and of impressing them with one's own character and ideals, was very dear to me. However, the fates were against us. A serious epidemic broke out in the school and three of the boys died. It never recovered from the blow, and much of my capital was irretrievably swallowed up. And yet, if it were not for the loss of the charming companionship of the boys, I could rejoice over my own misfortune, for, with my strong tastes for botany and zoology, I find an unlimited field of work here, and my sister is as devoted to Nature as I am. All this, Dr. Watson, has been brought upon your head by your expression as you surveyed the moor out of our window."

"It certainly did cross my mind that it might be a little dull—less for you, perhaps, than for your sister."

"No, no, I am never dull," said she, quickly.

"We have books, we have our studies, and we have interesting neighbours. Dr. Mortimer is a most learned man in his own line. Poor Sir Charles was also an admirable companion. We knew him well, and miss him more than I can tell. Do you think that I should intrude if I were to call this afternoon and make the acquaintance of Sir Henry?"

"I am sure that he would be delighted."

"Then perhaps you would mention that I propose to do so. We may in our humble way do something to make things more easy for him until he becomes accustomed to his new surroundings. Will you come upstairs, Dr. Watson, and inspect my collection of Lepidoptera? I think it is the most complete one in the south-west of England. By the time that you have looked through them lunch will be almost ready."

But I was eager to get back to my charge. The melancholy of the moor, the death of the unfortunate pony, the weird sound which had been associated with the grim legend of the Baskervilles, all these things tinged my thoughts with sadness. Then on the top of these more or less vague impressions there had come the definite and distinct warning of Miss Stapleton, delivered with such intense earnestness that I could not doubt that some grave and deep reason lay behind it. I resisted all pressure to stay for lunch, and I set off at once upon my return journey, taking the grass-grown path by which we had come.

It seems, however, that there must have been some short cut for those who knew it, for before I had reached the road I was astounded to see Miss Stapleton sitting upon a rock by the side of the track. Her face was beautifully flushed with her exertions, and she held her hand to her side.

"I have run all the way in order to cut you off, Dr. Watson," said she. "I had not even time to put on my hat. I must not stop, or my brother may miss me. I wanted to say to you how sorry I am about the stupid mistake I made in thinking that you were Sir Henry. Please forget the words I said, which have no application whatever to you."

"But I can't forget them, Miss Stapleton," said I. "I am Sir Henry's friend, and his welfare is a very close concern of mine. Tell me why it was that you were so eager that Sir Henry should return to London."

"A woman's whim, Dr. Watson. When you know me better you will understand that I cannot always give reasons for what I say or do."

"No, no. I remember the thrill in your voice. I remember the look in your eyes. Please, please, be frank with me, Miss Stapleton, for ever since I have been here I have been conscious of shadows all round me. Life has become like that great Grimpen Mire, with little green patches everywhere into which one may sink and with no guide to point the track. Tell me then what it was that you meant, and I will promise to convey your warning to Sir Henry."

An expression of irresolution passed for an instant over her face, but her eyes had hardened again when she answered me.

"You make too much of it, Dr. Watson," said she. "My brother and I were very much shocked by the death of Sir Charles. We knew him very intimately, for his favourite walk was over the moor to our house. He was deeply impressed with the curse which hung over the family, and when this tragedy came I naturally felt that there must be some grounds for the fears which he had expressed. I was distressed therefore when another member of the family came down to live here, and I felt that he should be warned of the danger which he will run. That was all which I intended to convey.

"But what is the danger?"

"You know the story of the hound?"

"I do not believe in such nonsense."

"But I do. If you have any influence with Sir Henry, take him away from a place which has always been fatal to his family. The world is wide. Why should he wish to live at the place of danger?"

"Because it is the place of danger. That is Sir Henry's nature. I fear that unless you can give me some more definite information than this it would be impossible to get him to move."

"I cannot say anything definite, for I do not know anything definite."

"I would ask you one more question, Miss Stapleton. If you meant no more than this when you first spoke to me, why should you not wish your brother to overhear what you said? There is nothing to which he, or anyone else, could object."

"My brother is very anxious to have the Hall inhabited, for he thinks it is for the good of the poor folk upon the moor. He would be very angry if he knew that I have said anything which might induce Sir Henry to go away. But I have done my duty now and I will say no more. I must get back, or he will miss me and suspect that I have seen you. Good-bye!" She turned and had disappeared in a few minutes among the scattered boulders, while I, with my soul full of vague fears, pursued my way to Baskerville Hall.

CHAPTER VIII. FIRST REPORT OF DR. WATSON

From this point onward I will follow the course of events by transcribing my own letters to Mr. Sherlock Holmes which lie before me on the table. One page is missing, but otherwise they are exactly as written and show my feelings and suspicions of the moment more accurately than my memory, clear as it is upon these tragic events, can possibly do.

Baskerville Hall, October 13th.

MY DEAR HOLMES,—My previous letters and telegrams have kept you pretty well up to date as to all that has occurred in this most God-forsaken corner of the world. The longer one stays here the more does the spirit of the moor sink into one's soul, its vastness, and also its grim charm. When you are once out upon its bosom you have left all traces of modern England behind you but, on the other hand you are conscious everywhere of the homes and the work of the prehistoric people. On all sides of you as you walk are the houses of these forgotten folk, with their graves and the huge monoliths which are supposed to have marked their temples. As you look at their gray stone huts against the scarred hill-sides you leave your own age behind you, and if you were to see a skin-clad, hairy man crawl out from the low door fitting a flint-tipped arrow on to the string of his bow, you would feel that his presence there was more natural than your own. The strange thing is that they should have lived so thickly on what must always have been most unfruitful soil. I am no antiquarian, but I could imagine that they were some unwarlike and harried race who were forced to accept that which none other would occupy.

All this, however, is foreign to the mission on which you sent me and will probably be very uninteresting to your severely practical mind. I can still remember your complete indifference as to whether the sun moved round the earth or the earth round the sun. Let me, therefore, return to the facts concerning Sir Henry Baskerville.

If you have not had any report within the last few days it is because up to to-day there was nothing of importance to relate. Then a very surprising circumstance occurred, which I shall tell you in due course. But, first of all, I must keep you in touch with some of the other factors in the situation.

One of these, concerning which I have said little, is the escaped convict upon the moor. There is strong reason now to believe that he has got right away, which is a considerable relief to the lonely house holders of this district. A fortnight has passed since his flight, during which he has not been seen and nothing has been heard of him. It is surely inconceivable that he could have held out upon the moor during all that time. Of course, so far as his concealment goes there is no difficulty at all. Any one of these stone huts would give him a hiding-place. But there is nothing to eat unless he were to catch and slaughter one of the moor sheep. We think, therefore, that he has gone, and the outlying farmers sleep the better in consequence.

We are four able-bodied men in this household, so that we could take good care of ourselves, but I confess that I have had uneasy moments when I have thought of the Stapletons. They live miles from any help. There are one maid, an old manservant, the sister, and the brother, the latter not a very strong man. They would be helpless in the hands of a desperate fellow like this Notting Hill criminal, if he could once effect an entrance. Both Sir Henry and I were concerned at their situation, and it was suggested that Perkins the groom should go over to sleep there, but Stapleton would not hear of it.

The fact is that our friend, the baronet, begins to display a considerable interest in our fair neighbour. It is not to be wondered at, for time hangs heavily in this lonely spot to an active man like him, and she is a very fascinating and beautiful woman. There is something tropical and exotic about her which forms a singular contrast to her cool and unemotional brother. Yet he also gives the idea of hidden fires. He has certainly a very marked influence over her, for I have seen her continually glance at him as she talked as if seeking approbation for what she said. I trust that he is kind to her. There is a dry glitter in his eyes, and a firm set of his thin lips, which goes with a positive and possibly a harsh nature. You would find him an interesting study.

He came over to call upon Baskerville on that first day, and the very next morning he took us both to show us the spot where the legend of the wicked

Hugo is supposed to have had its origin. It was an excursion of some miles across the moor to a place which is so dismal that it might have suggested the story. We found a short valley between rugged tors which led to an open, grassy space flecked over with the white cotton grass. In the middle of it rose two great stones, worn and sharpened at the upper end, until they looked like the huge corroding fangs of some monstrous beast. In every way it corresponded with the scene of the old tragedy. Sir Henry was much interested and asked Stapleton more than once whether he did really believe in the possibility of the interference of the supernatural in the affairs of men. He spoke lightly, but it was evident that

he was very much in earnest. Stapleton was guarded in his replies, but it was easy to see that he said less than he might, and that he would not express his whole opinion out of consideration for the feelings of the baronet. He told us of similar cases, where families had suffered from some evil influence, and he left us with the impression that he shared the popular view upon the matter.

On our way back we stayed for lunch at Merripit House, and it was there that Sir Henry made the acquaintance of Miss Stapleton. From the first moment that he saw her he appeared to be strongly attracted by her, and I am much mistaken if the feeling was not mutual. He referred to her again and again on our walk home, and since then hardly a day has passed that we have not seen something of the brother and sister. They dine here to-night, and there is some talk of our going to them next week. One would imagine that such a match would be very welcome to Stapleton, and yet I have more than once caught a look of the strongest disapprobation in his face when Sir Henry has been paying some attention to his sister. He is much attached to her, no doubt, and would lead a lonely life without her, but it would seem the height of selfishness if he were to stand in the way of her making so brilliant a marriage. Yet I am certain that he does not wish their intimacy to ripen into love, and I have several times observed that he has taken pains to prevent them from being tête-à-tête. By the way, your instructions to me never to allow Sir Henry to go out alone will become very much more oner-ous if a love affair were to be added to our other difficulties. My popularity would soon suffer if I were to carry out your orders to the letter.

The other day—Thursday, to be more exact—Dr. Mortimer lunched with us. He has been excavating a barrow at Long Down, and has got a prehis-toric skull which fills him with great joy. Never was there such a single-minded enthusiast as he! The Stapletons came in afterwards, and the good doctor took us all to the Yew Alley, at Sir Henry's request, to show us exactly

how everything occurred upon that fatal night. It is a long, dismal walk, the Yew Alley, between two high walls of clipped hedge, with a nar-row band of grass upon either side. At the far end is an old tumble-down summer-house. Half-way down is the moor-gate, where the old gentle-man left his cigar-ash. It is a white wooden gate with a latch. Beyond it lies the wide moor. I remembered your theory of the affair and tried to picture all that had oc-curred. As the old man stood there he saw something com-ing across the moor, some-thing which terrified him so that he lost his wits, and ran and ran until he died of sheer horror and exhaustion. There was the long, gloomy tunnel down which he fled. And from what? A sheep-dog of the moor? Or a spectral hound, black, silent, and monstrous? Was there a human agency in the matter? Did the pale, watchful Barrymore know more than he cared to say? It was all dim and vague, but always there is the dark shadow of crime behind it.

One other neighbour I have met since I wrote last. This is Mr. Frankland, of Lafter Hall, who lives some four miles to the south of us. He is an elderly man, red-faced, white-haired, and choleric. His passion is for the British law, and he has spent a large fortune in litigation. He fights for the mere pleasure of fighting and is equally ready to take up either side of a question, so that it is no wonder that he has found it a costly amusement. Sometimes he will shut up a right of way and defy the parish to make him open it. At others he will with his own hands tear down some other man's gate and declare that a path has existed there from time immemorial, defying the owner to prosecute him for trespass. He is learned in old manorial and communal rights, and he applies his knowledge sometimes in favour of the villagers of Fernworthy and sometimes against them, so that he is periodically either carried in triumph down the village street or else burned in effigy, according to his latest exploit. He is said to have about seven lawsuits upon his hands at present, which will probably swallow up the remainder of his fortune and so draw his sting and leave him harmless for the future. Apart from the law he seems a kindly, good-natured person, and I only mention him because you were particular that I should send some description of the people who surround us. He is curiously employed at present, for, being an amateur astronomer, he has an excellent telescope, with which he lies upon the roof of his own house and sweeps the moor all day in the hope of catching a glimpse of the escaped convict. If he would confine his energies to this all would be well, but there are rumours that he intends to prosecute Dr. Mortimer for opening a grave without the consent of the next-of-kin, because he dug up the neolithic skull in the barrow on Long Down. He helps to keep our lives from being monotonous and gives a little comic relief where it is badly needed.

And now, having brought you up to date in the escaped convict, the Stapletons, Dr. Mortimer, and Frankland, of Lafter Hall, let me end on that which is most important and tell you more about the Barrymores, and especially about the surprising development of last night.

First of all about the test telegram, which you sent from London in order to make sure that Barrymore was really here. I have already explained that the testimony of the postmaster shows that the test was worthless and that we have no proof one way or the other. I told Sir Henry how the matter stood, and he at once, in his downright fashion, had Barrymore up and asked him whether he had received the telegram himself. Barrymore said that he had.

"Did the boy deliver it into your own hands?" asked Sir Henry.

Barrymore looked surprised, and considered for a little time.

"No," said he, "I was in the box-room at the time, and my wife brought it up to me."

"Did you answer it yourself?"

"No; I told my wife what to answer and she went down to write it."

In the evening he recurred to the subject of his own accord.

"I could not quite understand the object of your questions this morning, Sir Henry," said he. "I trust that they do not mean that I have done anything to forfeit your confidence?"

Sir Henry had to assure him that it was not so and pacify him by giving him a considerable part of his old wardrobe, the London outfit having now all arrived.

Mrs. Barrymore is of interest to me. She is a heavy, solid person, very limited, intensely respectable, and inclined to be puritanical. You could hardly conceive a less emotional subject. Yet I have told you how, on the first night here, I heard her sobbing bitterly, and since then I have more than once observed traces of tears upon her face. Some deep sorrow gnaws ever at her heart. Sometimes I wonder if she has a guilty memory which haunts her, and sometimes I suspect Barrymore of being a domestic tyrant. I have always felt that there was something singular and questionable in this man's character, but the adventure of last night brings all my suspicions to a head.

And yet it may seem a small matter in itself. You are aware that I am not a very sound sleeper, and since I have been on guard in this house my slumbers have been lighter than ever. Last night, about two in the morning, I was aroused by a stealthy step passing my room. I rose, opened my door, and peeped out. A long black shadow was trailing down the corridor. It was thrown by a man who walked softly down the passage with a candle held in his hand. He was in shirt and trousers, with no covering to his feet. I could merely see the outline, but his height told me that it was Barrymore. He walked very slowly and circumspectly, and there was something indescribably guilty and furtive in his whole appearance.

I have told you that the corridor is broken by the balcony which runs round the hall, but that it is resumed upon the farther side. I waited until he had passed out of sight and then I followed him. When I came round the balcony he had reached the end of the farther corridor, and I could see from the glimmer of light through an open door that he had entered one of the rooms. Now, all these rooms are unfurnished and unoccupied, so that his expedition became more mysterious than ever. The light shone steadily as if he were standing motionless. I crept down the passage as noiselessly as I could and peeped round the corner of the door.

Barrymore was crouching at the window with the candle held against the glass. His profile was half turned towards me, and his face seemed to be rigid with expectation as he stared out into the blackness of the moor. For some minutes he stood watching intently. Then he gave a deep groan and with an impatient gesture he put out the light. Instantly I made my way back to my room, and very shortly came the stealthy steps passing once more upon their return journey. Long afterwards when I had fallen into a light sleep I heard a key turn somewhere in a lock, but I could not tell whence the sound came. What it all means I cannot guess, but there is some secret business going on in this house of gloom which sooner or later we shall get to the bottom of. I do not trouble you with my theories, for you

asked me to furnish you only with facts. I have had a long talk with Sir Henry this morning, and we have made a plan of campaign founded upon my observations of last night. I will not speak about it just now, but it should make my next report interesting reading.

CHAPTER IX. (SECOND REPORT OF DR. WATSON)
THE LIGHT UPON THE MOOR

Baskerville Hall, Oct. 15th.

MY DEAR HOLMES,—If I was compelled to leave you without much news during the early days of my mission you must acknowledge that I am making up for lost time, and that events are now crowding thick and fast upon us. In my last report I ended upon my top note with Barrymore at the window, and now I have quite a budget already which will, unless I am much mistaken, considerably surprise you. Things have taken a turn which I could not have anticipated. In some ways they have within the last forty-eight hours become much clearer and in some ways they have become more complicated. But I will tell you all and you shall judge for yourself.

Before breakfast on the morning following my adventure I went down the corridor and examined the room in which Barrymore had been on the night before. The western window through which he had stared so intently has, I noticed, one peculiarity above all other windows in the house—it commands the nearest outlook on the moor. There is an opening between two trees which enables one from this point of view to look right down upon it, while from all the other windows it is only a distant glimpse which can be obtained. It follows, therefore, that Barrymore, since only this window would serve the purpose, must have been looking out for something or somebody upon the moor. The night was very dark, so that I can hardly imagine how he could have hoped to see anyone. It had struck me that it was possible that some love intrigue was on foot. That would have accounted for his stealthy movements and also for the uneasiness of his wife. The man is a striking-looking fellow, very well equipped to steal the heart of a country girl, so that this theory seemed to have something to support it. That opening of the door which I had heard after I had returned to my room might mean that he had gone out to keep some clandestine appointment. So I reasoned with myself in the morning, and I tell you the direction of my suspicions, however much the result may have shown that they were unfounded.

But whatever the true explanation of Barrymore's movements might be, I felt that the responsibility of keeping them to myself until I could explain them was more than I could bear. I had an interview with the baronet in his study after breakfast, and I told him all that I had seen. He was less surprised than I had expected.

"I knew that Barrymore walked about nights, and I had a mind to speak to him about it," said he. "Two or three times I have heard his steps in the passage, coming and going, just about the hour you name."

"Perhaps then he pays a visit every night to that particular window," I suggested.

"Perhaps he does. If so, we should be able to shadow him, and see what it is that he is after. I wonder what your friend Holmes would do, if he were here."

"I believe that he would do exactly what you now suggest," said I. "He would follow Barrymore and see what he did."

"Then we shall do it together."

"But surely he would hear us."

"The man is rather deaf, and in any case we must take our chance of that. We'll sit up in my room to-night and wait until he passes." Sir Henry rubbed his hands with pleasure, and it was evident that he hailed the adventure as a relief to his somewhat quiet life upon the moor.

The baronet has been in communication with the architect who prepared the plans for Sir Charles, and with a contractor from London, so that we may expect great changes to begin here soon. There have been decorators and furnishers up from Plymouth, and it is evident that our friend has large ideas, and means to spare no pains or expense to restore the grandeur of his family. When the house is renovated and refurnished, all that he will need will be a wife to make it complete. Between ourselves there are pretty clear signs that this will not be wanting if the lady is willing, for I have seldom seen a man more infatuated with a woman than he is with our beautiful neighbour, Miss Stapleton. And yet the course of true love does not run quite as smoothly as one would under the circumstances expect. To-day, for example, its surface was broken by a very unexpected ripple, which has caused our friend considerable perplexity and annoyance.

After the conversation which I have quoted about Barrymore, Sir Henry put on his hat and prepared to go out. As a matter of course I did the same.

"What, are you coming, Watson?" he asked, looking at me in a curious way.

"That depends on whether you are going on the moor," said I.

"Yes, I am."

"Well, you know what my instructions are. I am sorry to intrude, but you heard how earnestly Holmes insisted that I should not leave you, and especially that you should not go alone upon the moor."

Sir Henry put his hand upon my shoulder with a pleasant smile.

"My dear fellow," said he, "Holmes, with all his wisdom, did not foresee some things which have happened since I have been on the moor. You understand me? I am sure that you are the last man in the world who would wish to be a spoil-sport. I must go out alone."

It put me in a most awkward position. I was at a loss what to say or what to do, and before I had made up my mind he picked up his cane and was gone.

But when I came to think the matter over my conscience reproached me bitterly for having on any pretext allowed him to go out of my sight. I imagined what my feelings would be if I had to return to you and to confess that some misfortune had occurred through my disregard for your instructions. I assure you my cheeks flushed at the very thought. It might not even now be too late to overtake him, so I set off at once in the direction of Merripit House.

I hurried along the road at the top of my speed without seeing anything of Sir Henry, until I came to the point where the moor path branches off. There, fearing that perhaps I had come in the wrong direction after all, I mounted a hill from which I could command a view—the same hill which is cut into the dark quarry. Thence I saw him at once. He was on the moor path, about a quarter of a mile off, and a lady was by his side who could only be Miss Stapleton. It was clear that there was already an understanding between them and that they had met by appointment. They were walking slowly along in deep conversation, and I saw her making quick little movements of her hands as if she were very earnest in what she was saying, while he listened intently, and once or twice shook his head in strong dissent. I stood among the rocks watching them, very much puzzled as to what I should do next. To follow them and break into their intimate conversation seemed to be an outrage, and yet my clear duty was never for an instant to let him out of my sight. To act the spy upon a friend was a hateful task. Still, I could see no better course than to observe him from the hill, and to clear my conscience by confessing to him afterwards what I had done. It is true that if any sudden danger had threatened him I was too far away to be of use, and yet I am sure that you will agree with me that the position was very difficult, and that there was nothing more which I could do.

Our friend, Sir Henry, and the lady had halted on the path and were standing deeply absorbed in their conversation, when I was suddenly aware that I was not the only witness of their interview. A wisp of green floating in the air caught my eye, and another glance showed me that it was carried on a stick by a man who was moving among the broken ground. It was Stapleton with his butterfly-net. He was very much closer to the pair than I was, and he appeared to be moving in their direction. At this instant Sir Henry suddenly drew Miss Stapleton to his side. His arm was round her, but it seemed to me that she was straining away from him with her face averted. He stooped his head to hers, and she raised one hand as if in protest. Next moment I saw them spring apart and turn hurriedly round. Stapleton was the cause of the interruption. He was running wildly towards them, his absurd net dangling behind him. He gesticulated and almost danced with excitement in front of the lovers. What the scene meant I could not imagine, but it seemed to me that Stapleton was abusing Sir Henry, who offered explanations, which became more angry as the other refused to accept them. The lady stood by in haughty silence. Finally Stapleton turned upon his heel and beckoned in a peremptory way to his sister, who, after an irresolute glance at Sir Henry, walked off by the side of her brother. The naturalist's angry gestures showed that the lady was included in his displeasure. The baronet stood for a minute looking after them, and then he walked slowly back the way that he had come, his head hanging, the very picture of dejection.

What all this meant I could not imagine, but I was deeply ashamed to have witnessed so intimate a scene without my friend's knowledge. I ran down the hill therefore and met the baronet at the bottom. His face was flushed with anger and his brows were wrinkled, like one who is at his wit's ends what to do.

"Halloa, Watson! Where have you dropped from?" said he."You don't mean to say that you came after me in spite of all?"

I explained everything to him: how I had found it impossible to remain behind, how I had followed him, and how I had witnessed all that had occurred. For an instant his eyes blazed at me, but my frankness disarmed his anger, and he broke at last into a rather rueful laugh.

"You would have thought the middle of that prairie a fairly safe place for a man to be private," said he, "but, by thunder, the whole countryside seems to have been out to see me do my wooing—and a mighty poor wooing at that! Where had you engaged a seat?"

"I was on that hill."

"Quite in the back row, eh? But her brother was well up to the front. Did you see him come out on us?"

"Yes, I did."

"Did he ever strike you as being crazy—this brother of hers?"

"I can't say that he ever did."

"I dare say not. I always thought him sane enough until to-day, but you can take it from me that either he or I ought to be in a strait-jacket. What's the matter with me, anyhow? You've lived near me for some weeks, Watson. Tell me straight, now! Is there anything that would prevent me from making a good husband to a woman that I loved?"

"I should say not."

"He can't object to my worldly position, so it must be myself that he has this down on. What has he against me? I never hurt man or woman in my life that I know of. And yet he would not so much as let me touch the tips of her fingers."

"Did he say so?"

"That, and a deal more. I tell you, Watson, I've only known her these few weeks, but from the first I just felt that she was made for me, and she, too— she was happy when she was with me, and that I'll swear. There's a light in a woman's eyes that speaks louder than words. But he has never let us get together, and it was only to-day for the first time that I saw a chance of having a few words with her alone. She was glad to meet me, but when she did it was not love that she would talk about, and she wouldn't have let me talk about it either if she could have stopped it. She kept coming back to it that this was a place of danger, and that she would never be happy until I had left it. I told her that since I had seen her I was in no hurry to leave it, and that if she really wanted me to go, the only way to work it was for her to arrange to go with me. With that I offered in as many words to marry her, but before she could answer down came this brother of hers, running at us with a face on him like a madman. He was just white with rage, and those light eyes of his were blazing with fury. What was I doing with the lady? How dared I offer her attentions which were distasteful to her? Did I think that because I was a baronet I could do what I liked? If he had not been her brother I should have known better how to answer him. As it was I told him that my feelings towards his sister were such as I was not ashamed of, and that I hoped that she might honour me by becoming my wife. That seemed to make the matter no better, so then I lost my temper too, and I answered him rather more hotly than I should perhaps, considering that she was standing by. So it ended by his going off with her, as you saw, and here am I as badly puzzled a man as any in this county. Just tell me what it all means, Watson, and I'll owe you more than ever I can hope to pay."

I tried one or two explanations, but, indeed, I was completely puzzled myself. Our friend's title, his fortune, his age, his character, and his appearance are all in his favour, and I know nothing against him unless it be this dark fate which runs in his family. That his advances should be rejected so brusquely without any reference to the lady's own wishes, and that the lady should accept the situation without protest, is very amazing. However, our conjectures were set at rest by a visit from Stapleton himself that very afternoon. He had come to offer apologies for his rudeness of the morning, and after a long private interview with Sir Henry in his study, the upshot of their conversation was that the breach is quite healed, and that we are to dine at Merripit House next Friday as a sign of it.

"I don't say now that he isn't a crazy man," said Sir Henry; "I can't forget the look in his eyes when he ran at me this morning, but I must allow that no man could make a more handsome apology than he has done."

"Did he give any explanation of his conduct?"

"His sister is everything in his life, he says. That is natural enough, and I am glad that he should understand her value. They have always been together, and according to his account he has been a very lonely man with only her as a companion, so that the thought of losing her was really terrible to him. He had not understood, he said, that I was becoming attached to her, but when he saw with his own eyes that it was really so, and that she might be taken away from him, it gave him such a shock that for a time he was not responsible for what he said or did. He was very sorry for all that had passed, and he recognized how foolish and how selfish it was that he should imagine that he could hold a beautiful woman like his sister to himself for her whole life. If she had to leave him he had rather it was to a neighbour like myself than to anyone else. But in any case it was a blow to him, and it would take him some time before he could prepare himself to meet it. He would withdraw all opposition upon his part if I would promise for three months to let the matter rest and to be content with cultivating the lady's friendship during that time without claiming her love. This I promised, and so the matter rests."

So there is one of our small mysteries cleared up. It is something to have touched bottom anywhere in this bog in which we are floundering. We know now why Stapleton looked with disfavour upon his sister's suitor—even when that suitor was so eligible a one as Sir Henry. And now I pass on to another thread which I have extricated out of the tangled skein, the mystery of the sobs in the night, of the tear-stained face of Mrs. Barrymore, of the secret journey of the butler to the western lattice window. Congratulate me, my dear Holmes, and tell me that I have not disappointed you as an agent—that you do not regret the confidence which you showed in me when you sent me down. All these things have by one night's work been thoroughly cleared.

I have said "by one night's work," but, in truth, it was by two nights' work, for on the first we drew entirely blank. I sat up with Sir Henry in his rooms until nearly three o'clock in the morning, but no sound of any sort did we hear except the chiming clock upon the stairs. It was a most melancholy vigil, and ended by each of us falling asleep in our chairs. Fortunately we were not discouraged, and we determined to try again. The next night we lowered the lamp, and sat smoking cigarettes without making the least sound. It was incredible how slowly the hours crawled by, and yet we were helped through it by the same sort of patient interest which the hunter must feel as he watches the trap into which he hopes the game may wander. One struck, and two, and we had almost for the second time given it up in despair, when in an instant we both sat bolt upright in our chairs, with all our weary senses keenly on the alert once more. We had heard the creak of a step in the passage.

Very stealthily we heard it pass along until it died away in the distance. Then the baronet gently opened his door and we set out in pursuit. Already our man had gone round the gallery, and the corridor was all in darkness. Softly we stole along until we had come into the other wing. We were just in time to catch a glimpse of the tall, black-bearded figure, his shoulders rounded, as he tip-toed down the passage. Then he passed through the same door as before, and the light of the candle framed it in the darkness and shot one single yellow beam across the gloom of the corridor. We shuffled cautiously towards it, trying every plank before we dared to put our whole weight upon it. We had taken the precaution of leaving our boots behind us, but, even so, the old boards snapped and creaked beneath our tread. Sometimes it seemed impossible that he should fail to hear our approach. However, the man is fortunately rather deaf, and he was entirely preoccupied in that which he was doing. When at last we reached the door and peeped through we found him crouching at the window, candle in hand, his white, intent face pressed against the pane, exactly as I had seen him two nights before.

We had arranged no plan of campaign, but the baronet is a man to whom the most direct way is always the most natural. He walked into the room, and as he did so Barrymore sprang up from the window with a sharp hiss of his breath and stood, livid and trembling, before us. His dark eyes, glaring out of the white mask of his face, were full of horror and astonishment as he gazed from Sir Henry to me.

"What are you doing here, Barrymore?"

"Nothing, sir." His agitation was so great that he could hardly speak, and the shadows sprang up and down from the shaking of his candle. "It was the window, sir. I go round at night to see that they are fastened."

"On the second floor?"

"Yes, sir, all the windows."

"Look here, Barrymore," said Sir Henry, sternly; "we have made up our minds to have the truth out of you, so it will save you trouble to tell it sooner rather than later. Come, now! No lies! What were you doing at that window?"

The fellow looked at us in a helpless way, and he wrung his hands together like one who is in the last extremity of doubt and misery.

"I was doing no harm, sir. I was holding a candle to the window."

"And why were you holding a candle to the window?"

"Don't ask me, Sir Henry—don't ask me! I give you my word, sir, that it is not my secret, and that I cannot tell it. If it concerned no one but myself I would not try to keep it from you."

A sudden idea occurred to me, and I took the candle from the trembling hand of the butler.

"He must have been holding it as a signal," said I. "Let us see if there is any answer." I held it as he had done, and stared out into the darkness of the night. Vaguely I could discern the black bank of the trees and the lighter expanse of the moor, for the moon was behind the clouds. And then I gave a cry of exultation, for a tiny pin-point of yellow light had suddenly transfixed the dark veil, and glowed steadily in the centre of the black square framed by the window.

"There it is!" I cried.

"No, no, sir, it is nothing—nothing at all!" the butler broke in; "I assure you, sir ——"

"Move your light across the window, Watson!" cried the baronet. "See, the other moves also! Now, you rascal, do you deny that it is a signal? Come, speak up! Who is your confederate out yonder, and what is this conspiracy that is going on?"

The man's face became openly defiant.

"It is my business, and not yours. I will not tell."

"Then you leave my employment right away."

"Very good, sir. If I must I must."

"And you go in disgrace. By thunder, you may well be ashamed of yourself. Your family has lived with mine for over a hundred years under this roof, and here I find you deep in some dark plot against me."

"No, no, sir; no, not against you!" It was a woman's voice, and Mrs.

Barrymore, paler and more horror-struck than her husband, was standing at the door. Her bulky figure in a shawl and skirt might have been comic were it not for the intensity of feeling upon her face.

"We have to go, Eliza. This is the end of it. You can pack our things," said the butler.

"Oh, John, John, have I brought you to this? It is my doing, Sir Henry—all mine. He has done nothing except for my sake and because I asked him."

"Speak out, then! What does it mean?"

"My unhappy brother is starving on the moor. We cannot let him perish at our very gates. The light is a signal to him that food is ready for him, and his light out yonder is to show the spot to which to bring it."

"Then your brother is —"

"The escaped convict, sir—Selden, the criminal."

"That's the truth, sir," said Barrymore. "I said that it was not my secret and that I could not tell it to you. But now you have heard it, and you will see that if there was a plot it was not against you."

This, then, was the explanation of the stealthy expeditions at night and the light at the window. Sir Henry and I both stared at the woman in amazement. Was it possible that this stolidly respectable person was of the same blood as one of the most notorious criminals in the country?

"Yes, sir, my name was Selden, and he is my younger brother. We humoured him too much when he was a lad, and gave him his own way in everything until he came to think that the world was made for his pleasure, and that he could do what he liked in it. Then as he grew older he met wicked companions, and the devil entered into him until he broke my mother's heart and dragged our name in the dirt. From crime to crime he sank lower and lower, until it is only the mercy of God which has snatched him from the scaffold; but to me, sir, he was always the little curly-headed boy that I had nursed and played with, as an elder sister would. That was why he broke prison, sir. He knew that I was here and that we could not refuse to help him. When he dragged himself here one night, weary and starving, with the warders hard at his heels, what could we do? We took him in and fed him and cared for him. Then you returned, sir, and my brother thought he would be safer on the moor than anywhere else until the hue and cry was over, so he lay in hiding there. But every second night we made sure if he was still there by putting a light in the window, and if there was an answer my husband took out some bread and meat to him. Every day we hoped that he was gone, but as long as he was there we could not desert him. That is the whole truth, as I am an honest Christian woman, and you will see that if there is blame in the matter it does not lie with my husband, but with me, for whose sake he has done all that he has."

The woman's words came with an intense earnestness which carried conviction with them.

"Is this true, Barrymore?"

"Yes, Sir Henry. Every word of it."

"Well, I cannot blame you for standing by your own wife. Forget what I have said. Go to your room, you two, and we shall talk further about this matter in the morning."

When they were gone we looked out of the window again. Sir Henry had flung it open, and the cold night wind beat in upon our faces. Far away in the black distance there still glowed that one tiny point of yellow light.

"I wonder he dares," said Sir Henry.

"It may be so placed as to be only visible from here."

"Very likely. How far do you think it is?"

"Out by the Cleft Tor, I think."

"Not more than a mile or two off."

"Hardly that."

"Well, it cannot be far if Barrymore had to carry out the food to it. And he is waiting, this villain, beside that candle. By thunder, Watson, I am going out to take that man!"

The same thought had crossed my own mind. It was not as if the Barrymores had taken us into their confidence. Their secret had been forced from them. The man was a danger to the community, an unmitigated scoundrel for whom there was neither pity nor excuse. We were only doing our duty in taking this chance of putting him back where he could do no harm. With his brutal and violent nature, others would have to pay the price if we held our hands. Any night, for example, our neighbours the Stapletons might be attacked by him, and it may have been the thought of this which made Sir Henry so keen upon the adventure.

"I will come," said I.

"Then get your revolver and put on your boots. The sooner we start the better, as the fellow may put out his light and be off."

In five minutes we were outside the door, starting upon our expedition. We hurried through the dark shrubbery, amid the dull moaning of the autumn wind and the rustle of the falling leaves. The night air was heavy with the smell of damp and decay. Now and again the moon peeped out for an instant, but clouds were driving over the face of the sky, and just as we came out on the moor a thin rain began to fall. The light still burned steadily in front.

"Are you armed?" I asked.

"I have a hunting-crop."

"We must close in on him rapidly, for he is said to be a desperate fellow. We shall take him by surprise and have him at our mercy before he can resist."

"I say, Watson," said the baronet, "what would Holmes say to this? How about that hour of darkness in which the power of evil is exalted?"

As if in answer to his words there rose suddenly out of the vast gloom of the moor that strange cry which I had already heard upon the borders of the great Grimpen Mire. It came with the wind through the silence of the night, a long, deep mutter, then a rising howl, and then the sad moan in which it died away. Again and again it sounded, the whole air throbbing with it, strident, wild, and menacing. The baronet caught my sleeve and his face glimmered white through the darkness.

"My God, what's that, Watson?"

"I don't know. It's a sound they have on the moor. I heard it once before."

It died away, and an absolute silence closed in upon us. We stood straining our ears, but nothing came.

"Watson," said the baronet, "it was the cry of a hound."

My blood ran cold in my veins, for there was a break in his voice which told of the sudden horror which had seized him.

"What do they call this sound?" he asked.

"Who?"

"The folk on the country-side."

"Oh, they are ignorant people. Why should you mind what they call it?"

"Tell me, Watson. What do they say of it?"

I hesitated but could not escape the question.

"They say it is the cry of the Hound of the Baskervilles."

He groaned and was silent for a few moments.

"A hound it was," he said, at last, "but it seemed to come from miles away, over yonder, I think."

"It was hard to say whence it came."

"It rose and fell with the wind. Isn't that the direction of the great Grimpen Mire?"

"Yes, it is."

"Well, it was up there. Come now, Watson, didn't you think yourself that it was the cry of a hound? I am not a child. You need not fear to speak the truth."

"Stapleton was with me when I heard it last. He said that it might be the calling of a strange bird."

"No, no, it was a hound. My God, can there be some truth in all these stories? Is it possible that I am really in danger from so dark a cause? You don't believe it, do you, Watson?"

"No, no."

"And yet it was one thing to laugh about it in London, and it is another to stand out here in the darkness of the moor and to hear such a cry as that. And my uncle! There was the footprint of the hound beside him as he lay. It all fits together. I don't think that I am a coward, Watson, but that sound seemed to freeze my very blood. Feel my hand!"

It was as cold as a block of marble.

"You'll be all right to-morrow."

"I don't think I'll get that cry out of my head. What do you advise that we do now?"

"Shall we turn back?"

"No, by thunder; we have come out to get our man, and we will do it. We after the convict, and a hell-hound, as likely as not, after us. Come on! We'll see it through if all the fiends of the pit were loose upon the moor."

We stumbled slowly along in the darkness, with the black loom of the craggy hills around us, and the yellow speck of light burning steadily in front. There is nothing so deceptive as the distance of a light upon a pitch-dark night, and sometimes the glimmer seemed to be far away upon the horizon and sometimes it might have been within a few yards of us. But at last we could see whence it came, and then we knew that we were indeed very close. A guttering candle was stuck in a crevice of the rocks which flanked it on each side so as to keep the wind from it and also to prevent it from being visible, save in the direction of Baskerville Hall. A boulder of granite concealed our approach, and crouching behind it we gazed over it at the signal light. It was strange to see this single candle burning there in the middle of the moor, with no sign of life near it—just the one straight yellow flame and the gleam of the rock on each side of it.

"What shall we do now?" whispered Sir Henry.

"Wait here. He must be near his light. Let us see if we can get a glimpse of him."

The words were hardly out of my mouth when we both saw him. Over the rocks, in the crevice of which the candle burned, there was thrust out an evil

yellow face, a terrible animal face, all seamed and scored with vile passions. Foul with mire, with a bristling beard, and hung with matted hair, it might well have belonged to one of those old savages who dwelt in the burrows on the hillsides. The light beneath him was reflected in his small, cunning eyes which peered fiercely to right and left through the darkness, like a crafty and savage animal who has heard the steps of the hunters.

Something had evidently aroused his suspicions. It may have been that Barrymore had some private signal which we had neglected to give, or the fellow may have had some other reason for thinking that all was not well, but I could read his fears upon his wicked face. Any instant he might dash out the light and vanish in the darkness. I sprang forward therefore, and Sir Henry did the same. At the same moment the convict screamed out a curse at us and hurled a rock which splintered up against the boulder which had sheltered us. I caught one glimpse of his short, squat, stronglybuilt figure as he sprang to his feet and turned to run. At the same moment by a lucky chance the moon broke through the clouds. We rushed over the brow of the hill, and there was our man running with great speed down the other side, springing over the stones in his way with the activity of a mountain goat. A lucky long shot of my revolver might have crippled him, but I had brought it only to defend myself if attacked, and not to shoot an unarmed man who was running away.

We were both swift runners and in fairly good training, but we soon found

193

that we had no chance of over taking him. We saw him for a long time in the moonlight until he was only a small speck moving swiftly among the boulders upon the side of a distant hill. We ran and ran until we were completely blown, but the space between us grew ever wider. Finally we stopped and sat panting on two rocks, while we watched him disappearing in the distance.

And it was at this moment that there occurred a most strange and unexpected thing. We had risen from our rocks and were turning to go home, having abandoned the hopeless chase. The moon was low upon the right, and the jagged pinnacle of a granite tor stood up against the lower curve of its silver disc. There, outlined as black as an ebony statue on that shining back-ground, I saw the figure of a man upon the tor. Do not think that it was

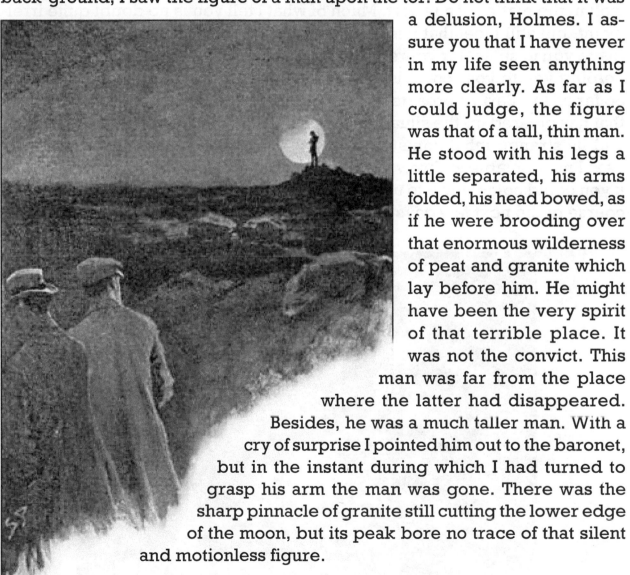

a delusion, Holmes. I assure you that I have never in my life seen anything more clearly. As far as I could judge, the figure was that of a tall, thin man. He stood with his legs a little separated, his arms folded, his head bowed, as if he were brooding over that enormous wilderness of peat and granite which lay before him. He might have been the very spirit of that terrible place. It was not the convict. This man was far from the place where the latter had disappeared. Besides, he was a much taller man. With a cry of surprise I pointed him out to the baronet, but in the instant during which I had turned to grasp his arm the man was gone. There was the sharp pinnacle of granite still cutting the lower edge of the moon, but its peak bore no trace of that silent and motionless figure.

I wished to go in that direction and to search the tor, but it was some distance away. The baronet's nerves were still quivering from that cry, which recalled the dark story of his family, and he was not in the mood for fresh adventures. He had not seen this lonely man upon the tor and could not feel the thrill which his strange presence and his commanding attitude had given to me. "A warder, no doubt," said he. "The moor has been thick with them since this fellow escaped." Well, perhaps his explanation may be the right one, but I should like to have some further proof of it. To-day we mean to communicate to the Princetown people where they should look for their missing man, but it is hard lines that we have not actually had the triumph of bringing him back as our own prisoner. Such are the adventures of last night, and you must acknowledge, my dear Holmes, that I have done you very well in the matter of a report. Much of what I tell you is no doubt quite irrelevant, but still I feel that it is best that I should let you have all the facts and leave you to select for yourself those which will be of most service to you in helping you to your conclusions. We are certainly making some progress. So far as the Barrymores go we have found the motive of their actions, and that has cleared up the situation very much. But the moor with its mysteries and its strange inhabitants remains as inscrutable as ever. Perhaps in my next I may be able to throw some light upon this also. Best of all would it be if you could come down to us. In any case you will hear from me again in the course of the next few days.

CHAPTER X. EXTRACT FROM THE DIARY OF DR. WATSON

So far I have been able to quote from the reports which I have forwarded during these early days to Sherlock Holmes. Now, however, I have arrived at a point in my narrative where I am compelled to abandon this method and to trust once more to my recollections, aided by the diary which I kept at the time. A few extracts from the latter will carry me on to those scenes which are indelibly fixed in every detail upon my memory. I proceed, then, from the morning which followed our abortive chase of the convict and our other strange experiences upon the moor.

OCTOBER 16TH.—A dull and foggy day with a drizzle of rain. The house is banked in with rolling clouds, which rise now and then to show the dreary curves of the moor, with thin, silver veins upon the sides of the hills, and the distant boulders gleaming where the light strikes upon their wet faces. It is melancholy outside and in. The baronet is in a black reaction after the excitements of the night. I am conscious myself of a weight at my heart and a feeling of impending danger—ever present danger, which is the more terrible because I am unable to define it.

And have I not cause for such a feeling? Consider the long sequence of incidents which have all pointed to some sinister influence which is at work around us. There is the death of the last occupant of the Hall, fulfilling so exactly the conditions of the family legend, and there are the repeated reports from peasants of the appearance of a strange creature upon the moor. Twice I have with my own ears heard the sound which resembled the distant baying of a hound. It is incredible, impossible, that it should really be outside the ordinary laws of nature. A spectral hound which leaves material footmarks and fills the air with its howling is surely not to be thought of. Stapleton may fall in with such a superstition, and Mortimer also; but if I have one quality upon earth it is common-sense, and nothing will persuade me to believe in such a thing. To do so would be to descend to the level of these poor peasants, who are not content with a mere fiend dog but must needs describe him with hell-fire shooting from his mouth and eyes. Holmes would not listen to such fancies, and I am his agent. But facts are facts, and I have twice heard this crying upon the moor. Suppose that there were really some huge hound loose upon it; that would go far to explain everything. But where could such a hound lie concealed, where did it get its food, where did it come from, how was it that no one saw it by day? It must be confessed that the natural explanation offers almost as many difficulties as the other. And always, apart from the hound, there is the fact of the human agency in London, the man in the cab, and the letter which warned Sir Henry against the moor. This at least was real, but it might have been the work of a protecting friend as easily as of an enemy. Where is that friend or enemy now? Has he remained in London, or has he followed us down here? Could he—could he be the stranger whom I saw upon the tor?

It is true that I have had only the one glance at him, and yet there are some things to which I am ready to swear. He is no one whom I have seen down here, and I have now met all the neighbours. The figure was far taller than that of Stapleton, far thinner than that of Frankland. Barrymore it might possibly have been, but we had left him behind us, and I am certain that he could not have followed us. A stranger then is still dogging us, just as a stranger dogged us in London. We have never shaken him off. If I could lay my hands upon that man, then at last we might find ourselves at the end of all our difficulties. To this one purpose I must now devote all my energies.

My first impulse was to tell Sir Henry all my plans. My second and wisest one is to play my own game and speak as little as possible to anyone. He is silent and distrait. His nerves have been strangely shaken by that sound upon the moor. I will say nothing to add to his anxieties, but I will take my own steps to attain my own end.

We had a small scene this morning after breakfast. Barrymore asked leave to speak with Sir Henry, and they were closeted in his study some little time. Sitting in the billiard-room I more than once heard the sound of voices raised, and I had a pretty good idea what the point was which was under discussion. After a time the baronet opened his door and called for me.

"Barrymore considers that he has a grievance," he said. "He thinks that it was unfair on our part to hunt his brother-in-law down when he, of his own free will, had told us the secret."

The butler was standing very pale but very collected before us.

"I may have spoken too warmly, sir," said he, "and if I have, I am sure that I beg your pardon. At the same time, I was very much surprised when I heard you two gentlemen come back this morning and learned that you had been chasing Selden. The poor fellow has enough to fight against without my putting more upon his track."

"If you had told us of your own free will it would have been a different thing," said the baronet, "you only told us, or rather your wife only told us, when it was forced from you and you could not help yourself."

"I didn't think you would have taken advantage of it, Sir Henry—indeed I didn't."

"The man is a public danger. There are lonely houses scattered over the moor, and he is a fellow who would stick at nothing. You only want to get a glimpse of his face to see that. Look at Mr. Stapleton's house, for example, with no one but himself to defend it. There's no safety for anyone until he is under lock and key."

"He'll break into no house, sir. I give you my solemn word upon that. But he will never trouble anyone in this country again. I assure you, Sir Henry, that in a very few days the necessary arrangements will have been made and he will be on his way to South America. For God's sake, sir, I beg of you not to let the police know that he is still on the moor. They have given up the chase there, and he can lie quiet until the ship is ready for him. You can't tell on him without getting my wife and me into trouble. I beg you, sir, to say nothing to the police."

"What do you say, Watson?"

I shrugged my shoulders. "If he were safely out of the country it would relieve the tax-payer of a burden."

"But how about the chance of his holding someone up before he goes?"

"He would not do anything so mad, sir. We have provided him with all that he can want. To commit a crime would be to show where he was hiding."

"That is true," said Sir Henry. "Well, Barrymore —"

"God bless you, sir, and thank you from my heart! It would have killed my poor wife had he been taken again."

"I guess we are aiding and abetting a felony, Watson? But, after what we have heard I don't feel as if I could give the man up, so there is an end of it. All right, Barrymore, you can go."

With a few broken words of gratitude the man turned, but he hesitated and then came back.

"You've been so kind to us, sir, that I should like to do the best I can for you in return. I know something, Sir Henry, and perhaps I should have said it before, but it was long after the inquest that I found it out. I've never breathed a word about it yet to mortal man. It's about poor Sir Charles's death."

The baronet and I were both upon our feet. "Do you know how he died?"

"No, sir, I don't know that."

"What then?"

"I know why he was at the gate at that hour. It was to meet a woman."

"To meet a woman! He?"

"Yes, sir."

"And the woman's name?"

"I can't give you the name, sir, but I can give you the initials. Her initials were L. L."

"How do you know this, Barrymore?"

"Well, Sir Henry, your uncle had a letter that morning. He had usually a great many letters, for he was a public man and well known for his kind heart, so that everyone who was in trouble was glad to turn to him. But that morning, as it chanced, there was only this one letter, so I took the more notice of it. It was from Coombe Tracey, and it was addressed in a woman's hand."

"Well?"

"Well, sir, I thought no more of the matter, and never would have done had it not been for my wife. Only a few weeks ago she was cleaning out Sir Charles's study—it had never been touched since his death—and she found the ashes of a burned letter in the back of the grate. The greater part of it was charred to pieces, but one little slip, the end of a page, hung together, and the writing could still be read, though it was gray on a black ground. It seemed to us to be a postscript at the end of the letter, and it said: 'Please, please, as you are a gentleman, burn this letter, and be at the gate by ten o clock. Beneath it were signed the initials L. L."

"Have you got that slip?"

"No, sir, it crumbled all to bits after we moved it."

"Had Sir Charles received any other letters in the same writing?"

"Well, sir, I took no particular notice of his letters. I should not have noticed this one, only it happened to come alone."

"And you have no idea who L. L. is?"

"No, sir. No more than you have. But I expect if we could lay our hands upon that lady we should know more about Sir Charles's death."

"I cannot understand, Barrymore, how you came to conceal this important information."

"Well, sir, it was immediately after that our own trouble came to us. And then again, sir, we were both of us very fond of Sir Charles, as we well might be considering all that he has done for us. To rake this up couldn't help our poor master, and it's well to go carefully when there's a lady in the case. Even the best of us ——"

"You thought it might injure his reputation?"

"Well, sir, I thought no good could come of it. But now you have been kind to us, and I feel as if it would be treating you unfairly not to tell you all that I know about the matter."

"Very good, Barrymore; you can go." When the butler had left us Sir Henry turned to me. "Well, Watson, what do you think of this new light?"

"It seems to leave the darkness rather blacker than before."

"So I think. But if we can only trace L. L. it should clear up the whole business. We have gained that much. We know that there is someone who has the facts if we can only find her. What do you think we should do?"

"Let Holmes know all about it at once. It will give him the clue for which he has been seeking. I am much mistaken if it does not bring him down."

I went at once to my room and drew up my report of the morning's conversation for Holmes. It was evident to me that he had been very busy of late, for the notes which I had from Baker Street were few and short, with no comments upon the information which I had supplied and hardly any reference to my mission. No doubt his blackmailing case is absorbing all his faculties. And yet this new factor must surely arrest his attention and renew his interest. I wish that he were here.

OCTOBER 17th.—All day to-day the rain poured down, rustling on the ivy and dripping from the eaves. I thought of the convict out upon the bleak, cold, shelterless moor. Poor devil! Whatever his crimes, he has suffered something to atone for them. And then I thought of that other one—the face in the cab, the figure against the moon. Was he also out in that deluged—the unseen watcher, the man of darkness? In the evening I put on my waterproof and I walked far upon the sodden moor, full of dark imaginings, the rain beating upon my face and the wind whistling about my ears. God help those who wander into the great mire now, for even the firm uplands are becoming a morass. I found the black tor upon which I had seen the solitary watcher, and from its craggy summit I looked out myself across the melancholy downs. Rain squalls drifted across their russet face, and the heavy, slate-coloured clouds hung low over the landscape, trailing in gray wreaths down the sides of the fantastic hills. In the distant hollow on the left, half hidden by the mist, the two thin towers of Baskerville Hall rose above the trees. They were the only signs of human life which I could see, save only those prehistoric huts which lay thickly upon the slopes of the hills. Nowhere was there any trace of that lonely man whom I had seen on the same spot two nights before.

As I walked back I was overtaken by Dr. Mortimer driving in his dog-cart over a rough moorland track which led from the outlying farmhouse of Foulmire. He has been very attentive to us, and hardly a day has passed that he has not called at the Hall to see how we were getting on. He insisted upon my climbing into his dog-cart, and he gave me a lift homeward. I found him much troubled over the disappearance of his little spaniel. It had wandered on to the moor and had never come back. I gave him such consolation as I might, but I thought of the pony on the Grimpen Mire, and I do not fancy that he will see his little dog again.

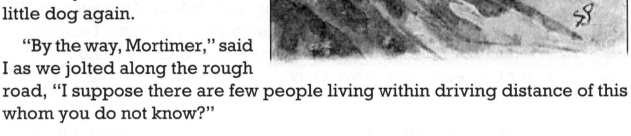

"By the way, Mortimer," said I as we jolted along the rough road, "I suppose there are few people living within driving distance of this whom you do not know?"

"Hardly any, I think."

"Can you, then, tell me the name of any woman whose initials are L. L.?"

He thought for a few minutes.

"No," said he. "There are a few gipsies and labouring folk for whom I can't answer, but among the farmers or gentry there is no one whose initials are those. Wait a bit though," he added after a pause. "There is Laura Lyons—her initials are L. L.—but she lives in Coombe Tracey."

"Who is she?" I asked.

"She is Frankland's daughter."

"What! Old Frankland the crank?"

"Exactly. She married an artist named Lyons, who came sketching on the moor. He proved to be a blackguard and deserted her. The fault from what I hear may not have been entirely on one side. Her father refused to have anything to do with her because she had married without his consent, and perhaps for one or two other reasons as well. So, between the old sinner and the young one the girl has had a pretty bad time."

"How does she live?"

"I fancy old Frankland allows her a pittance, but it cannot be more, for his own affairs are considerably involved. Whatever she may have deserved one could not allow her to go hopelessly to the bad. Her story got about, and several of the people here did something to enable her to earn an honest living. Stapleton did for one, and Sir Charles for another. I gave a trifle myself. It was to set her up in a typewriting business."

He wanted to know the object of my inquiries, but I managed to satisfy his curiosity without telling him too much, for there is no reason why we should take anyone into our confidence. To-morrow morning I shall find my way to Coombe Tracey, and if I can see this Mrs. Laura Lyons, of equivocal reputation, a long step will have been made towards clearing one incident in this chain of mysteries. I am certainly developing the wisdom of the serpent, for when Mortimer pressed his questions to an inconvenient extent I asked him casually to what type Frankland's skull belonged, and so heard nothing but craniology for the rest of our drive. I have not lived for years with Sherlock Holmes for nothing.

I have only one other incident to record upon this tempestuous and melancholy day. This was my conversation with Barrymore just now, which gives me one more strong card which I can play in due time.

Mortimer had stayed to dinner, and he and the baronet played écarté afterwards. The butler brought me my coffee into the library, and I took the chance to ask him a few questions.

"Well," said I, "has this precious relation of yours departed, or is he still lurking out yonder?"

"I don't know, sir. I hope to heaven that he has gone, for he has brought nothing but trouble here! I've not heard of him since I left out food for him last, and that was three days ago."

"Did you see him then?"

"No, sir, but the food was gone when next I went that way."

"Then he was certainly there?"

"So you would think, sir, unless it was the other man who took it."

I sat with my coffee-cup halfway to my lips and stared at Barrymore.

"You know that there is another man then?"

"Yes, sir; there is another man upon the moor."

"Have you seen him?"

"No, sir."

"How do you know of him then?"

"Selden told me of him, sir, a week ago or more. He's in hiding, too, but he's not a convict as far as I can make out. I don't like it, Dr. Watson—I tell you straight, sir, that I don't like it." He spoke with a sudden passion of earnestness.

"Now, listen to me, Barrymore! I have no interest in this matter but that of your master. I have come here with no object except to help him. Tell me, frankly, what it is that you don't like."

Barrymore hesitated for a moment, as if he regretted his outburst, or found it difficult to express his own feelings in words.

"It's all these goings-on, sir," he cried at last, waving his hand towards the rain-lashed window which faced the moor."There's foul play somewhere, and there's black villainy brewing, to that I'll swear! Very glad I should be, sir, to see Sir Henry on his way back to London again!"

"But what is it that alarms you?"

"Look at Sir Charles's death! That was bad enough, for all that the coroner said. Look at the noises on the moor at night. There's not a man would cross it after sundown if he was paid for it. Look at this stranger hiding out yonder, and watching and waiting! What's he waiting for? What does it mean? It means no good to anyone of the name of Baskerville, and very glad I shall be to be quit of it all on the day that Sir Henry's new servants are ready to take over the Hall."

"But about this stranger," said I. "Can you tell me anything about him? What did Selden say? Did he find out where he hid, or what he was doing?"

"He saw him once or twice, but he is a deep one, and gives nothing away. At first he thought that he was the police, but soon he found that he had some lay of his own. A kind of gentleman he was, as far as he could see, but what he was doing he could not make out."

"And where did he say that he lived?"

"Among the old houses on the hillside—the stone huts where the old folk used to live."

"But how about his food?"

"Selden found out that he has got a lad who works for him and brings him all he needs. I daresay he goes to Coombe Tracey for what he wants."

"Very good, Barrymore. We may talk further of this some other time." When the butler had gone I walked over to the black window, and I looked through a blurred pane at the driving clouds and at the tossing outline of the wind-swept trees. It is a wild night indoors, and what must it be in a stone hut upon the moor. What passion of hatred can it be which leads a man to lurk in such a place at such a time! And what deep and earnest purpose can he have which calls for such a trial! There, in that hut upon the moor, seems to lie the very centre of that problem which has vexed me so sorely. I swear that another day shall not have passed before I have done all that man can do to reach the heart of the mystery.

CHAPTER XI. THE MAN ON THE TOR

The extract from my private diary which forms the last chapter has brought my narrative up to the 18th of October, a time when these strange events began to move swiftly towards their terrible conclusion. The incidents of the next few days are indelibly graven upon my recollection, and I can tell them without reference to the notes made at the time. I start then from the day which succeeded that upon which I had established two facts of great importance, the one that Mrs. Laura Lyons of Coombe Tracey had written to Sir Charles Baskerville and made an appointment with him at the very place and hour that he met his death, the other that the lurking man upon the moor was to be found among the stone huts upon the hill-side. With these two facts in my possession I felt that either my intelligence or my courage must be deficient if I could not throw some further light upon these dark places.

I had no opportunity to tell the baronet what I had learned about Mrs. Lyons upon the evening before, for Dr. Mortimer remained with him at cards until it was very late. At breakfast, however, I informed him about my discovery, and asked him whether he would care to accompany me to Coombe Tracey. At first he was very eager to come, but on second thoughts it seemed to both of us that if I went alone the results might be better. The more formal we made the visit the less information we might obtain. I left Sir Henry behind, therefore, not without some prickings of conscience, and drove off upon my new quest.

When I reached Coombe Tracey I told Perkins to put up the horses, and I made inquiries for the lady whom I had come to interrogate. I had no difficulty in finding her rooms, which were central and well appointed. A maid showed me in without ceremony, and as I entered the sitting-room a lady, who was sitting before a Remington typewriter, sprang up with a pleasant smile of welcome. Her face fell, however, when she saw that I was a stranger, and she sat down again and asked me the object of my visit.

The first impression left by Mrs. Lyons was one of extreme beauty. Her eyes and hair were of the same rich hazel colour, and her cheeks, though considerably freckled, were flushed with the exquisite bloom of the brunette, the dainty pink which lurks at the heart of the sulphur rose. Admiration was, I repeat, the first impression. But the second was criticism. There was something subtly wrong with the face, some coarseness of expression, some hardness, perhaps, of eye, some looseness of lip which marred its perfect beauty. But these, of course, are after-thoughts. At the moment I was simply conscious that I was in the presence of a very handsome woman, and that she was asking me the reasons for my visit. I had not quite understood until that instant how delicate my mission was.

"I have the pleasure," said I, "of knowing your father." It was a clumsy introduction, and the lady made me feel it.

"There is nothing in common between my father and me," she said. "I owe him nothing, and his friends are not mine. If it were not for the late Sir Charles Baskerville and some other kind hearts I might have starved for all that my father cared."

"It was about the late Sir Charles Baskerville that I have come here to see you."

The freckles started out on the lady's face.

"What can I tell you about him?" she asked, and her fingers played nervously over the stops of her typewriter.

"You knew him, did you not?"

"I have already said that I owe a great deal to his kindness. If I am able to support myself it is largely due to the interest which he took in my unhappy situation."

"Did you correspond with him?"

The lady looked quickly up with an angry gleam in her hazel eyes.

"What is the object of these questions?" she asked sharply.

"The object is to avoid a public scandal. It is better that I should ask them here than that the matter should pass outside our control."

She was silent and her face was still very pale. At last she looked up with something reckless and defiant in her manner.

"Well, I'll answer," she said. "What are your questions?"

"Did you correspond with Sir Charles?"

"I certainly wrote to him once or twice to acknowledge his delicacy and his generosity."

"Have you the dates of those letters?"

"No."

"Have you ever met him?"

"Yes, once or twice, when he came into Coombe Tracey. He was a very retiring man, and he preferred to do good by stealth."

"But if you saw him so seldom and wrote so seldom, how did he know enough about your affairs to be able to help you, as you say that he has done?"

She met my difficulty with the utmost readiness.

"There were several gentlemen who knew my sad history and united to help me. One was Mr. Stapleton, a neighbour and intimate friend of Sir Charles's. He was exceedingly kind, and it was through him that Sir Charles learned about my affairs."

I knew already that Sir Charles Baskerville had made Stapleton his almoner upon several occasions, so the lady's statement bore the impress of truth upon it.

"Did you ever write to Sir Charles asking him to meet you?" I continued.

Mrs. Lyons flushed with anger again.

"Really, sir, this is a very extraordinary question."

"I am sorry, madam, but I must repeat it."

"Then I answer, certainly not."

"Not on the very day of Sir Charles's death?"

The flush had faded in an instant, and a deathly face was before me. Her dry lips could not speak the "No" which I saw rather than heard.

"Surely your memory deceives you," said I. "I could even quote a passage of your letter. It ran 'Please, please, as you are a gentleman, burn this letter, and be at the gate by ten o'clock.'"

I thought that she had fainted, but she recovered herself by a supreme effort.

"Is there no such thing as a gentleman?" she gasped.

"You do Sir Charles an injustice. He did burn the letter. But sometimes a letter may be legible even when burned. You acknowledge now that you wrote it?"

"Yes, I did write it," she cried, pouring out her soul in a torrent of words. "I did write it. Why should I deny it? I have no reason to be ashamed of it. I wished him to help me. I believed that if I had an interview I could gain his help, so I asked him to meet me."

"But why at such an hour?"

"Because I had only just learned that he was going to London next day and might be away for months. There were reasons why I could not get there earlier."

"But why a rendezvous in the garden instead of a visit to the house?"

"Do you think a woman could go alone at that hour to a bachelor's house?"

"Well, what happened when you did get there?"

"I never went."

"Mrs. Lyons!"

"No, I swear it to you on all I hold sacred. I never went. Something intervened to prevent my going."

"What was that?"

"That is a private matter. I cannot tell it."

"You acknowledge then that you made an appointment with Sir Charles at the very hour and place at which he met his death, but you deny that you kept the appointment."

"That is the truth."

Again and again I cross-questioned her, but I could never get past that point.

"Mrs. Lyons," said I, as I rose from this long and inconclusive interview, "you are taking a very great responsibility and putting yourself in a very false position by not making an absolutely clean breast of all that you know. If I have to call in the aid of the police you will find how seriously you are compromised. If your position is innocent, why did you in the first instance deny having written to Sir Charles upon that date?"

"Because I feared that some false conclusion might be drawn from it and that I might find myself involved in a scandal."

"And why were you so pressing that Sir Charles should destroy your letter?"

"If you have read the letter you will know."

"I did not say that I had read all the letter."

"You quoted some of it."

"I quoted the postscript. The letter had, as I said, been burned and it was not all legible. I ask you once again why it was that you were so pressing that Sir Charles should destroy this letter which he received on the day of his death."

"The matter is a very private one."

"The more reason why you should avoid a public investigation."

"I will tell you, then. If you have heard anything of my unhappy history you will know that I made a rash marriage and had reason to regret it."

"I have heard so much."

"My life has been one incessant persecution from a husband whom I abhor. The law is upon his side, and every day I am faced by the possibility that he may force me to live with him. At the time that I wrote this letter to Sir Charles I had learned that there was a prospect of my regaining my freedom if certain expenses could be met. It meant everything to me—peace of mind, happiness, self-respect—everything. I knew Sir Charles's generosity, and I thought that if he heard the story from my own lips he would help me."

"Then how is it that you did not go?"

"Because I received help in the interval from another source."

"Why then, did you not write to Sir Charles and explain this?"

"So I should have done had I not seen his death in the paper next morning."

The woman's story hung coherently together, and all my questions were unable to shake it. I could only check it by finding if she had, indeed, instituted divorce proceedings against her husband at or about the time of the tragedy.

It was unlikely that she would dare to say that she had not been to Baskerville Hall if she really had been, for a trap would be necessary to take her there, and could not have returned to Coombe Tracey until the early hours of the morning. Such an excursion could not be kept secret. The probability was, therefore, that she was telling the truth, or, at least, a part of the truth. I came away baffled and disheartened. Once again I had reached that dead wall which seemed to be built across every path by which I tried to get at the object of my mission. And yet the more I thought of the lady's face and of her manner the more I felt that something was being held back from me. Why should she turn so pale? Why should she fight against every admission until it was forced from her? Why should she have been so reticent at the time of the tragedy? Surely the explanation of all this could not be as innocent as she would have me believe. For the moment I could proceed no farther in that direction, but must turn back to that other clue which was to be sought for among the stone huts upon the moor.

And that was a most vague direction. I realized it as I drove back and noted how hill after hill showed traces of the ancient people. Barrymore's only indication had been that the stranger lived in one of these abandoned huts, and many hundreds of them are scattered throughout the length and breadth of the moor. But I had my own experience for a guide since it had shown me the man himself standing upon the summit of the Black Tor. That then should be the centre of my search. From there I should explore every hut upon the moor until I lighted upon the right one. If this man were inside it I should find out from his own lips, at the point of my revolver if necessary, who he was and why he had dogged us so long. He might slip away from us in the crowd of Regent Street, but it would puzzle him to do so upon the lonely moor. On the other hand, if I should find the hut and its tenant should not be within it I must remain there, however long the vigil, until he returned. Holmes had missed him in London. It would indeed be a triumph for me if I could run him to earth, where my master had failed.

Luck had been against us again and again in this inquiry, but now at last it came to my aid. And the messenger of good fortune was none other than Mr. Frankland, who was standing, gray whiskered and red-faced, outside the gate of his garden, which opened on to the high road along which I travelled.

"Good-day, Dr. Watson," cried he with unwonted good humour, "you must really give your horses a rest, and come in to have a glass of wine and to congratulate me."

My feelings towards him were very far from being friendly after what I had heard of his treatment of his daughter, but I was anxious to send Perkins and the wagonette home, and the opportunity was a good one. I alighted and sent a message to Sir Henry that I should walk over in time for dinner. Then I followed Frankland into his dining-room.

"It is a great day for me, sir—one of the red-letter days of my life," he cried with many chuckles. "I have brought off a double event. I mean to teach them in these parts that law is law, and that there is a man here who does not fear to invoke it. I have established a right of way through the centre of old Middleton's park, slap across it, sir, within a hundred yards of his own front door. What do you think of that? We'll teach these magnates that they cannot ride rough shod over the rights of the commoners, confound them! And I've closed the wood where the Fernworthy folk used to picnic. These infernal people seem to think that there are no rights of property, and that they can swarm where they like with their papers and their bottles. Both cases decided, Dr. Watson, and both in my favour. I haven't had such a day since I had Sir John Morland for trespass, because he shot in his own warren."

"How on earth did you do that?"

"Look it up in the books, sir. It will repay reading—Frankland v. Morland, Court of Queen's Bench. It cost me 200 pounds, but I got my verdict."

"Did it do you any good?"

"None, sir, none. I am proud to say that I had no interest in the matter. I act entirely from a sense of public duty. I have no doubt, for example, that the Fernworthy people will burn me in effigy to-night. I told the police last time they did it that they should stop these disgraceful exhibitions. The County Constabulary is in a scandalous state, sir, and it has not afforded me the protection to which I am entitled. The case of Frankland v. Regina will bring the matter before the attention of the public. I told them that they would have occasion to regret their treatment of me, and already my words have come true."

"How so?" I asked.

The old man put on a very knowing expression.

"Because I could tell them what they are dying to know; but nothing would induce me to help the rascals in any way."

I had been casting round for some excuse by which I could get away from his gossip, but now I began to wish to hear more of it. I had seen enough of the contrary nature of the old sinner to understand that any strong sign of interest would be the surest way to stop his confidences.

"Some poaching case, no doubt?" said I, with an indifferent manner.

"Ha, ha, my boy, a very much more important matter than that! What about the convict on the moor?"

I started. "You don't mean that you know where he is?" said I.

"I may not know exactly where he is, but I am quite sure that I could help the police to lay their hands on him. Has it never struck you that the way to catch that man was to find out where he got his food, and so trace it to him?"

He certainly seemed to be getting uncomfortably near the truth. "No doubt," said I; "but how do you know that he is anywhere upon the moor?"

"I know it because I have seen with my own eyes the messenger who takes him his food."

My heart sank for Barrymore. It was a serious thing to be in the power of this spiteful old busybody. But his next remark took a weight from my mind.

"You'll be surprised to hear that his food is taken to him by a child. I see him every day through my telescope upon the roof. He passes along the same path at the same hour, and to whom should he be going except to the convict?"

Here was luck indeed! And yet I suppressed all appearance of interest. A child! Barrymore had said that our unknown was supplied by a boy. It was on his track, and not upon the convict's, that Frankland had stumbled. If I could get his knowledge it might save me a long and weary hunt. But incredulity and indifference were evidently my strongest cards.

"I should say that it was much more likely that it was the son of one of the moorland shepherds taking out his father's dinner."

The least appearance of opposition struck fire out of the old autocrat. His eyes looked malignantly at me, and his gray whiskers bristled like those of an angry cat.

"Indeed, sir!" said he, pointing out over the wide-stretching moor. "Do you see that Black Tor over yonder? Well, do you see the low hill beyond with the thornbush upon it? It is the stoniest part of the whole moor. Is that a place where a shepherd would be likely to take his station? Your suggestion, sir, is a most absurd one."

I meekly answered that I had spoken without knowing all the facts. My submission pleased him and led him to further confidences.

"You may be sure, sir, that I have very good grounds before I come to an opinion. I have seen the boy again and again with his bundle. Every day, and sometimes twice a day, I have been able—but wait a moment, Dr. Watson. Do my eyes deceive me, or is there at the present moment something moving upon that hillside ?"

It was several miles off, but I could distinctly see a small dark dot against the dull green and gray.

"Come, sir, come!" cried Frankland, rushing upstairs. "You will see with your own eyes and judge for yourself."

The telescope, a formidable instrument mounted upon a tripod, stood upon the flat leads of the house. Frankland clapped his eye to it and gave a cry of satisfaction.

"Quick, Dr. Watson, quick, before he passes over the hill!"

There he was, sure enough, a small urchin with a little bundle upon his shoulder, toiling slowly up the hill. When he reached the crest I saw the ragged uncouth figure outlined for an instant against the cold blue sky. He looked round him with a furtive and stealthy air, as one who dreads pursuit. Then he vanished over the hill.

"Well! Am I right?"

"Certainly, there is a boy who seems to have some secret errand."

"And what the errand is even a county constable could guess. But not one word shall they have from me, and I bind you to secrecy also, Dr. Watson. Not a word! You understand!"

"Just as you wish."

"They have treated me shamefully—shamefully. When the facts come out in Frankland v. Regina I venture to think that a thrill of indignation will run through the country. Nothing would induce me to help the police in any way. For all they cared it might have been me, instead of my effigy, which these rascals burned at the stake. Surely you are not going! You will help me to empty the decanter in honour of this great occasion!"

But I resisted all his solicitations and succeeded in dissuading him from his announced intention of walking home with me. I kept the road as long as his eye was on me, and then I struck off across the moor and made for the stony hill over which the boy had disappeared. Everything was working in my favour, and I swore that it should not be through lack of energy or perseverance that I should miss the chance which fortune had thrown in my way.

The sun was already sinking when I reached the summit of the hill, and the long slopes beneath me were all golden-green on one side and gray shadow on the other. A haze lay low upon the farthest sky-line, out of which jutted the fantastic shapes of Belliver and Vixen Tor. Over the wide expanse there was no sound and no movement. One great gray bird, a gull or curlew, soared aloft in the blue Heaven. He and I seemed to be the only living things between the huge arch of the sky and the desert beneath it. The barren scene, the sense of loneliness, and the mystery and urgency of my task all struck a chill into my heart. The boy was nowhere to be seen. But down beneath me in a cleft of the hills there was a circle of the old stone huts, and in the middle of them there was one which retained sufficient roof to act as a screen against the weather. My heart leaped within me as I saw it. This must be the burrow where the stranger lurked. At last my foot was on the threshold of his hiding place—his secret was within my grasp.

As I approached the hut, walking as warily as Stapleton would do when with poised net he drew near the settled butterfly, I satisfied myself that the place had indeed been used as a habitation. A vague pathway among the boulders led to the dilapidated opening which served as a door. All was silent within. The unknown might be lurking there, or he might be prowling on the moor. My nerves tingled with the sense of adventure. Throwing aside my cigarette, I closed my hand upon the butt of my revolver and, walking swiftly up to the door, I looked in. The place was empty.

But there were ample signs that I had not come upon a false scent. This was certainly where the man lived. Some blankets rolled in a waterproof lay upon that very stone slab upon which neolithic man had once slumbered. The ashes of a fire were heaped in a rude grate. Beside it lay some cooking utensils and a bucket half-full of water. A litter of empty tins showed that the place had been occupied for some time, and I saw, as my eyes became accustomed to the checkered light, a pannikin and a half-full bottle of spirits standing in the corner. In the middle of the hut a flat stone served the purpose of a table, and upon this stood a small cloth bundle—the same, no doubt, which I had seen through the telescope upon the shoulder of the boy. It contained a loaf of bread, a tinned tongue, and two tins of preserved peaches. As I set it down again, after having examined it, my heart leaped to see that beneath it there lay a sheet of paper with writing upon it. I raised it, and this was what I read, roughly scrawled in pencil:—

Dr. Watson has gone to Coombe Tracey.

For a minute I stood there with the paper in my hands thinking out the meaning of this curt message. It was I, then, and not Sir Henry, who was being dogged by this secret man. He had not followed me himself, but he had set an agent—the boy, perhaps—upon my track, and this was his report. Possibly I had taken no step since I had been upon the moor which had not been observed and repeated. Always there was this feeling of an unseen force, a fine net drawn round us with infinite skill and delicacy, holding us so lightly that it was only at some supreme moment that one realized that one was indeed entangled in its meshes.

If there was one report there might be others, so I looked round the hut in search of them. There was no trace, however, of anything of the kind, nor could I discover any sign which might indicate the character or intentions of the man who lived in this singular place, save that he must be of Spartan habits and cared little for the comforts of life. When I thought of the heavy rains and looked at the gaping roof I understood how strong and immutable must be the purpose which had kept him in that inhospitable abode. Was he our malignant enemy, or was he by chance our guardian angel? I swore that I would not leave the hut until I knew.

Outside the sun was sinking low and the west was blazing with scarlet and gold. Its reflection was shot back in ruddy patches by the distant pools which lay amid the great Grimpen Mire. There were the two towers of Baskerville Hall, and there a distant blur of smoke which marked the village of Grimpen. Between the two, behind the hill, was the house of the Stapletons. All was sweet and mellow and peaceful in the golden evening light, and yet as I looked at them my soul shared none of the peace of nature but quivered at the vagueness and the terror of that interview which every instant was bringing nearer. With tingling nerves, but a fixed purpose, I sat in the dark recess of the hut and waited with sombre patience for the coming of its tenant.

And then at last I heard him. Far away came the sharp clink of a boot striking upon a stone. Then another and yet another, coming nearer and nearer. I shrank back into the darkest corner, and cocked the pistol in my pocket, determined not to discover myself until I had an opportunity of seeing something of the stranger. There was a long pause which showed that he had stopped. Then once more the footsteps approached and a shadow fell across the opening of the hut.

"It is a lovely evening, my dear Watson," said a well-known voice. "I really think that you will be more comfortable outside than in."

CHAPTER XII. DEATH ON THE MOOR

For a moment or two I sat breathless, hardly able to believe my ears. Then my senses and my voice came back to me, while a crushing weight of responsibility seemed in an instant to be lifted from my soul. That cold, incisive, ironical voice could belong to but one man in all the world.

"Holmes!" I cried—"Holmes!"

"Come out," said he, "and please be careful with the revolver."

I stooped under the rude lintel, and there he sat upon a stone outside, his gray eyes dancing with amusement as they fell upon my astonished features. He was thin and worn, but clear and alert, his keen face bronzed by the sun and roughened by the wind. In his tweed suit and cloth cap he looked like any other tourist upon the moor, and he had contrived, with that cat-like love of personal cleanliness which was one of his characteristics, that his chin should be as smooth and his linen as perfect as if he were in Baker Street.

"I never was more glad to see anyone in my life," said I, as I wrung him by the hand.

"Or more astonished, eh?"

"Well, I must confess to it."

"The surprise was not all on one side, I assure you. I had no idea that you had found my occasional retreat, still less that you were inside it, until I was within twenty paces of the door."

"My footprint, I presume?"

"No, Watson; I fear that I could not undertake to recognize your footprint amid all the footprints of the world. If you seriously desire to deceive me you must change your tobacconist; for when I see the stub of a cigarette marked Bradley, Oxford Street, I know that my friend Watson is in the neighbourhood. You will see it there beside the path. You threw it down, no doubt, at that supreme moment when you charged into the empty hut."

"Exactly."

"I thought as much—and knowing your admirable tenacity I was convinced that you were sitting in ambush, a weapon within reach, waiting for the tenant to return. So you actually thought that I was the criminal?"

"I did not know who you were, but I was determined to find out."

"Excellent, Watson! And how did you localize me? You saw me, perhaps, on the night of the convict hunt, when I was so imprudent as to allow the moon to rise behind me?"

"Yes, I saw you then."

"And have no doubt searched all the huts until you came to this one?"

"No, your boy had been observed, and that gave me a guide where to look."

"The old gentleman with the telescope, no doubt. I could not make it out when first I saw the light flashing upon the lens." He rose and peeped into the hut. "Ha, I see that Cartwright has brought up some supplies. What's this paper? So you have been to Coombe Tracey, have you?"

"Yes."

"To see Mrs. Laura Lyons?"

"Exactly."

"Well done! Our researches have evidently been running on parallel lines, and when we unite our results I expect we shall have a fairly full knowledge of the case."

"Well, I am glad from my heart that you are here, for indeed the responsibility and the mystery were both becoming too much for my nerves. But how in the name of wonder did you come here, and what have you been doing? I thought that you were in Baker Street working out that case of blackmailing."

"That was what I wished you to think."

"Then you use me, and yet do not trust me!" I cried with some bitterness. "I think that I have deserved better at your hands, Holmes."

"My dear fellow, you have been invaluable to me in this as in many other cases, and I beg that you will forgive me if I have seemed to play a trick upon you. In truth, it was partly for your own sake that I did it, and it was my appreciation of the danger which you ran which led me to come down and examine the matter for myself. Had I been with Sir Henry and you it is confident that my point of view would have been the same as yours, and my presence would have warned our very formidable opponents to be on their guard. As it is, I have been able to get about as I could not possibly have done had I been living in the Hall, and I remain an unknown factor in the business, ready to throw in all my weight at a critical moment."

"But why keep me in the dark?"

"For you to know could not have helped us, and might possibly have led to my discovery. You would have wished to tell me something, or in your kindness you would have brought me out some comfort or other, and so an unnecessary risk would be run. I brought Cartwright down with me—you remember the little chap at the express office—and he has seen after my simple wants: a loaf of bread and a clean collar. What does man want more? He has given me an extra pair of eyes upon a very active pair of feet, and both have been invaluable."

"Then my reports have all been wasted!"—My voice trembled as I recalled the pains and the pride with which I had composed them.

Holmes took a bundle of papers from his pocket.

"Here are your reports, my dear fellow, and very well thumbed, I assure you. I made excellent arrangements, and they are only delayed one day upon their way. I must compliment you exceedingly upon the zeal and the intelligence which you have shown over an extraordinarily difficult case."

I was still rather raw over the deception which had been practised upon me, but the warmth of Holmes's praise drove my anger from my mind. I felt also in my heart that he was right in what he said and that it was really best for our purpose that I should not have known that he was upon the moor.

"That's better," said he, seeing the shadow rise from my face. "And now tell me the result of your visit to Mrs. Laura Lyons—it was not difficult for me to guess that it was to see her that you had gone, for I am already aware that she is the one person in Coombe Tracey who might be of service to us in the matter. In fact, if you had not gone to-day it is exceedingly probable that I should have gone to-morrow."

The sun had set and dusk was settling over the moor. The air had turned chill and we withdrew into the hut for warmth. There, sitting together in the twilight, I told Holmes of my conversation with the lady. So interested was he that I had to repeat some of it twice before he was satisfied.

"This is most important," said he when I had concluded. "It fills up a gap which I had been unable to bridge, in this most complex affair. You are aware, perhaps, that a close intimacy exists between this lady and the man Stapleton?"

"I did not know of a close intimacy."

"There can be no doubt about the matter. They meet, they write, there is a complete understanding between them. Now, this puts a very powerful weapon into our hands. If I could only use it to detach his wife——"

"His wife?"

"I am giving you some information now, in return for all that you have given me. The lady who has passed here as Miss Stapleton is in reality his wife."

"Good heavens, Holmes! Are you sure of what you say? How could he have permitted Sir Henry to fall in love with her?"

"Sir Henry's falling in love could do no harm to anyone except Sir Henry. He took particular care that Sir Henry did not make love to her, as you have yourself observed. I repeat that the lady is his wife and not his sister."

"But why this elaborate deception?"

"Because he foresaw that she would be very much more useful to him in the character of a free woman."

All my unspoken instincts, my vague suspicions, suddenly took shape and centred upon the naturalist. In that impassive, colourless man, with his straw hat and his butterfly-net, I seemed to see something terrible—a creature of infinite patience and craft, with a smiling face and a murderous heart.

"It is he, then, who is our enemy—it is he who dogged us in London?"

"So I read the riddle."

"And the warning—it must have come from her!"

"Exactly."

The shape of some monstrous villainy, half seen, half guessed, loomed through the darkness which had girt me so long.

"But are you sure of this, Holmes? How do you know that the woman is his wife?"

"Because he so far forgot himself as to tell you a true piece of autobiography upon the occasion when he first met you, and I daresay he has many a time regretted it since. He was once a schoolmaster in the north of England. Now, there is no one more easy to trace than a schoolmaster. There are scholastic agencies by which one may identify any man who has been in the profession. A little investigation showed me that a school had come to grief under atrocious circumstances, and that the man who had owned it—the name was different—had disappeared with his wife. The descriptions agreed. When I learned that the missing man was devoted to entomology the identification was complete."

The darkness was rising, but much was still hidden by the shadows.

"If this woman is in truth his wife, where does Mrs. Laura Lyons come in?" I asked.

"That is one of the points upon which your own researches have shed a light. Your interview with the lady has cleared the situation very much. I did not know about a projected divorce between herself and her husband. In that case, regarding Stapleton as an unmarried man, she counted no doubt upon becoming his wife."

"And when she is undeceived?"

"Why, then we may find the lady of service. It must be our first duty to see her—both of us—to-morrow. Don't you think, Watson, that you are away from your charge rather long? Your place should be at Baskerville Hall."

The last red streaks had faded away in the west and night had settled upon the moor. A few faint stars were gleaming in a violet sky.

"One last question, Holmes," I said, as I rose. "Surely there is no need of secrecy between you and me. What is the meaning of it all? What is he after?"

Holmes's voice sank as he answered:——

"It is murder, Watson—refined, cold-blooded, deliberate murder. Do not ask me for particulars. My nets are closing upon him, even as his are upon Sir Henry, and with your help he is already almost at my mercy. There is but one danger which can threaten us. It is that he should strike before we are ready to do so. Another day—two at the most—and I have my case complete, but until then guard your charge as closely as ever a fond mother watched her ailing child. Your mission to-day has justified itself, and yet I could almost wish that you had not left his side. Hark!"

A terrible scream—a prolonged yell of horror and anguish—burst out of the silence of the moor. That frightful cry turned the blood to ice in my veins.

"Oh, my God!" I gasped. "What is it? What does it mean?"

Holmes had sprung to his feet, and I saw his dark, athletic outline at the door of the hut, his shoulders stooping, his head thrust forward, his face peering into the darkness.

"Hush!" he whispered. "Hush!"

The cry had been loud on account of its vehemence, but it had pealed out from somewhere far off on the shadowy plain. Now it burst upon our ears, nearer, louder, more urgent than before.

"Where is it?" Holmes whispered; and I knew from the thrill of his voice that he, the man of iron, was shaken to the soul." Where is it, Watson?"

"There, I think." I pointed into the darkness.

"No, there!"

Again the agonized cry swept through the silent night, louder and much nearer than ever. And a new sound mingled with it, a deep, muttered rumble, musical and yet menacing, rising and falling like the low, constant murmur of the sea.

"The hound!" cried Holmes. "Come, Watson, come! Great heavens, if we are too late!"

He had started running swiftly over the moor, and I had followed at his heels. But now from somewhere among the broken ground immediately in front of us there came one last despairing yell, and then a dull, heavy thud. We halted and listened. Not another sound broke the heavy silence of the windless night.

I saw Holmes put his hand to his forehead like a man distracted. He stamped his feet upon the ground.

"He has beaten us, Watson. We are too late."

"No, no, surely not!"

"Fool that I was to hold my hand. And you, Watson, see what comes of abandoning your charge! But, by Heaven, if the worst has happened, we'll avenge him!"

Blindly we ran through the gloom, blundering against boulders, forcing our way through gorse bushes, panting up hills and rushing down slopes, heading always in the direction whence those dreadful sounds had come. At every rise Holmes looked eagerly round him, but the shadows were thick upon the moor, and nothing moved upon its dreary face.

"Can you see anything?"

"Nothing."

"But, hark, what is that?"

A low moan had fallen upon our ears. There it was again upon our left! On that side a ridge of rocks ended in a sheer cliff which overlooked a stone-strewn slope. On its jagged face was spread-eagled some dark, irregular object. As we ran towards it the vague outline hardened into a definite shape. It was a prostrate man face downward upon the ground, the head doubled under him at a horrible angle, the shoulders rounded and the body hunched together as if in the act of throwing a somersault. So grotesque was the attitude that I could not for the instant realise that that moan had been the passing of his soul. Not a whisper, not a rustle, rose now from the dark figure over which we stooped. Holmes laid his hand upon him, and held it up again, with an exclamation of horror. The gleam of the match which he struck shone upon his clotted fingers and upon the ghastly pool which widened slowly from the crushed skull of the victim. And it shone upon something else which turned our hearts sick and faint within us—the body of Sir Henry Baskerville!

There was no chance of either of us forgetting that peculiar ruddy tweed suit—the very one which he had worn on the first morning that we had seen him in Baker Street. We caught the one clear glimpse of it, and then the match flickered and went out, even as the hope had gone out of our souls. Holmes groaned, and his face glimmered white through the darkness.

"The brute! the brute!" I cried with clenched hands. "Oh Holmes, I shall never forgive myself for having left him to his fate."

"I am more to blame than you, Watson. In order to have my case well rounded and complete, I have thrown away the life of my client. It is the greatest blow which has befallen me in my career. But how could I know—how could l know—that he would risk his life alone upon the moor in the face of all my warnings?"

"That we should have heard his screams—my God, those screams!—and yet have been unable to save him! Where is this brute of a hound which drove him to his death? It may be lurking among these rocks at this instant. And Stapleton, where is he? He shall answer for this deed."

"He shall. I will see to that. Uncle and nephew have been murdered—the one frightened to death by the very sight of a beast which he thought to be supernatural, the other driven to his end in his wild flight to escape from it. But now we have to prove the connection between the man and the beast. Save from what we heard, we cannot even swear to the existence of the latter, since Sir Henry has evidently died from the fall. But, by heavens, cunning as he is, the fellow shall be in my power before another day is past!"

We stood with bitter hearts on either side of the mangled body, overwhelmed by this sudden and irrevocable disaster which had brought all our long and weary labours to so piteous an end. Then, as the moon rose we climbed to the top of the rocks over which our poor friend had fallen, and from the summit we gazed out over the shadowy moor, half silver and half gloom. Faraway, miles off, in the direction of Grimpen, a single steady yellow light was shining. It could only come from the lonely abode of the Stapletons. With a bitter curse I shook my fist at it as I gazed.

"Why should we not seize him at once?"

"Our case is not complete. The fellow is wary and cunning to the last degree. It is not what we know, but what we can prove. If we make one false move the villain may escape us yet."

"What can we do?"

"There will be plenty for us to do to-morrow. To-night we can only perform the last offices to our poor friend."

Together we made our way down the precipitous slope and approached the body, black and clear against the silvered stones. The agony of those contorted limbs struck me with a spasm of pain and blurred my eyes with tears.

"We must send for help, Holmes! We cannot carry him all the way to the Hall. Good heavens, are you mad?"

He had uttered a cry and bent over the body. Now he was dancing and laughing and wringing my hand. Could this be my stern, self-contained friend? These were hidden fires, indeed!

"A beard! A beard! The man has a beard!"

"A beard?"

"It is not the baronet—it is—why, it is my neighbour, the convict!"

With feverish haste we had turned the body over, and that dripping beard was pointing up to the cold, clear moon. There could be no doubt about the beetling forehead, the sunken animal eyes. It was indeed the same face which had glared upon me in the light of the candle from over the rock—the face of Selden, the criminal.

Then in an instant it was all clear to me. I remembered how the baronet had told me that he had handed his old wardrobe to Barrymore. Barrymore had passed it on in order to help Selden in his escape. Boots, shirt, cap—it was all Sir Henry's. The tragedy was still black enough, but this man had at least deserved death by the laws of his country. I told Holmes how the matter stood, my heart bubbling over with thankfulness and joy.

"Then the clothes have been the poor devil's death," said he. "It is clear enough that the hound has been laid on from some article of Sir Henry's— the boot which was abstracted in the hotel, in all probability— and so ran this man down. There is one very singular thing, however: How came Selden, in the darkness, to know that the hound was on his trail?"

"He heard him."

"To hear a hound upon the moor would not work a hard man like this convict into such a paroxysm of terror that he would risk recapture by screaming wildly for help. By his cries he must have run a long way after he knew the animal was on his track. How did he know?"

"A greater mystery to me is why this hound, presuming that all our conjectures are correct —"

"I presume nothing."

"Well, then, why this hound should be loose to-night. I suppose that it does not always run loose upon the moor. Stapleton would not let it go unless he had reason to think that Sir Henry would be there."

"My difficulty is the more formidable of the two, for I think that we shall very shortly get an explanation of yours, while mine may remain for ever a mystery. The question now is, what shall we do with this poor wretch's body? We cannot leave it here to the foxes and the ravens."

"I suggest that we put it in one of the huts until we can communicate with the police."

"Exactly. I have no doubt that you and I could carry it so far. Halloa, Watson, what's this? It's the man himself, by all that's wonderful and audacious! Not a word to show your suspicions—not a word, or my plans crumble to the ground."

A figure was approaching us over the moor, and I saw the dull red glow of a cigar. The moon shone upon him, and I could distinguish the dapper shape and jaunty walk of the naturalist. He stopped when he saw us, and then came on again.

"Why, Dr. Watson, that's not you, is it? You are the last man that I should have expected to see out on the moor at this time of night. But, dear me, what's this? Somebody hurt? Not—don't tell me that it is our friend Sir Henry!" He hurried past me and stooped over the dead man. I heard a sharp intake of his breath and the cigar fell from his fingers.

"Who—who's this?" he stammered.

"It is Selden, the man who escaped from Princetown."

Stapleton turned a ghastly face upon us, but by a supreme effort he had overcome his amazement and his disappointment. He looked sharply from Holmes to me.

"Dear me! What a very shocking affair! How did he die?"

"He appears to have broken his neck by falling over these rocks. My friend and I were strolling on the moor when we heard a cry."

"I heard a cry also. That was what brought me out. I was uneasy about Sir Henry."

"Why about Sir Henry in particular?" I could not help asking.

"Because I had suggested that he should come over. When he did not come I was surprised, and I naturally became alarmed for his safety when I heard cries upon the moor. By the way"—his eyes darted again from my face to Holmes's—"did you hear anything else besides a cry?"

"No," said Holmes; "did you?"

"No."

"What do you mean, then?"

"Oh, you know the stories that the peasants tell about a phantom hound, and so on. It is said to be heard at night upon the moor. I was wondering if there were any evidence of such a sound to-night."

"We heard nothing of the kind," said I.

"And what is your theory of this poor fellow's death?"

"I have no doubt that anxiety and exposure have driven him off his head. He has rushed about the moor in a crazy state and eventually fallen over here and broken his neck."

"That seems the most reasonable theory," said Stapleton, and he gave a sigh which I took to indicate his relief. "What do you think about it, Mr. Sherlock Holmes?"

My friend bowed his compliments.

"You are quick at identification," said he.

"We have been expecting you in these parts since Dr. Watson came down. You are in time to see a tragedy."

"Yes, indeed. I have no doubt that my friend's explanation will cover the facts. I will take an unpleasant remembrance back to London with me to-morrow."

"Oh, you return to-morrow?"

"That is my intention."

"I hope your visit has cast some light upon those occurrences which have puzzled us?"

Holmes shrugged his shoulders.

"One cannot always have the success for which one hopes. An investigator needs facts, and not legends or rumours. It has not been a satisfactory case."

My friend spoke in his frankest and most unconcerned manner. Stapleton still looked hard at him. Then he turned to me.

"I would suggest carrying this poor fellow to my house, but it would give my sister such a fright that I do not feel justified in doing it. I think that if we put something over his face he will be safe until morning."

And so it was arranged. Resisting Stapleton's offer of hospitality, Holmes and I set off to Baskerville Hall, leaving the naturalist to return alone. Looking back we saw the figure moving slowly away over the broad moor, and behind him that one black smudge on the silvered slope which showed where the man was lying who had come so horribly to his end.

CHAPTER XIII. FIXING THE NETS

"We're at close grips at last," said Holmes as we walked together across the moor. "What a nerve the fellow has! How he pulled himself together in the face of what must have been a paralyzing shock when he found that the wrong man had fallen a victim to his plot. I told you in London, Watson, and I tell you now again, that we have never had a foeman more worthy of our steel."

"I am sorry that he has seen you."

"And so was I at first. But there was no getting out of it."

"What effect do you think it will have upon his plans now that he knows you are here?"

"It may cause him to be more cautious, or it may drive him to desperate measures at once. Like most clever criminals, he may be too confident in his own cleverness and imagine that he has completely deceived us."

"Why should we not arrest him at once?"

"My dear Watson, you were born to be a man of action. Your instinct is always to do something energetic. But supposing, for argument's sake, that we had him arrested to-night, what on earth the better off should we be for that? We could prove nothing against him. There's the devilish cunning of it! If he were acting through a human agent we could get some evidence, but if we were to drag this great dog to the light of day it would not help us in putting a rope round the neck of its master."

"Surely we have a case."

"Not a shadow of one—only surmise and conjecture. We should be laughed out of court if we came with such a story and such evidence."

"There is Sir Charles's death."

"Found dead without a mark upon him. You and I know that he died of sheer fright, and we know also what frightened him; but how are we to get twelve stolid jurymen to know it? What signs are there of a hound? Where are the marks of its fangs? Of course we know that a hound does not bite a dead body and that Sir Charles was dead before ever the brute overtook him. But we have to prove all this, and we are not in a position to do it."

"Well, then, to-night?"

"We are not much better off to-night. Again, there was no direct connection between the hound and the man's death. We never saw the hound. We heard it; but we could not prove that it was running upon this man's trail. There is a complete absence of motive. No, my dear fellow; we must reconcile ourselves to the fact that we have no case at present, and that it is worth our while to run any risk in order to establish one."

"And how do you propose to do so?"

"I have great hopes of what Mrs. Laura Lyons may do for us when the position of affairs is made clear to her. And I have my own plan as well. Sufficient for to-morrow is the evil thereof; but I hope before the day is past to have the upper hand at last."

I could draw nothing further from him, and he walked, lost in thought, as far as the Baskerville gates.

"Are you coming up?"

"Yes; I see no reason for further concealment. But one last word, Watson. Say nothing of the hound to Sir Henry. Let him think that Selden's death was as Stapleton would have us believe. He will have a better nerve for the ordeal which he will have to undergo to-morrow, when he is engaged, if I remember your report aright, to dine with these people."

"And so am I."

"Then you must excuse yourself and he must go alone. That will be easily arranged. And now, if we are too late for dinner, I think that we are both ready for our suppers."

Sir Henry was more pleased than surprised to see Sherlock Holmes, for he had for some days been expecting that recent events would bring him down from London. He did raise his eyebrows, however, when he found that my friend had neither any luggage nor any explanations for its absence. Between us we soon supplied his wants, and then over a belated supper we explained to the baronet as much of our experience as it seemed desirable that he should know. But first I had the unpleasant duty of breaking the news to Barrymore and his wife. To him it may have been an unmitigated relief, but she wept bitterly in her apron. To all the world he was the man of violence, half animal and half demon; but to her he always remained the little wilful boy of her own girlhood, the child who had clung to her hand. Evil indeed is the man who has not one woman to mourn him.

"I've been moping in the house all day since Watson went off in the morning," said the baronet. "I guess I should have some credit, for I have kept my promise. If I hadn't sworn not to go about alone I might have had a more lively evening, for I had a message from Stapleton asking me over there."

"I have no doubt that you would have had a more lively evening," said Holmes drily. "By the way, I don't suppose you appreciate that we have been mourning over you as having broken your neck?"

Sir Henry opened his eyes. "How was that?"

"This poor wretch was dressed in your clothes. I fear your servant who gave them to him may get into trouble with the police."

"That is unlikely. There was no mark on any of them, as far as I know."

"That's lucky for him—in fact, it's lucky for all of you, since you are all on the wrong side of the law in this matter. I am not sure that as a conscientious detective my first duty is not to arrest the whole household. Watson's reports are most incriminating documents."

"But how about the case?" asked the baronet. "Have you made anything out of the tangle? I don't know that Watson and I are much the wiser since we came down."

"I think that I shall be in a position to make the situation rather more clear to you before long. It has been an exceedingly difficult and most complicated business. There are several points upon which we still want light—but it is coming all the same."

"We've had one experience, as Watson has no doubt told you. We heard the hound on the moor, so I can swear that it is not all empty superstition. I had something to do with dogs when I was out West, and I know one when I hear one. If you can muzzle that one and put him on a chain I'll be ready to swear you are the greatest detective of all time."

"I think I will muzzle him and chain him all right if you will give me your help."

"Whatever you tell me to do I will do."

"Very good; and I will ask you also to do it blindly, without always asking the reason."

"Just as you like."

"If you will do this I think the chances are that our little problem will soon be solved. I have no doubt——"

He stopped suddenly and stared fixedly up over my head into the air. The lamp beat upon his face, and so intent was it and so still that it might have been that of a clear-cut classical statue, a personification of alertness and expectation.

"What is it?" we both cried.

I could see as he looked down that he was repressing some internal emotion. His features were still composed, but his eyes shone with amused exultation.

"Excuse the admiration of a connoisseur," said he as he waved his hand towards the line of portraits which covered the opposite wall. "Watson won't allow that I know anything of art, but that is mere jealousy, because our views upon the subject differ. Now, these are a really very fine series of portraits."

"Well, I'm glad to hear you say so," said Sir Henry, glancing with some surprise at my friend. "I don't pretend to know much about these things, and I'd be a better judge of a horse or a steer than of a picture. I didn't know that you found time for such things. "

"I know what is good when I see it, and I see it now. That's a Kneller, I'll swear, that lady in the blue silk over yonder, and the stout gentleman with the wig ought to be a Reynolds. They are all family portraits, I presume?"

"Every one."

"Do you know the names?"

"Barrymore has been coaching me in them, and I think I can say my lessons fairly well."

"Who is the gentleman with the telescope?"

"That is Rear-Admiral Baskerville, who served under Rodney in the West Indies. The man with the blue coat and the roll of paper is Sir William Baskerville, who was Chairman of Committees of the House of Commons under Pitt."

"And this Cavalier opposite to me—the one with the black velvet and the lace?"

"Ah, you have a right to know about him. That is the cause of all the mischief, the wicked Hugo, who started the Hound of the Baskervilles. We're not likely to forget him."

I gazed with interest and some surprise upon the portrait.

"Dear me!" said Holmes, "he seems a quiet, meek-mannered man enough, but I dare say that there was a lurking devil in his eyes. I had pictured him as a more robust and ruffianly person."

"There's no doubt about the authenticity, for the name and the date, 1647, are on the back of the canvas."

Holmes said little more, but the picture of the old roysterer seemed to have a fascination for him, and his eyes were continually fixed upon it during supper. It was not until later, when Sir Henry had gone to his room, that I was able to follow the trend of his thoughts. He led me back into the banqueting-hall, his bedroom candle in his hand, and he held it up against the time-stained portrait on the wall.

"Do you see anything there?"

I looked at the broad plumed hat, the curling love-locks, the white lace collar, and the straight, severe face which was framed between them. It was not a brutal countenance, but it was prim, hard, and stern, with a firm-set, thin-lipped mouth, and a coldly intolerant eye.

"Is it like anyone you know?"

"There is something of Sir Henry about the jaw."

"Just a suggestion, perhaps. But wait an instant!" He stood upon a chair, and, holding up the light in his left hand, he curved his right arm over the broad hat and round the long ringlets.

"Good heavens!" I cried, in amazement.

The face of Stapleton had sprung out of the canvas.

"Ha, you see it now. My eyes have been trained to examine faces and not their trimmings. It is the first quality of a criminal investigator that he should see through a disguise."

"But this is marvellous. It might be his portrait."

"Yes, it is an interesting instance of a throwback, which appears to be both physical and spiritual. A study of family portraits is enough to convert a man to the doctrine of reincarnation. The fellow is a Baskerville—that is evident."

"With designs upon the succession."

"Exactly. This chance of the picture has supplied us with one of our most obvious missing links. We have him, Watson, we have him, and I dare swear that before to-morrow night he will be fluttering in our net as helpless as one of his own butterflies. A pin, a cork, and a card, and we add him to the Baker Street collection!" He burst into one of his rare fits of laughter as he turned away from the picture. I have not heard him laugh often, and it has always boded ill to somebody.

I was up betimes in the morning, but Holmes was afoot earlier still, for I saw him as I dressed, coming up the drive.

"Yes, we should have a full day to-day," he remarked, and he rubbed his hands with the joy of action. "The nets are all in place, and the drag is about to begin. We'll know before the day is out whether we have caught our big, lean-jawed pike, or whether he has got through the meshes."

"Have you been on the moor already?"

"I have sent a report from Grimpen to Princetown as to the death of Selden. I think I can promise that none of you will be troubled in the matter. And I have also communicated with my faithful Cartwright, who would certainly have pined away at the door of my hut, as a dog does at his master's grave, if I had not set his mind at rest about my safety."

"What is the next move?"

"To see Sir Henry. Ah, here he is!"

"Good morning, Holmes," said the baronet. "You look like a general who is planning a battle with his chief of the staff."

"That is the exact situation. Watson was asking for orders."

"And so do I."

"Very good. You are engaged, as I understand, to dine with our friends the Stapletons to-night."

"I hope that you will come also. They are very hospitable people, and I am sure that they would be very glad to see you."

"I fear that Watson and I must go to London."

"To London?"

"Yes, I think that we should be more useful there at the present juncture."

The baronet's face perceptibly lengthened.

"I hoped that you were going to see me through this business. The Hall and the moor are not very pleasant places when one is alone."

"My dear fellow, you must trust me implicitly and do exactly what I tell you. You can tell your friends that we should have been happy to have come with you, but that urgent business required us to be in town. We hope very soon to return to Devonshire. Will you remember to give them that message?"

"If you insist upon it."

"There is no alternative, I assure you."

I saw by the baronet's clouded brow that he was deeply hurt by what he regarded as our desertion.

"When do you desire to go?" he asked coldly.

"Immediately after breakfast. We will drive in to Coombe Tracey, but Watson will leave his things as a pledge that he will come back to you. Watson, you will send a note to Stapleton to tell him that you regret that you cannot come."

"I have a good mind to go to London with you," said the baronet. "Why should I stay here alone?"

"Because it is your post of duty. Because you gave me your word that you would do as you were told, and I tell you to stay."

"All right, then, I'll stay."

"One more direction! I wish you to drive to Merripit House. Send back your trap, however, and let them know that you intend to walk home."

"To walk across the moor?"

"Yes."

"But that is the very thing which you have so often cautioned me not to do."

"This time you may do it with safety. If I had not every confidence in your nerve and courage I would not suggest it, but it is essential that you should do it."

"Then I will do it."

"And as you value your life do not go across the moor in any direction save along the straight path which leads from Merripit House to the Grimpen Road, and is your natural way home."

"I will do just what you say."

"Very good. I should be glad to get away as soon after breakfast as possible, so as to reach London in the afternoon."

I was much astounded by this programme, though I remembered that Holmes had said to Stapleton on the night before that his visit would terminate next day. It had not crossed my mind, however, that he would wish me to go with him, nor could I understand how we could both be absent at a moment which he himself declared to be critical. There was nothing for it, however, but implicit obedience; so we bade good-bye to our rueful friend, and a couple of hours afterwards we were at the station of Coombe Tracey and had dispatched the trap upon its return journey. A small boy was waiting upon the platform.

"Any orders, sir?"

"You will take this train to town, Cartwright. The moment you arrive you will send a wire to Sir Henry Baskerville, in my name, to say that if he finds the pocket-book which I have dropped he is to send it by registered post to Baker Street."

"Yes, sir."

"And ask at the station office if there is a message for me."

The boy returned with a telegram, which Holmes handed to me. It ran: "Wire received. Coming down with unsigned warrant. Arrive five-forty.— LESTRADE."

"That is in answer to mine of this morning. He is the best of the professionals, I think, and we may need his assistance. Now, Watson, I think that we cannot employ our time better than by calling upon your acquaintance, Mrs. Laura Lyons."

His plan of campaign was beginning to be evident. He would use the baronet in order to convince the Stapletons that we were really gone, while we should actually return at the instant when we were likely to be needed. That telegram from London, if mentioned by Sir Henry to the Stapletons, must remove the last suspicions from their minds. Already I seemed to see our nets drawing closer around that lean-jawed pike.

Mrs. Laura Lyons was in her office, and Sherlock Holmes opened his interview with a frankness and directness which considerably amazed her.

"I am investigating the circumstances which attended the death of the late Sir Charles Baskerville," said he. "My friend here, Dr. Watson, has informed me of what you have communicated, and also of what you have withheld in connection with that matter."

"What have I withheld?" she asked defiantly.

"You have confessed that you asked Sir Charles to be at the gate at ten o'clock. We know that that was the place and hour of his death. You have with held what the connection is between these events."

"There is no connection."

"In that case the coincidence must indeed be an extraordinary one. But I think that we shall succeed in establishing a connection after all. I wish to be perfectly frank with you, Mrs. Lyons. We regard this case as one of murder, and the evidence may implicate not only your friend Mr. Stapleton, but his wife as well."

The lady sprang from her chair.

"His wife!" she cried.

"The fact is no longer a secret. The person who has passed for his sister is really his wife."

Mrs. Lyons had resumed her seat. Her hands were grasping the arms of her chair, and I saw that the pink nails had turned white with the pressure of her grip.

"His wife!" she said again. "His wife! He is not a married man."

Sherlock Holmes shrugged his shoulders.

"Prove it to me! Prove it to me! And if you can do so —!" The fierce flash of her eyes said more than any words.

"I have come prepared to do so," said Holmes, drawing several papers from his pocket. "Here is a photograph of the couple taken in York four years ago. It is indorsed 'Mr. and Mrs. Vandeleur,' but you will have no difficulty in recognizing him, and her also, if you know her by sight. Here are three written descriptions by trustworthy witnesses of Mr. and Mrs. Vandeleur, who at that time kept St. Oliver's private school. Read them and see if you can doubt the identity of these people."

She glanced at them, and then looked up at us with the set, rigid face of a desperate woman.

"Mr. Holmes," she said, "this man had offered me marriage on condition that I could get a divorce from my husband. He has lied to me, the villain, in every conceivable way. Not one word of truth has he ever told me. And why—why? I imagined that all was for my own sake. But now I see that I was never anything but a tool in his hands. Why should I preserve faith with him who never kept any with me? Why should I try to shield him from the consequences of his own wicked acts? Ask me what you like, and there is nothing which I shall hold back. One thing I swear to you, and that is that when I wrote the letter I never dreamed of any harm to the old gentleman, who had been my kindest friend."

"I entirely believe you, madam," said Sherlock Holmes. "The recital of these events must be very painful to you, and perhaps it will make it easier if I tell you what occurred, and you can check me if I make any material mistake. The sending of this letter was suggested to you by Stapleton?"

"He dictated it."

"I presume that the reason he gave was that you would receive help from Sir Charles for the legal expenses connected with your divorce?"

"Exactly."

"And then after you had sent the letter he dissuaded you from keeping the appointment?"

"He told me that it would hurt his self-respect that any other man should find the money for such an object, and that though he was a poor man himself he would devote his last penny to removing the obstacles which divided us."

"He appears to be a very consistent character. And then you heard nothing until you read the reports of the death in the paper?"

"No."

"And he made you swear to say nothing about your appointment with Sir Charles?"

"He did. He said that the death was a very mysterious one, and that I should certainly be suspected if the facts came out. He frightened me into remaining silent."

"Quite so. But you had your suspicions?"

She hesitated and looked down.

"I knew him," she said. "But if he had kept faith with me I should always have done so with him."

"I think that on the whole you have had a fortunate escape," said Sherlock Holmes. "You have had him in your power and he knew it, and yet you are alive. You have been walking for some months very near to the edge of a precipice. We must wish you good-morning now, Mrs. Lyons, and it is probable that you will very shortly hear from us again."

"Our case becomes rounded off, and difficulty after difficulty thins away in front of us," said Holmes as we stood waiting for the arrival of the express from town. "I shall soon be in the position of being able to put into a single connected narrative one of the most singular and sensational crimes of modern times. Students of criminology will remember the analogous incidents in Godno, in Little Russia, in the year '66, and of course there are the Anderson murders in North Carolina, but this case possesses some features which are entirely its own. Even now we have no clear case against this very wily man. But I shall be very much surprised if it is not clear enough before we go to bed this night."

The London express came roaring into the station, and a small, wiry bulldog of a man had sprung from a first-class carriage. We all three shook hands, and I saw at once from the reverential way in which Lestrade gazed at my companion that he had learned a good deal since the days when they had first worked together. I could well remember the scorn which the theories of the reasoner used then to excite in the practical man.

"Anything good?" he asked.

"The biggest thing for years," said Holmes. "We have two hours before we need think of starting. I think we might employ it in getting some dinner and then, Lestrade, we will take the London fog out of your throat by giving you a breath of the pure night air of Dartmoor. Never been there? Ah, well, I don't suppose you will forget your first visit."

CHAPTER XIV. THE HOUND OF THE BASKERVILLES

One of Sherlock Holmes's defects—if, indeed, one may call it a defect—was that he was exceedingly loath to communicate his full plans to any other person until the instant of their fulfilment. Partly it came no doubt from his own masterful nature, which loved to dominate and surprise those who were around him. Partly also from his professional caution, which urged him never to take any chances. The result, however, was very trying for those who were acting as his agents and assistants. I had often suffered under it, but never more so than during that long drive in the darkness. The great ordeal was in front of us; at last we were about to make our final effort, and yet Holmes had said nothing, and I could only surmise what his course of action would be. My nerves thrilled with anticipation when at last the cold wind upon our faces and the dark, void spaces on either side of the narrow road told me that we were back upon the moor once again. Every stride of the horses and every turn of the wheels was taking us nearer to our supreme adventure.

Our conversation was hampered by the presence of the driver of the hired wagonette, so that we were forced to talk of trivial matters when our nerves were tense with emotion and anticipation. It was a relief to me, after that unnatural restraint, when we at last passed Frankland's house and knew that we were drawing near to the Hall and to the scene of action. We did not drive up to the door but got down near the gate of the avenue. The wagonette was paid off and ordered to return to Coombe Tracey forthwith, while we started to walk to Merripit House.

"Are you armed, Lestrade?"

The little detective smiled.

"As long as I have my trousers I have a hip-pocket, and as long as I have my hip-pocket I have something in it."

"Good! My friend and I are also ready for emergencies."

"You're mighty close about this affair, Mr. Holmes. What's the game now?"

"A waiting game."

"My word, it does not seem a very cheerful place," said the detective with a shiver, glancing round him at the gloomy slopes of the hill and at the huge lake of fog which lay over the Grimpen Mire. "I see the lights of a house ahead of us."

"That is Merripit House and the end of our journey. I must request you to walk on tiptoe and not to talk above a whisper."

We moved cautiously along the track as if we were bound for the house, but Holmes halted us when we were about two hundred yards from it.

"This will do," said he. "These rocks upon the right make an admirable screen."

"We are to wait here?"

"Yes, we shall make our little ambush here. Get into this hollow, Lestrade. You have been inside the house, have you not, Watson? Can you tell the position of the rooms? What are those latticed windows at this end?"

"I think they are the kitchen windows."

"And the one beyond, which shines so brightly?"

"That is certainly the dining-room."

"The blinds are up. You know the lie of the land best. Creep forward quietly and see what they are doing—but for heaven's sake don't let them know that they are watched!"

I tiptoed down the path and stooped behind the low wall which surrounded the stunted orchard. Creeping in its shadow I reached a point whence I could look straight through the uncurtained window.

There were only two men in the room, Sir Henry and Stapleton. They sat with their profiles towards me on either side of the round table. Both of them were smoking cigars, and coffee and wine were in front of them. Stapleton was talking with animation, but the baronet looked pale and distrait. Perhaps the thought of that lonely walk across the ill-omened moor was weighing heavily upon his mind.

As I watched them Stapleton rose and left the room, while Sir Henry filled his glass again and leaned back in his chair, puffing at his cigar. I heard the creak of a door and the crisp sound of boots upon gravel. The steps passed along the path on the other side of the wall under which I crouched. Looking  over, I saw the naturalist pause at the door of an out-house in the corner of the orchard. A key turned in a lock, and as he passed in there was a curious scuffling noise from within. He was only a minute or so inside, and then I heard the key turn once more and he passed me and re-entered the house. I saw him rejoin his guest, and I crept quietly back to where my companions were waiting to tell them what I had seen.

"You say, Watson, that the lady is not there?" Holmes asked, when I had finished my report.

"No."

"Where can she be, then, since there is no light in any other room except the kitchen?"

"I cannot think where she is."

I have said that over the great Grimpen Mire there hung a dense, white fog. It was drifting slowly in our direction, and banked itself up like a wall on that side of us, low, but thick and well defined. The moon shone on it, and it looked like a great shimmering ice-field, with the heads of the distant tors as rocks borne upon its surface. Holmes's face was turned towards it, and he muttered impatiently as he watched its sluggish drift.

"It's moving towards us, Watson."

"Is that serious?"

"Very serious, indeed—the one thing upon earth which could have disarranged my plans. He can't be very long, now. It is already ten o'clock. Our success and even his life may depend upon his coming out before the fog is over the path."

The night was clear and fine above us. The stars shone cold and bright, while a half-moon bathed the whole scene in a soft, uncertain light. Before us lay the dark bulk of the house, its serrated roof and bristling chimneys hard outlined against the silver-spangled sky. Broad bars of golden light from the lower windows stretched across the orchard and the moor. One of them was suddenly shut off. The servants had left the kitchen. There only remained the lamp in the dining-room where the two men, the murderous host and the unconscious guest, still chatted over their cigars.

Every minute that white woolly plain which covered one half of the moor was drifting closer and closer to the house. Already the first thin wisps of it were curling across the golden square of the lighted window. The farther wall of the orchard was already invisible, and the trees were standing out of a swirl of white vapour. As we watched it the fog-wreaths came crawling round both corners of the house and rolled slowly into one dense bank, on which the upper floor and the roof floated like a strange ship upon a shadowy sea. Holmes struck his hand passionately upon the rock in front of us and stamped his feet in his impatience.

"If he isn't out in a quarter of an hour the path will be covered. In half an hour we won't be able to see our hands in front of us."

"Shall we move farther back upon higher ground?"

"Yes, I think it would be as well."

So as the fog-bank flowed onward we fell back before it until we were half a mile from the house, and still that dense white sea, with the moon silvering its upper edge, swept slowly and inexorably on.

"We are going too far," said Holmes. "We dare not take the chance of his being overtaken before he can reach us. At all costs we must hold our ground where we are." He dropped on his knees and clapped his ear to the ground. "Thank God, I think that I hear him coming."

A sound of quick steps broke the silence of the moor. Crouching among the stones we stared intently at the silver-tipped bank in front of us. The steps grew louder, and through the fog, as through a curtain, there stepped

the man whom we were awaiting. He looked round him in surprise as he emerged into the clear, starlit night. Then he came swiftly along the path, passed close to where we lay, and went on up the long slope behind us. As he walked he glanced continually over either shoulder, like a man who is ill at ease.

"Hist!" cried Holmes, and I heard the sharp click of a cocking pistol. "Look out! It's coming!"

There was a thin, crisp, continuous patter from somewhere in the heart of that crawling bank. The cloud was within fifty yards of where we lay, and we glared at it, all three, uncertain what horror was about to break from the heart of it. I was at Holmes's elbow, and I glanced for an instant at his face. It was pale and exultant, his eyes shining brightly in the moonlight. But suddenly they started forward in a rigid, fixed stare, and his lips parted in amazement. At the same instant Lestrade gave a yell of terror and threw himself face downward upon the ground. I sprang to my feet, my inert hand grasping my pistol, my mind paralyzed by the dreadful shape which had sprung out upon us from the shadows of the fog. A hound it was, an enormous coal-black hound, but not such a hound as mortal eyes have ever seen. Fire burst from its open mouth, its eyes glowed with a smouldering glare, its muzzle and hackles and dewlap were outlined in flickering flame. Never in the delirious dream of a disordered brain could anything more savage, more appalling, more hellish be conceived than that dark form and savage face which broke upon us out of the wall of fog.

With long bounds the huge black creature was leaping down the track, following hard upon the footsteps of our friend. So paralyzed were we by

the apparition that we allowed him to pass before we had recovered our nerve. Then Holmes and I both fired together, and the creature gave a hideous howl, which showed that one at least had hit him. He did not pause, however, but bounded onward. Far away on the path we saw Sir Henry looking back, his face white in the moonlight, his hands raised in horror, glaring helplessly at the frightful thing which was hunting him down.

But that cry of pain from the hound had blown all our fears to the winds. If he was vulnerable he was mortal, and if we could wound him we could kill him. Never have I seen a man run as Holmes ran that night. I am reckoned fleet of foot, but he outpaced me as much as I outpaced the little professional. In front of us as we flew up the track we heard scream after scream from Sir Henry and the deep roar of the hound. I was in time to see the beast spring upon its victim, hurl him to the ground, and worry at his throat. But the next instant Holmes had emptied five barrels of his revolver into the creature's flank. With a last howl of agony and a vicious snap in the air, it rolled upon its back, four feet pawing furiously, and then fell limp upon its side. I stooped, panting, and pressed my pistol to the dreadful, shimmering head, but it was useless to press the trigger. The giant hound was dead.

Sir Henry lay insensible where he had fallen. We tore away his collar, and Holmes breathed a prayer of gratitude when we saw that there was no sign of a wound and that the rescue had been in time. Already our friend's eyelids shivered and he made a feeble effort to move. Lestrade thrust his brandy-flask between the baronet's teeth, and two frightened eyes were looking up at us.

"My God!" he whispered. "What was it? What, in heaven's name, was it?"

"It's dead, whatever it is," said Holmes. "We've laid the family ghost once and for-ever."

In mere size and strength it was a terrible creature which was lying stretched before us. It was not a pure bloodhound and it was not a pure mastiff; but it appeared to be a combination of the two—gaunt, savage, and as large as a small lioness. Even now, in the stillness of death, the huge jaws seemed to be dripping with a bluish flame and the small, deep-set, cruel eyes were ringed with fire. I placed my hand upon the glowing muzzle, and as I held them up my own fingers smouldered and gleamed in the darkness.

"Phosphorus," I said.

"A cunning preparation of it," said Holmes, sniffing at the dead animal. "There is no smell which might have interfered with his power of scent. We owe you a deep apology, Sir Henry, for having exposed you to this fright. I was prepared for a hound, but not for such a creature as this. And the fog gave us little time to receive him."

"You have saved my life."

"Having first endangered it. Are you strong enough to stand?"

"Give me another mouthful of that brandy and I shall be ready for anything. So! Now, if you will help me up. What do you propose to do?"

"To leave you here. You are not fit for further adventures to-night. If you will wait, one or other of us will go back with you to the Hall."

He tried to stagger to his feet; but he was still ghastly pale and trembling in every limb. We helped him to a rock, where he sat shivering with his face buried in his hands.

"We must leave you now," said Holmes. "The rest of our work must be done, and every moment is of importance. We have our case, and now we only want our man.

"It's a thousand to one against our finding him at the house," he continued as we retraced our steps swiftly down the path. "Those shots must have told him that the game was up."

"We were some distance off, and this fog may have deadened them."

"He followed the hound to call him off—of that you may be certain. No, no, he's gone by this time! But we'll search the house and make sure."

The front door was open, so we rushed in and hurried from room to room to the amazement of a doddering old manservant, who met us in the passage. There was no light save in the dining-room, but Holmes caught up the lamp and left no corner of the house unexplored. No sign could we see of the man whom we were chasing. On the upper floor, however, one of the bedroom doors was locked.

"There's someone in here," cried Lestrade. "I can hear a movement. Open this door!"

A faint moaning and rustling came from within. Holmes struck the door just over the lock with the flat of his foot and it flew open. Pistol in hand, we all three rushed into the room.

But there was no sign within it of that desperate and defiant villain whom we expected to see. Instead we were faced by an object so strange and so unexpected that we stood for a moment staring at it in amazement.

The room had been fashioned into a small museum, and the walls were lined by a number of glass-topped cases full of that collection of butterflies and moths the formation of which had been the relaxation of this complex and dangerous man. In the centre of this room there was an upright beam, which had been placed at some period as a support for the old worm-eaten baulk of timber which spanned the roof. To this post a figure was tied, so swathed and muffled in the sheets which had been used to secure it that one could not for the moment tell whether it was that of a man or a woman. One towel passed round the throat and was secured at the back of the pillar.

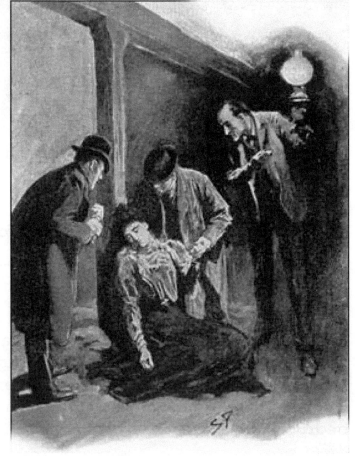

Another covered the lower part of the face, and over it two dark eyes—eyes full of grief and shame and a dreadful questioning—stared back at us. In a minute we had torn off the gag, unswathed the bonds, and Mrs. Stapleton sank upon the floor in front of us. As her beautiful head fell upon her chest I saw the clear red weal of a whiplash across her neck.

"The brute!" cried Holmes. "Here, Lestrade, your brandy-bottle! Put her in the chair! She has fainted from ill-usage and exhaustion."

She opened her eyes again.

"Is he safe?" she asked. "Has

he escaped?"

"He cannot escape us, madam."

"No, no, I did not mean my husband. Sir Henry? Is he safe?"

"Yes."

"And the hound?"

"It is dead."

She gave a long sigh of satisfaction.

"Thank God! Thank God! Oh, this villain! See how he has treated me!" She shot her arms out from her sleeves, and we saw with horror that they were all mottled with bruises. "But this is nothing—nothing! It is my mind and soul that he has tortured and defiled. I could endure it all, ill-usage, solitude, a life of deception, everything, as long as I could still cling to the hope that I had his love, but now I know that in this also I have been his dupe and his tool." She broke into passionate sobbing as she spoke.

"You bear him no good will, madam," said Holmes. "Tell us then where we shall find him. If you have ever aided him in evil, help us now and so atone."

"There is but one place where he can have fled," she answered. "There is an old tin mine on an island in the heart of the mire. It was there that he kept his hound and there also he had made preparations so that he might have a refuge. That is where he would fly."

The fog-bank lay like white wool against the window. Holmes held the lamp towards it.

"See," said he. "No one could find his way into the Grimpen Mire to-night."

She laughed and clapped her hands. Her eyes and teeth gleamed with fierce merriment

"He may find his way in, but never out," she cried. "How can he see the guiding wands to-night? We planted them together, he and I, to mark the pathway through the mire. Oh, if I could only have plucked them out to-day. Then indeed you would have had him at your mercy!"

It was evident to us that all pursuit was in vain until the fog had lifted. Meanwhile we left Lestrade in possession of the house while Holmes and I went back with the baronet to Baskerville Hall. The story of the Stapletons could no longer be withheld from him, but he took the blow bravely when he learned the truth about the woman whom he had loved. But the shock of the night's adventures had shattered his nerves, and before morning he lay delirious in a high fever, under the care of Dr. Mortimer. The two of them were destined to travel together round the world before Sir Henry had become once more the hale, hearty man that he had been before he became master of that ill-omened estate.

And now I come rapidly to the conclusion of this singular narrative, in which I have tried to make the reader share those dark fears and vague surmises which clouded our lives so long and ended in so tragic a manner. On the morning after the death of the hound the fog had lifted and we were guided by Mrs.Stapleton to the point where they had found a pathway through the bog. It helped us to realize the horror of this woman's life when we saw the eagerness and joy with which she laid us on her husband's track. We left her standing upon the thin peninsula of firm, peaty soil which tapered out into the widespread bog. From the end of it a small wand planted here and there showed where the path zigzagged from tuft to tuft of rushes among those green-scummed pits and foul quagmires which barred the way to the stranger. Rank reeds and lush, slimy water-plants sent an odour of decay and a heavy miasmatic vapour onto our faces, while a false step plunged us more than once thigh-deep into the dark, quivering mire, which shook for yards in soft undulations around our feet. Its tenacious grip plucked at our heels as we walked, and when we sank into it it was as if some malignant hand was tugging us down into those obscene depths, so grim and purposeful was the clutch in which it held us. Once only we saw a trace that someone had passed that perilous way before us. From amid a tuft of cotton grass which bore it up out of the slime some dark thing was projecting. Holmes sank to his waist as he stepped from the path to seize it, and had we not been there to drag him out he could never have set his foot upon firm land again. He held an old black boot in the air. "Meyers, Toronto," was printed on the leather inside.

"It is worth a mud bath," said he. "It is our friend Sir Henry's missing boot."

"Thrown there by Stapleton in his flight."

"Exactly. He retained it in his hand after using it to set the hound upon the track. He fled when he knew the game was up, still clutching it. And he hurled it away at this point of his flight. We know at least that he came so far in safety."

But more than that we were never destined to know, though there was much which we might surmise. There was no chance of finding footsteps in the mire, for the rising mud oozed swiftly in upon them, but as we at last reached firmer ground beyond the morass we all looked eagerly for them. But no slightest sign of them ever met our eyes. If the earth told a true story, then Stapleton never reached that island of refuge towards which he struggled through the fog upon that last night. Somewhere in the heart of the great Grimpen Mire, down in

the foul slime of the huge morass which had sucked him in, this cold and cruel-hearted man is forever buried.

Many traces we found of him in the bog-girt island where he had hid his savage ally. A huge driving-wheel and a shaft half-filled with rubbish showed the position of an abandoned mine. Beside it were the crumbling remains of the cottages of the miners, driven away no doubt by the foul reek of the surrounding swamp. In one of these a staple and chain with a quantity of gnawed bones showed where the animal had been confined. A skeleton with a tangle of brown hair adhering to it lay among the debris.

"A dog!" said Holmes. "By Jove, a curly-haired spaniel. Poor Mortimer will never see his pet again. Well, I do not know that this place contains any secret which we have not already fathomed. He could hide his hound, but he could not hush its voice, and hence came those cries which even in daylight were not pleasant to hear. On an emergency he could keep the hound in the out-house at Merripit, but it was always a risk, and it was only on the supreme day, which he regarded as the end of all his efforts, that he dared do it. This paste in the tin is no doubt the luminous mixture with which the creature was daubed. It was suggested, of course, by the story of the family hell-hound, and by the desire to frighten old Sir Charles to death. No wonder the poor devil of a convict ran and screamed, even as our friend did, and as we ourselves might have done, when he saw such a creature bounding through the darkness of the moor upon his track. It was a cunning device, for, apart from the chance of driving your victim to his death, what peasant would venture to inquire too closely into such a creature should he get sight of it, as many have done, upon the moor? I said it in London, Watson, and I say it again now, that never yet have we helped to hunt down a more dangerous man than he who is lying yonder"—he swept his long arm towards the huge mottled expanse of green-splotched bog which stretched away until it merged into the russet slopes of the moor.

CHAPTER XV. A RETROSPECTION

It was the end of November and Holmes and I sat, upon a raw and foggy night, on either side of a blazing fire in our sitting-room in Baker Street. Since the tragic upshot of our visit to Devonshire he had been engaged in two affairs of the utmost importance, in the first of which he had exposed the atrocious conduct of Colonel Upwood in connection with the famous card scandal of the Nonpareil Club, while in the second he had defended the unfortunate Mme. Montpensier from the charge of murder which hung over her in connection with the death of her step-daughter, Mlle. Carere, the young lady who, as it will be remembered, was found six months later alive

and married in New York. My friend was in excellent spirits over the success which had attended a succession of difficult and important cases, so that I was able to induce him to discuss the details of the Baskerville mystery. I had waited patiently for the opportunity, for I was aware that he would never permit cases to overlap, and that his clear and logical mind would not be drawn from its present work to dwell upon memories of the past. Sir Henry and Dr. Mortimer were, however, in London, on their way to that long voyage which had been recommended for the restoration of his shattered nerves. They had called upon us that very afternoon, so that it was natural that the subject should come up for discussion.

"The whole course of events," said Holmes, "from the point of view of the man who called himself Stapleton was simple and direct, although to us, who had no means in the beginning of knowing the motives of his actions and could only learn part of the facts, it all appeared exceedingly complex. I have had the advantage of two conversations with Mrs. Stapleton, and the case has now been so entirely cleared up that I am not aware that there is anything which has remained a secret to us. You will find a few notes upon the matter under the heading B in my indexed list of cases."

"Perhaps you would kindly give me a sketch of the course of events from memory."

"Certainly, though I cannot guarantee that I carry all the facts in my mind. Intense mental concentration has a curious way of blotting out what has passed. The barrister who has his case at his fingers' end, and is able to argue with an expert upon his own subject finds that a week or two of the courts will drive it all out of his head once more. So each of my cases displaces the last, and Mlle. Carere has blurred my recollection of Baskerville Hall. To-morrow some other little problem may be submitted to my notice which will in turn dispossess the fair French lady and the infamous Upwood. So far as the case of the Hound goes, however, I will give you the course of events as nearly as I can, and you will suggest anything which I may have forgotten.

"My inquiries show beyond all question that the family portrait did not lie, and that this fellow was indeed a Baskerville. He was a son of that Rodger Baskerville, the younger brother of Sir Charles, who fled with a sinister reputation to South America, where he was said to have died unmarried. He did, as a matter of fact, marry, and had one child, this fellow, whose real name is the same as his father's. He married Beryl Garcia, one of the beauties of Costa Rica, and, having purloined a considerable sum of public money, he changed his name to Vandeleur and fled to England, where he established a school in the east of Yorkshire. His reason for attempting this special line of business was that he had struck up an acquaintance with a consumptive tutor upon the voyage home, and that he had used this man's ability to make the undertaking a success. Fraser, the tutor, died however, and the school which had begun well sank from disrepute into infamy. The Vandeleurs found it convenient to change their name to Stapleton, and he brought the remains of his fortune, his schemes for the future, and his taste for entomology to the south of England. I learned at the British Museum that he was a recognized authority upon the subject, and that the name of Vandeleur has been permanently attached to a certain moth which he had, in his Yorkshire days, been the first to describe.

"We now come to that portion of his life which has proved to be of such intense interest to us. The fellow had evidently made inquiry and found that only two lives intervened between him and a valuable estate. When he went to Devonshire his plans were, I believe, exceedingly hazy, but that he meant mischief from the first is evident from the way in which he took his wife with him in the character of his sister. The idea of using her as a decoy was clearly already in his mind, though he may not have been certain how the details of his plot were to be arranged. He meant in the end to have the estate, and he was ready to use any tool or run any risk for that end. His first act was to establish himself as near to his ancestral home as he could, and his second was to cultivate a friendship with Sir Charles Baskerville and with the neighbours.

"The baronet himself told him about the family hound, and so prepared the way for his own death. Stapleton, as I will continue to call him, knew that the old man's heart was weak and that a shock would kill him. So much he had learned from Dr. Mortimer. He had heard also that Sir Charles was superstitious and had taken this grim legend very seriously. His ingenious mind instantly suggested a way by which the baronet could be done to death, and yet it would be hardly possible to bring home the guilt to the real murderer.

"Having conceived the idea he proceeded to carry it out with considerable finesse. An ordinary schemer would have been content to work with a savage hound. The use of artificial means to make the creature diabolical was a flash of genius upon his part. The dog he bought in London from Ross and Mangles, the dealers in Fulham Road. It was the strongest and most savage in their possession. He brought it down by the North Devon line and walked a great distance over the moor so as to get it home without exciting any remarks. He had already on his insect hunts learned to penetrate the Grimpen Mire, and so had found a safe hiding-place for the creature. Here he kennelled it and waited his chance.

"But it was some time coming. The old gentleman could not be decoyed outside of his grounds at night. Several times Stapleton lurked about with his hound, but without avail. It was during these fruitless quests that he, or rather his ally, was seen by peasants, and that the legend of the demon dog received a new confirmation. He had hoped that his wife might lure Sir Charles to his ruin, but here she proved unexpectedly independent. She would not endeavour to entangle the old gentleman in a sentimental attachment which might deliver him over to his enemy. Threats and even, I am sorry to say, blows refused to move her. She would have nothing to do with it, and for a time Stapleton was at a deadlock.

"He found a way out of his difficulties through the chance that Sir Charles, who had conceived a friendship for him, made him the minister of his charity in the case of this unfortunate woman, Mrs. Laura Lyons. By representing himself as a single man he acquired complete influence over her, and he gave her to understand that in the event of her obtaining a divorce from her husband he would marry her. His plans were suddenly brought to a head by his knowledge that Sir Charles was about to leave the Hall on the advice of Dr. Mortimer, with whose opinion he himself pretended to coincide. He must act at once, or his victim might get beyond his power. He therefore put pressure upon Mrs. Lyons to write this letter, imploring the old man to give her an interview on the evening before his departure for London. He then, by a specious argument, prevented her from going, and so had the chance for which he had waited.

"Driving back in the evening from Coombe Tracey he was in time to get his hound, to treat it with his infernal paint, and to bring the beast round to the gate at which he had reason to expect that he would find the old gentleman waiting. The dog, incited by its master, sprang over the wicket-gate and pursued the unfortunate baronet, who fled screaming down the Yew Alley. In that gloomy tunnel it must indeed have been a dreadful sight to see that huge black creature, with its flaming jaws and blazing eyes, bounding after its victim. He fell dead at the end of the alley from heart disease and terror. The hound had kept upon the grassy border while the baronet had run down the path, so that no track but the man's was visible. On seeing him lying still the creature had probably approached to sniff at him, but finding him dead had turned away again. It was then that it left the print which was actually observed by Dr. Mortimer. The hound was called off and hurried away to its lair in the Grimpen Mire, and a mystery was left which puzzled the authorities, alarmed the country-side, and finally brought the case within the scope of our observation.

"So much for the death of Sir Charles Baskerville. You perceive the devilish cunning of it, for really it would be almost impossible to make a case against the real murderer. His only accomplice was one who could never give him away, and the grotesque, inconceivable nature of the device only served to make it more effective. Both of the women concerned in the case, Mrs. Stapleton and Mrs. Laura Lyons, were left with a strong suspicion against Stapleton. Mrs. Stapleton knew that he had designs upon the old man, and also of the existence of the hound. Mrs. Lyons knew neither of these things, but had been impressed by the death occurring at the time of an uncancelled appointment which was only known to him. However, both of them were under his influence, and he had nothing to fear from them. The first half of his task was successfully accomplished but the more difficult still remained.

"It is possible that Stapleton did not know of the existence of an heir in Canada. In any case he would very soon learn it from his friend Dr. Mortimer, and he was told by the latter all details about the arrival of Henry Baskerville. Stapleton's first idea was that this young stranger from Canada might possibly be done to death in London without coming down to Devonshire at all. He distrusted his wife ever since she had refused to help him in laying a trap for the old man, and he dared not leave her long out of his sight for fear he should lose his influence over her. It was for this reason that he took her to London with him. They lodged, I find, at the Mexborough Private Hotel, in Craven Street, which was actually one of those called upon by my agent in search of evidence. Here he kept his wife imprisoned in her room while he, disguised in a beard, followed Dr. Mortimer to Baker Street and afterwards to the station and to the Northumberland Hotel. His wife had some inkling of his plans; but she had such a fear of her husband—a fear founded upon brutal ill-treatment—that she dare not write to warn the man whom she knew to be in danger. If the letter should fall into Stapleton's hands her own life would not be safe. Eventually, as we know, she adopted the expedient of cutting out the words which would form the message, and addressing the letter in a disguised hand. It reached the baronet, and gave him the first warning of his danger.

"It was very essential for Stapleton to get some article of Sir Henry's attire so that, in case he was driven to use the dog, he might always have the means of setting him upon his track. With characteristic promptness and audacity he set about this at once, and we cannot doubt that the boots or chambermaid of the hotel was well bribed to help him in his design. By chance, however, the first boot which was procured for him was a new one and, therefore, useless for his purpose. He then had it returned and obtained another—a most instructive incident, since it proved conclusively to my mind that we were dealing with a real hound, as no other supposition could explain this anxiety to obtain an old boot and this indifference to a new one. The more outre and grotesque an incident is the more carefully it deserves to be examined, and the very point which appears to complicate a case is, when duly considered and scientifically handled, the one which is most likely to elucidate it.

"Then we had the visit from our friends next morning, shadowed always by Stapleton in the cab. From his knowledge of our rooms and of my appearance, as well as from his general conduct, I am inclined to think that Stapleton's career of crime has been by no means limited to this single Baskerville affair. It is suggestive that during the last three years there have been four considerable burglaries in the West Country, for none of which was any criminal ever arrested. The last of these, at Folkestone Court, in May, was remarkable for the cold-blooded pistoling of the page, who surprised the masked and solitary burglar. I cannot doubt that Stapleton recruited his waning resources in this fashion, and that for years he has been a desperate and dangerous man.

"We had an example of his readiness of resource that morning when he got away from us so successfully, and also of his audacity in sending back my own name to me through the cabman. From that moment he understood that I had taken over the case in London, and that therefore there was no chance for him there. He returned to Dartmoor and awaited the arrival of the baronet."

"One moment!" said I. "You have, no doubt, described the sequence of events correctly, but there is one point which you have left unexplained. What became of the hound when its master was in London?"

"I have given some attention to this matter and it is undoubtedly of importance. There can be no question that Stapleton had a confidant, though it is unlikely that he ever placed himself in his power by sharing all his plans with him. There was an old manservant at Merripit House, whose name was Anthony. His connection with the Stapletons can be traced for several years, as far back as the schoolmastering days, so that he must have been aware that his master and mistress were really husband and wife. This man has disappeared and has escaped from the country. It is suggestive that Anthony is not a common name in England, while Antonio is so in all Spanish or Spanish-American countries. The man, like Mrs. Stapleton herself, spoke good English, but with a curious lisping accent. I have myself seen this old man cross the Grimpen Mire by the path which Stapleton had marked out. It is very probable, therefore, that in the absence of his master it was he who cared for the hound, though he may never have known the purpose for which the beast was used.

"The Stapletons then went down to Devonshire, whither they were soon followed by Sir Henry and you. One word now as to how I stood myself at that time. It may possibly recur to your memory that when I examined the paper upon which the printed words were fastened I made a close inspection for the water-mark. In doing so I held it within a few inches of my eyes, and was conscious of a faint smell of the scent known as white jessamine. There are seventy-five perfumes, which it is very necessary that a criminal expert should be able to distinguish from each other, and cases have more than once within my own experience depended upon their prompt recognition. The scent suggested the presence of a lady, and already my thoughts began to turn towards the Stapletons. Thus I had made certain of the hound, and had guessed at the criminal before ever we went to the west country.

"It was my game to watch Stapleton. It was evident, however, that I could not do this if I were with you, since he would be keenly on his guard. I deceived everybody, therefore, yourself included, and I came down secretly when I was supposed to be in London. My hardships were not so great as you imagined, though such trifling details must never interfere with the investigation of a case. I stayed for the most part at Coombe Tracey, and only used the hut upon the moor when it was necessary to be near the scene of action. Cartwright had come down with me, and in his disguise as a country boy he was of great assistance to me. I was dependent upon him for food and clean linen. When I was watching Stapleton, Cartwright was frequently watching you, so that I was able to keep my hand upon all the strings.

"I have already told you that your reports reached me rapidly, being forwarded instantly from Baker Street to Coombe Tracey. They were of great service to me, and especially that one incidentally truthful piece of biography of Stapleton's. I was able to establish the identity of the man and the woman and knew at last exactly how I stood. The case had been considerably complicated through the incident of the escaped convict and the relations between him and the Barrymores. This also you cleared up in a very effective way, though I had already come to the same conclusions from my own observations.

"By the time that you discovered me upon the moor I had a complete knowledge of the whole business, but I had not a case which could go to a jury. Even Stapleton's attempt upon Sir Henry that night which ended in the death of the unfortunate convict did not help us much in proving murder against our man. There seemed to be no alternative but to catch him red-handed, and to do so we had to use Sir Henry, alone and apparently unprotected, as a bait. We did so, and at the cost of a severe shock to our client we succeeded in completing our case and driving Stapleton to his destruction. That Sir Henry should have been exposed to this is, I must confess, a reproach to my management of the case, but we had no means of foreseeing the terrible and paralyzing spectacle which the beast presented, nor could we predict the fog which enabled him to burst upon us at such short notice. We succeeded in our object at a cost which both the specialist and Dr. Mortimer assure me will be a temporary one. A long journey may enable our friend to recover not only from his shattered nerves but also from his wounded feelings. His love for the lady was deep and sincere, and to him the saddest part of all this black business was that he should have been deceived by her.

"It only remains to indicate the part which she had played throughout. There can be no doubt that Stapleton exercised an influence over her which may have been love or may have been fear, or very possibly both, since they are by no means incompatible emotions. It was, at least, absolutely effective. At his command she consented to pass as his sister, though he found the limits of his power over her when he endeavoured to make her the direct accessory to murder. She was ready to warn Sir Henry so far as she could without implicating her husband, and again and again she tried to do so. Stapleton himself seems to have been capable of jealousy, and when he saw the baronet paying court to the lady, even though it was part of his own plan, still he could not help interrupting with a passionate outburst which revealed the fiery soul which his self-contained manner so cleverly concealed. By encouraging the intimacy he made it certain that Sir Henry would frequently come to Merripit House and that he would sooner or later get the opportunity which he desired. On the day of the crisis, however, his wife turned suddenly against him. She had learned something of the death of the convict, and she knew that the hound was being kept in the out-house on the evening that Sir Henry was coming to dinner. She taxed her husband with his intended crime, and a furious scene followed, in which he showed her for the first time that she had a rival in his love. Her fidelity turned in an instant to bitter hatred and he saw that she would betray him. He tied her up, therefore, that she might have no chance of warning Sir Henry, and he hoped, no doubt, that when the whole countryside put down the baronet's death to the curse of his family, as they certainly would do, he could win his wife back to accept an accomplished fact and to keep silent upon what she knew. In this I fancy that in any case he made a miscalculation, and that, if we had not been there, his doom would none the less have been sealed. A woman of Spanish blood does not condone such an injury so lightly. And now, my dear Watson, without referring to my notes, I cannot give you a more detailed account of this curious case. I do not know that anything essential has been left unexplained."

"He could not hope to frighten Sir Henry to death as he had done the old uncle with his bogie hound."

"The beast was savage and half-starved. If its appearance did not frighten its victim to death, at least it would paralyze the resistance which might be offered."

"No doubt. There only remains one difficulty. If Stapleton came into the succession, how could he explain the fact that he, the heir, had been living unannounced under another name so close to the property? How could he claim it without causing suspicion and inquiry?"

"It is a formidable difficulty, and I fear that you ask too much when you expect me to solve it. The past and the present are within the field of my inquiry, but what a man may do in the future is a hard question to answer. Mrs. Stapleton has heard her husband discuss the problem on several occasions. There were three possible courses. He might claim the property from South America, establish his identity before the British authorities there and so obtain the fortune without ever coming to England at all; or he might adopt an elaborate disguise during the short time that he need be in London; or, again, he might furnish an accomplice with the proofs and papers, putting him in as heir, and retaining a claim upon some proportion of his income. We cannot doubt from what we know of him that he would have found some way out of the difficulty. And now, my dear Watson, we have had some weeks of severe work, and for one evening, I think, we may turn our thoughts into more pleasant channels. I have a box for 'Les Huguenots.' Have you heard the De Reszkes? Might I trouble you then to be ready in half an hour, and we can stop at Marcini's for a little dinner on the way?"

ABOUT THE CONTRIBUTORS

TIMOTHY GREEN BECKLEY

He's a friend of all things weird and un-known.

Since an early age his life has more or less revolved around the paranormal. His grandfather saw the apparition of a headless horseman. Beckley's life was saved by invisible beings around the age of three. The house he was raised in was thought to be haunted. Beckley also underwent out of body experiences at age six.

He saw his first of three UFOs when he was but ten, and has had two more sightings since – including an attempt to communicate with one of these objects.

Tim grew up listening to the only all night talk show in the country that revolved around the strange and unexplained. Long John Nebel's guests included the early UFO contactees who claimed to have visited other planets and built time machines in the desert. Tim was fascinated by everything that went bump in the night – or even in the daylight for that matter. Years later, Tim was to appear on Long John's show numerous times and over the years has been a frequent guest on hundreds of programs which have come and gone just like ghosts in the night.

He is one of the few Americans ever to be invited to speak before closed door meetings on UFOs presided over by the late Earl of Clancarty at the House of Lords in England. He visited Loch Ness in Scotland while in the UK and went home with a belief that Nessie was somehow connected with dragons of mythology as well as strange discs engraved on cathedrals and ghostly phenomena.

The Inner Light Publications and Global Communications' catalog of books and video titles now number over 200, including the works of Tim Swartz, T. Lobsang Rampa, Sean Casteel, Commander X, Brad Steiger, John Keel, Tracy Twyman, Wendelle Stevens and a host of many other authors. His own bestsellers include "Our Alien Planet," "Strange Saga," "Subterranean Worlds Inside Earth," and "John Lennon – We Knew You."

As the horror movie host Mr. Creepo, Beckley has made numerous films including "Skin Eating Jungle Vampires" and "Blood Sucking Vampire Freaks."

Web Sites:

www.ConspiracyJournal.Com

www.MrCreepo.Com

www.TeslaSecretLab.com

NICK REDFERN

Nick Redfern works full-time as an author, lecturer and journalist. He focuses upon a wide range of unsolved mysteries, including the increasingly tedious Roswell affair of 1947, the macabre Men in Black, Bigfoot, UFOs, the Loch Ness Monster, alien encounters, and government conspiracies. He writes for *UFO Magazine; Mysterious Universe*; *Fate*; *Cryptomundo*; and *Fortean Times*. He also has a regular, weekly, cryptozoology-themed column at Mania.com titled *Lair of the Beasts*.

His many previous books include *Space Girl Dead on Spaghetti Junction*; *The FBI Files*; *Man-Monkey*; *Monsters of Texas* (co-authored with Ken Gerhard); *Cosmic Crashes*; *Final Events*; *On the Trail of the Saucer Spies*; *Keep Out!*; *There's something in the Woods*; *Strange Secrets* (with Andy Roberts); *Memoirs of a Monster Hunter*; *Science Fiction Secrets*; *The NASA Con-*

spiracies; *A Covert Agenda*; *Celebrity Secrets*; and *The Real Men in Black*.

Nick has appeared on numerous television shows, including VH1's *Legend Hunters*; the BBC's *Out of this World*; Fox News; History Channel's *Ancient Aliens*, *MonsterQuest*, *America's Book of Secrets*; and *UFO Hunters*; National Geographic Channel's *The Truth about UFOs* and *Paranatural*; and SyFy Channel's *Proof Positive* – in which Nick and the Centre for Fortean Zoology's Jon Downes raced around Puerto Rico in a cool silver-coloured jeep in search of the blood-sucking nightmare known as the Chupacabra.

He lists his favourite things as late 1970s punk-rock and new-wave music, black t-shirts and black jeans, Carlsberg Special Brew, Tennents Super, zombies, chocolate, *Family Guy*, *The Walking Dead*, *Night of the Demon*, *Terrorvision*, the works of Jack Kerouac, the novels of Carlos Ruiz Zafon, *Rammstein*, *Motorhead*, Abby from *NCIS*, *Oasis*, a nice cup of tea with lots of milk and sugar, and burned toast with mountains of margarine.

Nick can be contacted at http://nickredfernfortean.blogspot.com

ANDREW GABLE

I've been a resident of southeastern Pennsylvania for my entire life. Folklore and mythology, as well as ghosts, UFOs and all manner of Forteana, and particularly cryptozoology, have interested me for well over two decades. However, it was several years before I actually wrote anything on the topic. A few friends of mine had been putting together a small publication, "The Cryptozoology Review," on the topic. I eventually wrote two articles for the magazine, "The Beast of Gevaudan and Other 'Maulers'" – maulers being my term for the strange, usually  canine, animals that attack man and animal alike – and "Two Possible Cryptids From Precolumbian Mesoamerica," which dealt with the ahuizotl, an Aztec water monster which could have been some sort of otter, and the traditions in Latin America of the Camazotz and other winged cryptids and the possible survival of Desmodus draculae, a giant form of vampire bat. Other articles were in various stages of planning when the magazine folded. In the following years, I began to focus more exclusively on more local cryptozoology – Pennsylvania, Maryland, and Delaware. This focus gave rise to the bits written for this book. I've written a book on "The Mystery Animals of Pennsylvania," which is still forthcoming from CFZ Press. A follow-up, "The Mystery Animals of Maryland," is currently in the works.

CLAUDIA CUNNINGHAM

I was born in Albany, NY and attended local schools in the area.

After high school, for a time I studied to be an X-ray technologist then dropped out of college to go to work for the New York Telephone and Telegraph Company in the mid-1960s. After a few years I decided to work in State government, and worked in several capacities at the New York State Department of Labor, retiring in 2002.

Through the years I was a keyboard player in a 60s rock band and later went on to play piano solo at several restaurants in the local upstate area. Music is my inspiration and passion, particularly mid-60s music, which I think of as the best ever!

I collect 1950s dolls and toys and love reading nonfiction (conspiracy/paranormal, mainly). I love to travel and never want to stop learning about the world around me. What's it all about is the question that drives me ever forward in my quest to understand my role in life.

I have done about eight radio shows with Timothy Green Beckley, including Coast to Coast AM, Church of Mabas, Paracast and others, regarding my experiences with the Men-in-Black and other phenomena. I have a years-long involvement with paranormal encounters, and I love to share my experiences with others, in the hopes I will always learn more. I am a paranormal sleuth at heart and I never tire of my quest to uncover the whys and wherefores of the great mysteries of life.

WILLIAM KERN

Served 20 years in U.S. Navy. Photojournalist with Great Lakes Bulletin; Documentary Motion Picture Cameraman. Participated in many NASA unmanned and manned space missions. Served 10 years in the intelligence community prior to and during and following the Vietnam conflict. He wrote and published six novels: "The Morningstar Conspiracy," "A Fine Raving Madness," "Loose Ends," "Space Enough And Time," "The Windmills of Mars," and "The Man Who Fell From A Clear Blue Sky." He is currently working on his 7th novel, "The Farside Chronicles." He has also compiled information for other books, including, "Secret Societies And The Founding Of America," "UFOs: Another Point of View," and "Analogue: The World's Strangest Conspiracies." He published "A Dangerous Book," "Mandy And The Wunk," and "Never Ever Drop," authored by Rodger Stevens, and "The Web of The Stars," authored by Midori Severi (pseudonym). All are available on CD-ROM. He is currently the layout artist and ad designer for "Conspiracy Journal", edited by Tim Beckley.

Born in Washington, Indiana in 1936, William C. Kern served 20 years as a Photographer in the United States Navy.

He served in USS Intrepid, (CVA-11), now a National Museum in New York. He was a photojournalist for the Great Lakes Bulletin, an award-winning military newspaper, and was the Official Photographer for the United States Navy Band.

In the early 1960s he was assigned to VAP-62, a heavy reconnaissance photo air group at NAS Jacksonville, Florida. Flying RA3B's, this squadron, with others, was charged with the responsibility of obtaining intelligence photos of Soviet missile emplacements in Cuba, evidence of which led directly to the "Cuban Missile Crisis."

Prior to the Vietnam conflict, he was assigned to the Naval Reconnaissance Technical Support Center in Suitland, Maryland and to Defense Intelligence Agency in Arlington, Virginia. DIA is the military counterpart of CIA. His duties while at these facilities is still classified. He was occassionally assigned courier duties to transport classified information to CIA Langley, Virginia.

During the height of the Vietnam conflict, he was assigned to the Fleet Intelligence Center, Pacific Facility, where over-flight intelligence information from SEATO was gathered and disseminated to friendly nations and to U. S. Intelligence Agencies. He received special training as a courier and qualified with both the .38 Service Revolver and the .45 Model 1911 semi-automatic Service Pistol; and qualified with the .30 caliber M1A-1 Carbine. He was authorized to use deadly force to safeguard highly classified overflight materials which he transported for dissemination to Civilian and Military Intelligence Agencies of the United States, Australia, New Zealand, Canada and United Kingdom.

He returned to CONUS in October, 1968 and was assigned to USS Constellation, CV64. One year later he arrived at NATTU Motion Picture School in Pensacola, Florida where he studied lighting, single and double system sound, casting, script writing, shooting techniques and camera operation and maintenance. He graduated 2nd in a class of 20 and was awarded a certificate of completion for his film on the hearing impaired.

From 1970 until he retired in 1975, he was assigned to the National Parachute Test Range (Naval Aerospace Recovery Facility), El Centro, California. His duties were as a Documentary Motion Picture Cameraman and he produced a number of excellent films, including RDT&E of the Bell Aerospace (Stratos Western) AeroCab egress system in Los Angeles, California, and the Desert Heat Evaluation of the C5-A Galaxy.

He was officially commended for these two films and others. He also filmed RDT&E features on the egress and retrograde systems of Apollo, Viking, Voyager and Pioneer manned and unmanned space projects.

For two years he was the "Voice of Mission Control" and military liaison during the development and testing of a number of sophisticated aircraft and missile designs, including the B-1 bomber and Tomahawk Cruise Missile.

He also did feature films on the Martin-Baker zero speed/ zero altitude jet aircraft egress systems; LAPES (Low Altitude Parachute Extraction System) used in Vietnam; Rogallo Wing; ParaWing; heli-borne man-tow insertion/retrieval system; mid-air "trapeze" recovery system for the *Discoverer/Corona/Keyhole* spy satellite; on-going RDT&E analysis of the egress systems for the space flight program, and other sophisticated classified aerospace systems and hardware, many of which are now in common use by military units and numerous civilian police forces.

ASSIGNMENTS:
USS Intrepid, CVA (S)-11, January 1955
Staff, NTC Glakes, IL
VAP-62, NAS Jax, FL (contemporary of Roger Chaffee-astronaut*)
NRTSC, Suitland, MD
DIA, Arlington, VA (Until Gulf of Tonkin Event)
FICPACFAC, RP (Vietnam Era)
USS Constellation, CV-64 (Vietnam Era)
MoPic School, NATTU, Pensacola, FL
NPTR (NARF), El Centro, CA, to February 1975
* Killed with Gus Grissom and Ed White during the Apollo
launchpad fire at Cape Canaveral.

AWARDS:
National Defense Ribbon
Occupation Forces, Europe
Navy Unit Citation, Cuban Blockade
Meritorious Unit Commendation, TET
Good Conduct-20 years
Honorable Transfer to Fleet Reserve
Honorable Discharge and Retirement

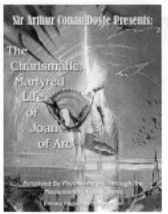